THINKING ABOUT JUSTICE

THINKING ABOUT JUSTICE

A BOOK OF READINGS

EDITED BY
KELLY GORKOFF & RICHARD JOCHELSON

FERNWOOD PUBLISHING · HALIFAX & WINNIPEG

Editing: Jessica Antony
Cover design: John van der Woude
Printed and bound in Canada by Hignell Book Printing

Published in Canada by Fernwood Publishing
32 Oceanvista Lane, Black Point, Nova Scotia, B0J 1B0
and 748 Broadway Avenue, Winnipeg, Manitoba, R3G 0X3
www.fernwoodpublishing.ca

Fernwood Publishing Company Limited gratefully acknowledges the financial support
of the Government of Canada through the Canada Book Fund and the Canada Council
for the Arts, the Nova Scotia Department of Communities, Culture and Heritage,
the Manitoba Department of Culture, Heritage and Tourism under the
Manitoba Publishers Marketing Assistance Program and the Province of Manitoba,
through the Book Publishing Tax Credit, for our publishing program.

Library and Archives Canada Cataloguing in Publication

Thinking about justice: a book of readings / edited by Kelly
Gorkoff & Richard Jochelson.

Includes bibliographical references.
ISBN 978-1-55266-472-8

1. Justice. I. Gorkoff, Kelly, 1965- II. Jochelson, Richard,
1974-

JC578.T45 2012   320.01'1   C2011-908397-3

CONTENTS

PART III — BRIDGING THE DIVIDE / 155

ACKNOWLEDGEMENTS

We would like to acknowledge the contributors to this volume, who have made this collection so diverse and thought provoking. You have endured through rigorous changes, modifications and critique, and you always managed to answer the call and had time for us as we developed the manuscript. Your contributions, patience and professionalism are most appreciated.

We also wish to thank our colleagues at the University of Winnipeg who were supportive of this project before this volume was conceived, when we were planning an obtusely titled conference, "Theorizing Justice: Interdisciplining the Divide." Four conferences later, their support has crystallized in the establishment of the Centre for Interdisciplinary Justice Studies, which now fosters the kind of dialogic knowledge mobilization we were aiming for in this volume. For their contributions to the Centre, we wish to thank Dr. Steven Kohm and the people who run <http://www.cijs.ca>.

We are also grateful to the good folks at Fernwood. Thanks go to Debbie Mathers for pre-production, Beverley Rach for production, John van der Woude for cover design, Jessica Antony for a thorough copy edit and especially to Wayne Antony for leading us through this journey. We would also like to thank the anonymous reviewers of the volume who helped to strengthen it from the early phases until completion. Double blind peer review is a complication in volumes such as this, but we are most grateful for the strengths these reviews brought to the final manuscript.

Thank you to Melanie Janelle Murchison for your technical support in the final phases of the project. Your contributions were indispensable.

Last, to our close friends and family, we could not have finished this volume without your support and love. In all our works, we owe you a tremendous debt of gratitude.

ABOUT THE AUTHORS

Steve Bittle is an assistant professor in the Department of Criminology at the University of Ottawa. His recent publications focus on the governance of corporate crime. His other research interests include the sociology of law and control and criminological theory.

Ronjon Paul Datta is an assistant professor of Social Theory and Cultural Studies at the University of Alberta. His research interests include contemporary and classical social theory, the philosophy of social science, political sociology and the sociology of religion. He is an associate editor of the *Canadian Journal of Sociology*.

Joshua Freistadt is a doctoral student in the Department of Sociology at the University of Alberta whose research interests include critical criminology and socio-legal studies, urban marginality, giving and generosity, the sociology of families and social theory.

Robert Froese studied at the honours level in politics at the University of Winnipeg. His honours research interests include the study of media and criminality, political theory and urban studies. He is currently in graduate studies at York University.

Kelly Gorkoff is a faculty member in the Department of Criminal Justice at the University of Winnipeg and a doctoral student in the Department of Sociology and Anthropology at Carleton University. She previously worked as a research associate with RESOLVE, publishing her scholarship with Fernwood (*Being Heard: The Experiences of Young Women in Prostitution*, 2003).

Bryan Hogeveen is associate professor of the Department of Sociology at the University of Alberta. He is widely published in the area of youth justice issues, and his research interests include social theory, youth and society and neo-liberal governance strategies.

Richard Jochelson is an associate professor in the Department of Criminal Justice at the University of Winnipeg and holds his PhD in law from Osgoode Hall. He is a member of the Bar of Manitoba and co-authored *Sex and the Supreme Court: Obscenity and Indecency Law in Canada*, with Kirsten Kramar (Fernwood 2011).

Steven A. Kohm is an associate professor in the Department of Criminal Justice at the University of Winnipeg. He is the author of internationally published works dealing with media representations of criminality and criminal justice, popular conceptions of justice in court television programs and the study of folklore and issues of justice.

Kirsten Kramar is an associate professor in and Chair of the Department of Sociology at the University of Winnipeg. She has published works dealing with socio-legal issues in infanticide, coroner's investigations and the regulation of sex in North America. She co-authored *Sex and the Supreme Court: Obscenity and Indecency Law in Canada* (Fernwood 2011) with Richard Jochelson.

Glen Luther is an associate professor in the Faculty of Law at the University of Saskatchewan. He holds a Master's degree in law and has extensive legal practice experience as a criminal lawyer. He has argued before the Supreme Court of Canada and has published in the area of legal procedure and psychiatry.

Trevor Markesteyn is a corrections psychologist for Manitoba Corrections and holds a PhD in psychology. He has authored public reports and articles in the field of corrections and is involved in adjunct teaching at the post-secondary level.

Ravi Malhotra is an associate professor in the Faculty of Law at the University of Ottawa. He is widely published in the field of critical disability studies, human rights and labour law, and has also developed expertise in the history of critical disability studies and labour law in North America.

Melanie Janelle Murchison is a graduate student in Legal Studies at Carleton University. She has published in the area of corrections, and her research interests include the empirical study of the judiciary and theorizing jury nullification.

Jeremy Patzer is a doctoral student in the Department of Sociology and Anthropology at Carleton University. His research interests, while varied, include the governance of indigeneity in Canadian law and the critical analysis of legal cases in the understanding of these issues.

Shannon Sampert is an associate professor in the Department of Politics at the University of Winnipeg. A former journalist, Dr. Sampert studies and disseminates research in feminism and the law, and the intersection between politics and media and the subsequent effects on democracy.

Frances M. Shaver is a professor in and chair of the Department of Sociology and Anthropology at Concordia University. She has developed expertise in and is widely published on the topic of people who work in the sex industry and is actively involved in advocacy in this regard.

Michael Weinrath is a professor in and chair of the Department of Criminal Justice at the University of Winnipeg. He is relatively unique among criminologists as he has served as a practitioner with Alberta Corrections. He has authored numerous public reports and journal articles in the field of corrections.

THINKING ABOUT JUSTICE

Kelly Gorkoff and Richard Jochelson

PROBLEMATIZING JUSTICE

Justice is an experience, a concept, a thought and an action as well as a
virtue of an individual or a state/government. Justice is poetic, legal, illegal
and political. It is a profoundly personal experience and, at the same time,
a source of treatises of legal and political philosophy. Raphael (2001) claims
it is a concept that pervades social thought to an unrivalled extent. We see
justice in calls for political change, in pleas to courts and in seeking mercy
from oppression. It is identifiable in a mother's cry of retribution for her
child's killer. It is concretized in pleas to mitigate punishment for criminals
who have lived marginalized and abused lives. It is in protest groups' calls
to hold accountable those corporations that pollute the ocean or deforest
expanses of land. Justice, in these examples, seems knowable. We feel it in the
triumph of "good" over "bad" through its seeming adherence to logic. Yet
justice is beyond this simplistic identification. It is, at the same time, inargu-
ably abstract. Although justice is noted through an appeal to its necessity and
reality, it is also noted in its apparent absence especially in critical times or
eras of social unrest. As a concept and as a goal, justice is opaque, but may
be realized in the operation of state or institutional apparatuses or by those
who seek to marshal the concept to achieve certain ends — in other words,
acts "in the name of justice."

To begin, we note that answers to the question of justice have straddled
many academic domains, from philosophy to law, politics to gender studies,
criminal justice to the classics. Philosophy has been a primary domain of the
study of the concept of justice. Most philosophical understandings consider
justice to be a balance, a morally correct state of things and being. It derives
from authorities, is both natural and constituted: from God to judiciaries, from
monarchs to prime ministers. In the context of law, politics and other studies
of the social, scholars claim justice is both blind and fair — it is a method, a
virtue and a process. While injustice is easy to spot, justice is not. Identifying
and achieving an act, experience or field of justice is contested. The most
well-worn debates in the study of the law ask whether justice exists naturally
or is (socially) created. If it is created, we can study it by asking questions such
as what do we hope to achieve with it, what is its purpose and goal? On the
other hand, if it is natural, how do we ensure we do not suffocate its possibility?

The naturalness of justice is encapsulated in perspectives that consider the diligence of authorities, lawmakers and politicians to minimally interfere with the flourishing of justice. In a practical sense, philosopher John Rawls (1971) claimed justice is the first virtue of social institutions. Institutions variously manifest rules of justice. They can be found in set rules and rights that apply to everyone (in this sense they illustrate the philosophy of Immauel Kant and are categorical) and are similar to Mill (1906), who thought of justice as a principle of action. Justice is akin to "truth" and "fact." Often, this is accomplished by guaranteeing that practices allow for the naturalness of justice to prevail. This naturalness has a meritocratic sense and merit is, on such accounts, natural.

Others are more utilitarian in that they focus less on the rule itself and turn attention toward the outcome or consequence of following the rule. Instead of rules reflecting a truth, utilitarians recognize that as humans create systems of order there is a need to be diligent in ensuring those systems do not advantage or disadvantage particular social groups. Therefore, the consequences of following these rules of justice are what matter most to such scholars.

Justice as created suggests it is achieved through authority, through the command of a sovereign power or a legislature where decisions regarding what justice is and how to create it lies. Garland (1990) claims that justice is a product of social structure and cultural values. Thus it does not have a natural sense, but is, over time, constituted through thought and action — its boundaries are thus delineated through the fluidity of the social. It is here where, in addition to the abstract, we find competing practices of justice from constitutions to policy, from punishment to reward.

Corrective and Distributive Justice

This contemporary debate has deep roots. In *Nicomachean Ethics*, Aristotle made a distinction between pivotal types of justice: corrective and distributive. Corrective justice is concerned with punishment, or righting a wrong. In the name of justice, it asks why we punish, who to punish and what punishment is received. Predicated on the notion that power must be administered fairly and reflective of a consensus of values within society, corrective justice is concerned with debates about what constitutes fair, and hence just, correction. It is backward-looking in that it responds to an act or event and seeks to restore or correct an imbalance. For example, a criminal act of theft is said to require an act of corrective justice. In this sense, damage must be repaired and someone held accountable. Corrective justice has both a conservative and reformative purpose, and can be utilitarian or retributive. Therefore, from a utilitarian perspective, correction can be thought of as a sacrifice of one for the good of the many, or conservatively, it can be thought of as necessary to uphold or restore natural orders. Debates of corrective justice focus on the practicality of correction through examination of the practices of correction. Debates on retribution versus restoration pit Western liberal legal approaches with more holistic, often indigenous-based, approaches.

Distributive justice is more forward-looking than corrective justice. It is concerned with the proper allocation of societal goods (for example, wealth and power) and how those goods should be distributed. Essentially, distributive justice is concerned with how social systems can be ordered to ensure justice is met through daily practice. It is not concerned with events, such as responding to an act, the way corrective justice is, but is more concerned with a template upon which daily living occurs. For example, when all people have enough to eat and drink, justice is achieved through a distributive lens and value of equality. As such, it can uphold the value consensus in society and the status quo or it can generate the ideas to reform the society. Questions arise regarding the societal distribution of power and goods. Do societies distribute to each according to their ability or to each according to their need? Socialist versus capitalist systems, and democratic versus fascist governments are common poles in macro-political/economic debates of distributive justice. Debates of this sort are found in numerous public policy arenas including health care and criminal justice, in regulating insurance industries and in political activism. However, distributive justice debates are especially abstract. Political and legal scholars recognize various ways to achieve justice from liberal (the individual) to social (the collective) and some have moved to the post-structural realm. This is a dense and productive field of justice studies. For instance, debates about distribution inform the arguments of those who advocate for social justice as apprised of "substantial political content," seeking the "alleviation of poverty and the reduction of inequalities 'as a matter of justice rather than charity'" (Jackson cited in Brodie 2007: 5).

In turn, the idea of redistribution as a function of social justice inspires, for some, a politics of recognition (see Benhabib 1992 and Benhabib et al. 1995). The politics of recognition as an argument of justice have moved not only beyond redistribution but also toward justice framed as the promise of identity politics or equality of representation regardless of one's identity. However, that very promise has the potential to make the idea of justice fall in on itself. Fraser writes (2000: para 2):

> Claims for the recognition of difference now drive many of the world's social conflicts, from campaigns for national sovereignty and subnational autonomy, to battles around multiculturalism, to the newly energized movements for international human rights, which seek to promote both universal respect for shared humanity and esteem for cultural distinctiveness. They have also become

predominant within social movements such as feminism, which had previously foregrounded the redistribution of resources. To be sure, such struggles cover a wide range of aspirations, from the patently emancipatory to the downright reprehensible (with most probably falling somewhere in between). Nevertheless, the recourse to a common grammar is worth considering. Why today, after the demise of Soviet-style communism and the acceleration of globalization, do so many conflicts take this form? Why do so many movements couch their claims in the idiom of recognition?

Zizek (2009) argues that the shift to identity politics has eliminated the possibility of systemic change by reformulating systemic problems into personal issues. This has trivialized justice into feelings of pity for others. He advocates a return to the abstractness of justice, politics and ethics. Badiou (2001) makes similar claims against the politics of humanitarianism and social justice, making reference to the "moral terrorism" of human rights, which, along with democracy, cannot sustain a universal principle of justice. What they mean by this is that we need to think about justice beyond the field of the individual (as we often do in systems of democracy) and be careful about moralizing, which is the imposition of one set of values, or truth, on everyone (for example, the tacit understanding of people as "bad" or "good"). In particular, Badiou opposes the problem of difference to a question of truths. In other words, we cannot simply fight to bring everyone up to the same level (as the method of social justice and totalizing calls for equality suggest), but we need to recognize a plurality of truths. These scholars call for an expansion of the concept of justice, a break from the conventional categories by removing justice from its usual groupings so engrained in Western systems. This includes a return to abstract thinking and philosophizing in place of empirical and universal truth claims of justice.

The above brief discussion is a mere and, by design, incomplete snapshot of introductory but central issues of justice. Clearly, the great debates about justice could never be summarized in a few pages. Just as surely, we do not contend to present the above discussion as a summary of debates inherent to the conception of justice.

Justice and the Academic Disciplines

Such debates about the nature and content of justice are readily accessible in the law, politics, sociology and the liberal arts generally. These disciplines tend to think about justice through the lenses particular to their field. For instance, in a criminal justice department, a researcher might be most interested in the way issues of justice manifest in institutions of criminal justice, such as corrections facilities. A geographer might raise questions of justice about the way social services for impoverished citizens are dispersed though an urban environment. A legal scholar might seek to give content to the meaning of justice within the confines of the constitutional law of the land, which purports to bind the long arm of the law. A critical sociologist might ask if justice is merely another means of oppressing the already marginalized and powerless members of society. These caricatures illustrate that often times it is the field of study itself that colours the discussion of justice. When these fields speak of justice they may indeed be speaking of entirely different concepts.

Given the multitude of experiences, thoughts and ideas about what justice is, it seems a futile question with endless pivot points. We do not think so. We think justice should not be taken for granted. Given this diversity, we claim there is a need to think about justice. Justice is worthy of explanation and explication. Indeed it is quite troublesome when one acts too quickly on an act of perceived injustice without thinking about ways to frame what justice is or is not. We think it is of utmost importance that we unravel threads, explore streams of thought and not simply accept or reject arguments, but rather think and learn about how particular arguments can extend our understanding of this elusive and important concept. Therefore, this book seeks to problematize justice and reveal boundaries for thinking about justice. We strive to develop a way to organize our discussions about justice. Simply put, problematizing something means to complicate it. We do not assume justice is one thing. Here, we treat justice as a problematic, a thing to be discussed, thought about and carefully considered.

How might we think about justice while merely conceiving of justice as an undefined collection of possibilities or, worse, immaterialities? Here we are inspired by the work of those scholars who speak of justice as requiring oblique study — that it, of necessity, must be studied indirectly since any direct study of justice would limit its potential (Derrida 2002: 237). Thus, the need, as Badiou and Zizek claim, is to understand justice beyond its concrete empirical, commonsensical or political iterations.

Crank (2003) implores us to study different types of knowledge, to study different ways of knowing and to acquire the methodological tools to understand these ways of knowing (3). This means we cannot contain the definition of justice. The idea of the problematic intrigues us because it "open(s) the field to claims of anyone, even when the authenticity of their view is yet to be discovered" (11).

Thus we are moved by these scholars' pleas to consider justice broadly, amongst numerous disciplines, methodologies and practices or, said otherwise, using a "big tent" approach. The problematic makes exploration worthy, tolerance of alterity (the ability to distinguish between self and not-self) primary and dialogue amongst the disciplines, methodologies and practices possible. We are therefore inspired by Crank's calls to observe, learn and tolerate competing perspectives of justice. We also heed Pearce's call for reading theory and text (2001). He claims that reading about something depends on an interdiscourse and intertextuality and is a transferential relationship. By this he suggests reading something is a process of positioning. We must acknowledge and understand that it matters how we position ourselves to a topic. We bring an orientation of personal and institutional (including academic) experiences as well as ethical and political commitments to any text. Crank and Pearce's position allows us to pivot the problematic of justice to a problematic of orientation. Here we are inspired by Douglas Litowitz's conceptions of law (1997) as internal and external.

Internal, External and Bridging Perspectives

Conceptions of justice differ not only through the lens of the academic field studying the conception but also between "internal" and "external" approaches to the study. Generally speaking, internal perspectives tend to study justice from the perspective of those officials who work or study within the (criminal) justice system, whereas external perspectives view the system from the outside, questioning the "truths" that the critical players in the system deem fundamental (Litowitz 1997: 21). Litowitz also admits that one need not contend that "internal and external approaches constitute separate universes of discourse" (1997: 24). In this regard, Litowitz gives the example of a Marxist convincing officials in the criminal justice system that some conceptions of criminality are caused by "monopoly capitalism" resulting in law reform (24–25). In other words, Litowitz postulates that there is a type of knowledge — a middle ground — that bridges the divide between the external and internal (what we will refer to as bridging). Principally, such perspectives might use an external systemic orientation to ameliorate internal conditions. They might also find the answers to their internal experiences so unsatisfactory that they find themselves asking more externally oriented questions.

We can also think about each approach as using a particular methodology. A methodology is a strategy for constructing knowledge about something. It is the logic behind any research or inquiry of or into something. Methodologies are broad approaches to producing knowledge that involve assumptions, conceptual definitions and specifications about how to approach research and generate knowledge. This is often referred to as an epistemology, which is a term that endeavours to ask how we create knowledge. The different perspectives outlined in this book are not only distinguished by their differences in approach, but also differences in epistemology.

This fairly simplistic means of understanding justice as internal, external or bridging can prove to be quite productive in helping us problematize justice. It is important to note that while we present these divisions in their pure form, within and between each perspective is a continuum. Internal approaches are not all the same; they differ in terms of the type of justice they assume and the scope of change for which they call. Similarly, in the external category, some perspectives are much more abstract than others. Some of the less abstract ones slide into the bridging category. While it might be easier to categorize these as discrete, we recognize the inability to do so. Thus, as with the very concept of justice, some of the chapters that represent each perspective are fuzzy and may at some point in their discussion acknowledge and slide into another perspective. As in life, abstract ideas cannot be completely contained.

Part I: Internal Perspectives

Internal perspectives tend to study justice from the approach of those who work or study within the (criminal) justice system. These types of studies are concerned with making justice tangible by changing policies based on particular assumptions of what justice could be or managing situations in which an assumed justice can occur. Internal perspectives tend to try to help justice institutions achieve their goals more effectively. These studies rarely question the goals of (criminal) justice institutions and simply assume the definitions and goals of the institution that they study. For instance, a study quantifying the recidivism rate of inmates who have been through a designated program would be an internal analytic. Implicit in this study is the goal of the criminal justice system to decrease crime; therefore crime reduction is an indicator of justice achieved. Similarly, a study that uses the experiences of victims in the system to critique it is internalist. Women's critiques of how police and criminal courts deal with domestic violence are an example. These studies suggest the system ought to be modified to meet the unique needs of victims of spousal assault so that conviction rates in these cases are similar to conviction rates of other crimes. This is justice achieved. These perspectives tend to be associated with corrective justice. That is, they seek to find ways to correct injustices in the best way possible. In that sense, they are uniquely focused on normative notions of "best types" of correction. Correction is achieved in a return to baseline norms.

Internal studies tend to employ a positivist methodology. Positivism is a methodology that is based in the scientific method that claims we can know something through observation and empirical evidence that is accumulated and compared over time and is a methodology that is objective and neutral in its gathering and claims-making. Positivism operates on a cause and effect model and assumes there is a truth that can be known if we study properly. For the most part, internal perspectives use evaluation, police accounting structures, statistical evidence, content analysis or other generally accepted methods to normatively evaluate the practices of justice. It is not surprising that much of this research has been funded by government and other interested parties to create facts about criminal justice. Positivistic research has been the basis for the generation of academic criminal justice knowledge (see Wellford 2007; Kraska 2011; Cullen 1995; Deflem 2002; and Farrell and Koch 1995). It is safe to say that the field is dominated by social scientific knowledge regarding etiologies of crime, jurisprudence and correctional programming.

Often, these internal analytics leave unquestioned the particular assumptions about justice contained in justice institutions, instead seeking to examine its practice within assumed concepts. In the context of legal theory, Alan Hunt has been highly critical of internalist perspectives:

> The dominant tradition of contemporary legal theory is epitomised by H.L.A. Hart and Ronald Dworkin, who despite their other differences insist upon the adoption of an internalist perspective…. Internal theories exhibit a predisposition to adopt the self-description of judges or lawyers as primary empirical material…. There is thus a naive acceptance of legal ideology as legal reality. Internal theory is simply too close to its subject matter. (Hunt 1987: 10)

Hunt's is a stinging critique of internal legal approaches, but it provides a worthwhile caution to those who theorize principally within an established regime. It warns of the insularity, loss of perspective and inherent bias that may occur when one is too close to the objects of one's interest.

One would be remiss to describe all internal work in this way. An approach that would dismiss all internal work as naïve or flawed dismisses the possibility of knowledge for knowledge's sake. It dismisses the possibility that empirical observation may be interesting, informative and useful — that internal studies can describe in intimate detail how justice institutions work on a day-to-day basis. It dismisses the possibility that some internal voices call for change from within a system. Even when such calls for change are described as naïve, improvements may be incremental but useful and important as a result of an internal orientation. For example, few would argue that a debate between rehabilitation or retribution in prisons today is unworthy. Lastly, internal approaches that call for change may at least attempt to sort out inconsistencies inherent in those systems. An analysis of law that is purely doctrinal, may, for example, point out that the courts have failed to live up to the constitutional promise of our *Charter of Rights and Freedoms*. A corrections evaluation may reveal that a particular ameliorative program is having little or no effect in achieving its ends.

The first three chapters — Part I of the book — dovetail with and illustrate the internal perspective. What draws these three chapters together is how they coalesce around questioning the practices of justice from the inside — therefore their conclusions and findings support the goals of the criminal justice system. Chapter One by Weinrath, Murchison and Markesteyn reports on Manitoba Corrections' seven week Minobimasdiziwin Gang Program, finding that despite some positive design features and participant response, there were no discernable program effects on reoffence. Contained in this research is its positivistic epistemology regarding the creation of knowledge to speak to those within the system. Therefore, findings of lack of effect on reoffence supports the normative goals of corrections being about reducing crime rates. Chapter Two is Luther's exploration of the Supreme Court of Canada's adoption of broad police power law-generating techniques (known as "ancillary powers"). The author criticizes the retroactive nature of judicial decision making in police powers cases. In making the argument, the author provides a case for a fundamental belief in the rule of law, which is a foundational normative aspect of the Canadian criminal justice system. In Chapter Three, Sampert and Froese explore the crime coverage of certain local and sensational cases of youth crime in the *Winnipeg Sun*, Winnipeg's popular tabloid newspaper. While the authors make many critical findings, their conclusions suggest the media's agenda setting is problematic and creates a barrier for normative, fair and equal justice.

Part II: External Perspectives

External perspectives tend to question the foundations of justice, denying any underlying "truths" of justice systems. Instead of assumptions of existing truths, external approaches use a broad-based critique of normative justice. As such, they are less concerned with corrective justice and more focused on understanding distributive justice and the way that power relations are allocated throughout the system. This includes attending to the abstractness of justice as well as thinking about normative justice as a tool of oppression. Thus they question the normative assumptions of the current order of justice and avoid approaching research of the criminal justice system needing particular changes to make the system work better. Instead, external approaches critique the basis of what we assume to be the truth about justice. Litowitz argues these theories are consigned to deconstructive and critical approaches of justice (1997: 21–40). Being broadly based, this approach emanates from outside of justice institutions and resists constructions of how a justice system should operate (Zizek 2002a). Many are responding to Derrida's call that justice be "deontologized," claiming that positivist (internal) attempts to rationalize justice through quantification ends up exposing its hollow core. He claims we need to re-ontologize justice; that is, justice should be based upon an ability to ignore the finer details of otherness, and to judge a situation abstractly and recognize that a subjectivity exists in the operation of law and justice. External studies abstract from the details and machinations of normative justice or, in the words of Derrida, ignore the camouflage of the human face and look straight at abstract justice (2002a:

10). For example, studies such as those conducted by Chambliss (1964) ask in whose interest law operates. This study utilizes a broad-based approach to indentify who benefits from the normalness of law. Other studies, like Badiou's ethics, ask specifically about the connection between justice and politics. He states: "Justice cannot be a State programme: justice is the qualification of an egalitarian political orientation in act" (2005: 54). Justice is more than its realization in the empirical world. Justice is not meant to be achieved, but rather conceptually interrogated. External positions tend not to advocate for specific change, instead calling for restrained action. These positions recognize that justice is an intentional concept which itself has values written into its use and practice.

Most external studies of justice utilize a critical social science methodology. This methodology argues to adopt a subjective position concerning the knowledge of justice, recognizing that the objectivity of positivism is inherently flawed. Critical social scientists argue that claims of objectivity are impossible because terms like justice are intentional and value laden. As such, any claims to objectivity are false. Therefore all work in a critical methodological framework is by its very nature subjective. Critical methodologies suggest reality is multi-layered and complex. This methodology does not use determinism and essentialism the way positivism does. Instead it suggests social reality is constituted through dialectics and a bounded autonomy. This means things are mutually transforming and dependent on multiplicity of circumstance. It critiques positivism's stance on social facts claiming these are interpretations of "the real" within a framework of pre-constructed values, theory and meaning (Kraska and Newman 2011: 58). Facts and theory are related, and external perspectives seek to unveil the theoretical assumptions at work and how these perspectives have constructed the notions of justice we currently have.

At its most external, such conceptions of justice might see a future of bleakness, futility and indeterminacy. Each and every current practice of justice is seen, from the most critical of external perspectives, as being meted out by fluid and relational power, where systems of justice either disguise power or mete out oppression under the guise of liberty (Golder and Fitzpatrick 2009: 1–39). A less bleak vision from this external view would see justice as a continuous process — a notion of justice that sees it as ever-changing and interacting with the social world. This type of justice would constitute meanings and subjects in the social world but also be influenced by the social world and its subjects. For instance, a campaign to end violence against children brings with it society's view of children as innocent and vulnerable. The innocence of children is, given the history of the world, relatively new and is a creation of the law, which forbade child labour and made nurturing the legal responsibility of parents. Therefore an external analytic does not examine child abuse as a contemporary right, but as a reflection of a series of historical interactions between law and age.

As such, external analysis provides an important counterpoint to the surety of the internal. Observations from outside the justice system can provide important contact points of examination and reflection of those inside the system who might question the normality and taken-for-granted nature of practices of justice. A corrections researcher may, through her research, start to problematize the institutions of corrections. A lawyer may question the justice of law when she repeatedly prosecutes those she believes to be morally innocent or comes to see navigating the legal terrain as a game lawyers play to further their careers rather than achieve justice. The external project allows a philosophical and political economic assessment of the self and the social, and allows for broader conceptions of justice to be considered. Depending on perspective, it allows an observer to unpack relational power to reveal the lack of justice in the social; it may redefine justice's boundaries, revealing the concept as a means of social, even governmental, control. The external approach reveals either the lie of justice or its complete absence. External approaches do not seek prescription, but rely on description and analyses (for examples see Rose et al. 2006, 1998; Rose 1999; Valverde 2003).

We see the hallmarks of externality in Chapters Four, Five, Six and Seven of this volume. These chapters coalesce around the indeterminacy of justice or at least its absence in the current socio-political order. All of them question in some way what we assume to be the truth about justice. In Chapter Four, Patzer explores issues of indigenous sovereignty, but in the process reveals the separation of law and justice, seeing law's justice as a practice of power that serves to silence the already marginalized. In Chapter Five, Datta explores critical realist and Foucaultian theoretical traditions to elucidate an approach to studying justice. His project is a meta-theoretical one, in the same way that Badiou calls us to question theoretically the tools we use to understand justice. Datta concludes that realist sociology provides the requisite tools for the study of justice. In Chapter Six, Bittle studies the criminal scheme that allows for the criminalization of organizations that fail to provide safe conditions for the workers and the public. Bittle reintroduces the importance of the state into a post-legal analysis examining the symbiotic relationship between the state and corporate capitalism, revealing surprising, contingent and constitutive power relations in the context of corporate crime. In Chapter Seven, Kramar uses Foucault's governmentality analytic to interrogate Canada's criminal law against infanticide. Kramar's work falls mainly in the world of the external analytic; however, her argument demonstrates affinity with bridging (described below) in that she recognizes the need for substantive gender equality over formal legal equality. Kramar's work, at the least then, enters the fray of a mediated but ever-changing social consensus in which equality as a concept is continually reinvented. What hinges all of these together in an external category is their methodological approach, which attends to how discussions of justice must be located in a theory of what we conceive justice is or can be. In this sense they remove themselves from the assumptions of normal justice and seek other goals in a broad-based analytic.

Part III: Bridging Perspectives
If we think about internal vs. external analytics of justice as watertight, we are likely mistaken. At times one leaks into the other. There are also specific analytics that find problem with both perspectives. In that sense they desire to make change in a system of justice, but not in the internal sense, because the shifts postulated by a bridging approach do not seek a correction of the system to return to baseline norms but rather calls for a redistribution of power relations. However, a strictly external analytic does not provide prescription for change. Using external critique to instigate significant change in our legal and political systems provides a powerful use of theory in the context of the study of justice. Those placing their work in this axis see critical analysis as vital to the deconstruction of justice systems. Externalism can be harnessed to bring about shifts in law and policy, at the least to strive towards justice, even if the content of that justice remains elusive. For example, we may seek to modify a current practice of justice and create new or multiple goals of the criminal justice system, ones not previously conceived. These approaches, while informed by the nihilistic predilections of unmitigated externalism, congregate around an optimistic leap of faith — that justice can be better or at least better understood and even given some content. For some, this might mean that social activism is possible and even desirable. For others, the task of the bridgers would merely be a more nuanced knowledge. The terrain of the bridgers is vast. It is a space occupied by the internalist, who has dared to pay attention to the external critique of the institution she researches. It is also space occupied by the externalist, who has accepted the complexity of power relations in society but seeks mediated social responses. So, a researcher who wants to help get youth prostitutes off the street may not be satisfied with a purely internal approach, which confines her to be bound by legal explications of age. She might instead search for material and realist grounds for change, unencumbered by the internal legal analyses.

This, however, represents a different type of change. It is not the change of the internalist, who seeks a return to foundational principles of justice (for instance, rule of law), but rather is more expansive and at times revolutionary. The bridger accepts broader societal shifts and the historical recognition that things change considerably over time. For instance, gender relations have transformed remarkably in the past decade. This broad type of change is what Ewald describes when he writes of the "whole range of practices aimed at allowing 'society' continually to reach a compromise with itself, to bring forth its own normativity" (Ewald 1988: 56–57; Golder and Fitzpatrick 2009: 106). Golder and Fitzpatrick describe this phenomena or bridging as one that sees modifications of justice as a justice of the norm; justice is something other than the social contract (between the state and citizen) — it is a "calibrated consensus" — it is self-managing and ever-changing, providing a "regular statement of society's relationship with itself" (106–07; Ewald 1987: 107). This means that there is some agency allowable by citizens. In social movement and in terms of social change, we can make things new again. Social relations can be modified. These include relations of justice. Methodologically speaking, research under this umbrella uses multiple methods. They may blend empiricism with a realism that is critical. Therefore the chapters in this section seek a realness to abstract conceptualizations.

Bridgers who originate from an external space may make constructive suggestions in the name of justice in order to take part in the continual dialogue of this mediated but ever-changing social consensus. Similarly, those who use internal methodologies may discover results so troubling that they see the need to seek substantial and systemic reform. The bridging space is a place of dialogue between the externalist and internalist, and is a space where profound change is proposed. It is a space in a continuum between the purely internal and the purely external. It is a space where ideas can be discussed by differently oriented theorists and practitioners. We believe it is a space being occupied by increasingly more scholars as they seek materiality, or a real change.

In Chapter Eight, Malhotra uses critical disability theory, based on the theories of Foucault and Goffman, to explore the famous Tracy Latimer case. What at first blush seems externalist becomes a bridging analytic in his argument for a pragmatic, even incremental, use of Canadian constitutional values to ameliorate the marginalization of disability communities. He justifies this equivocal call for legal change on the basis of potential gains and justice for disadvantaged communities.

In Chapter Nine, Kohm explores calls for social and economic justice for Winnipeg's inner city — home to the city's most marginalized and excluded. While Kohm begins his study with an internal, positivist orientation (he uses Census statistics and his own interviews) he ultimately calls for a "broader conversation" about justice informed by the voices of a vulnerable and victimized population.

In Chapter Ten, Shaver critically explores a number of regimes for regulating, criminalizing or legalizing sex work in Canada. Using a number of methodologies, including empirical research and comparative legal approaches, she argues for a pluralism, rather than an individual moralism, as the basis for dealing with sex work. Her search for rational and pragmatic solutions to the day-to-day material issues and problems facing sex workers ultimately endorses decriminalization. In the internalism of her methodology, Shaver manages to ask the reader to move beyond the moralistic stance towards sex trade workers entrenched in our Criminal Code. She asks us to look for a broader justice, one that seeks reliable empiricism to ground systemic change. Thus, an internal analytic founds the call for wholesale change of social policy.

Finally, in Chapter Eleven, Hogeveen and Friestadt problematize the question of justice for youth who come into contact with the justice system. In this study of the police practice of geographically excluding "othered" youths, the authors call for the fashioning of spaces of welcome for excluded youth. The authors interpret positivistic (hence, internalist) methodologies, such as interviews and media and statistical analyses, through a critical lens (one founded on the theories of Derrida). The mating of externalist theory, which claims justice cannot be estimated, with internalist empirical methods allows the authors to challenge institutions and practices which "(re)produce otherness." Reverence and respect for marginalized youth are advocated in what for these authors is an elusive search for justice.

CONCLUSION

In this book, we ask the reader to join us on a journey through three demarcation points on a spectrum of justice studies — through readings that reflect each point. Each perspective has strengths and weaknesses and each are recognizable by their epistemology. A current trend in the study of justice is to use the externalism to foster change or recognize, at the least, nascent evolution. The bridging approaches recognize the flaws of internalism, but recognize a need to do something. The new discourses are optimistic in tone, but critical in methodology. Those who bridge the divide between the internal and external may rely on the unpacking analytics of externalism, or the unyielding empiricism of the internal approach, but what unites them is a desire to engage in a broader discussion of justice, one where mediated alternatives are posited; one where profound change is possible or at least worth the experiment. These bridging spaces provide interesting points of contact for the external and the internal analytics of justice.

By placing these bridging works in this volume beside more internal and external works, we hope that more such discussions can take place, even if they exist only in the imagination of the cautious reader. We end this introductory chapter no closer to an elucidation of justice's content, but hopefully, with the reader's permission, we are closer to a more fulsome and rich discussion of justice in a social space, and better informed about the nature of those spaces.

References

Aristotle, N. 1962. *Nicomachean Ethics*. Trans. Martin Ostwald. New York: Macmillan Books.

Badiou, Alain. 2001. *Ethics: An Essay on the Understanding of Evil*. London: Verso Books.

___. 2005. *Infinite Thought: Truth and the Return to Philosophy*. London: Continuum Books.

Barnett, Randy. 1990. "The Internal and External Analysis of Concepts." *Cardozo Law Review* 11: 525.

Benhabib, Seyla. 1992. *Situating the Self: Gender, Community and Postmodernism in Contemporary Ethics*. New York: Routledge.

Benhabib, Seyla, Drucilla Cornell and Nancy Fraser (eds.). 1995. *Feminist Contentions*. London: Routledge.

Berkowitz, Peter. 1995. *Nietzsche: The Ethics of an Immoralist*. Cambridge: Harvard University Press.

Brodie, Janine. 2007. "Reforming Social Justice in Neoliberal Times." *Studies in Social Justice* 1, 2.

___. 2008. "Recasting the Social in Social Citizenship." In E. Isin (ed.), *Recasting the Social in Citizenship*. Toronto: University of Toronto Press.

Chambliss, William J. 1964. "The Law of Vagrancy." *Social Problems* 12.

Crank, John C. 2003. *Imagining Justice*. Boise State University: Anderson Publishing.

Cullen, Frank. 1995. "Fighting Back: Criminal Justice as an Academic Discipline." *Academy of Criminal Justice Sciences* 13, 4.

Dean, Mitchell. 1999. *Governmentality: Power and Rule in Modern Society*. London: Sage Publications.

Deflem, M. 2002. "Teaching Criminal Justice in Liberal Arts Education: A Sociologist's Confessions." *ACJS Today* XXII, 2.

Derrida, Jacques. 2002. "Force of Law: The 'Mystical Foundation of Authority.'" In Gil Anidjar (ed.), *Jacques Derrida: Acts of Religion*. London: Routledge.

Dworkin R. 1977. *The Philosophy of Law* (Oxford Readings in Philosophy). New York: Oxford University Press.

___. 1996 *Freedom's Law: The Moral Reading of the American Constitution*. Cambridge, MA: Harvard University Press.

Ewald, Francois. 1987. "Justice, Equality, Judgement: On Social Justice." Trans. Iain Fraser. In Gunther Teubner (ed.), *Juridification of Social Spheres: A Comparative Analysis in the Areas of Labor, Corporate, Antitrust And Social Welfare Law*. New York and Berlin: Wlater de Gruyter.

___. 1988 "A Concept of Social Law." Trans. Iain Fraser. In Gunther Teubner (ed.), *Dilemmas of Law in the Welfare State*. New York and Berlin: Wlater de Gruyter.

Farrell, Bill, and Larry Koch. 1995. "Criminal Justice, Sociology, and Academia." *The American Sociologist* 26, 1.

Fish, Stanley. 2008. *Save The World on Your Own Time*. Oxford: Oxford University Press.

Fraser, Nancy. 2000. "Rethinking Recognition." *New Left Review* 3.

Foucault, Michel. 1980. *The History of Sexuality. Volume 1: An Introduction*. Trans. Robert Hurley. New York: Vintage.

___. 1980. *Power/Knowledge: Selected Interviews and Other Writings 1972–1977*. Edited by Colin Gordon. London: Harvester.

___. 1991. "Governmentality." Trans. Rosi Braidotti and revised by Colin Gordon. In Graham Burchell, Colin Gordon and Peter Miller (eds.), *The Foucault Effect: Studies in Governmentality*. Chicago, IL: University of Chicago Press.

___. 1997. *Ethics: Subjectivity and Truth*. Edited by Paul Rabinow. New York: New Press.

Garland, D. 1990. *Punishment and Modern Society*. Oxford: Oxford University Press.

Golder, Ben, and Peter Fitzpatrick. 2009. *Foucault's Law*. London: Routledge.

Hart, H.L.A. 1961. *The Concept of Law*. Oxford: Clarendon Press.

Hunt, Alan. 1987. "The Critique of Law: What Is 'Critical' about Critical Legal Theory?" *Critical Legal Studies* 5.

Hunt, Alan, and Gary Wickham. 1994. *Foucault and Law: Towards a Sociology of Law and Governance*. London and Boulder, CO: Pluto Press.

Jackson, B. 2005. "The Conceptual History of Social Justice." *Political Studies Review*, 3.

Kraska, Peter B. 2011. "Criminal Justice Theory: It's Time to Ask Why?" In Peter B. Kraska and John Brent (eds.), *Theorizing Criminal Justice: Eight Essential Orientations*. Long Grove, IL: Waveland Press.

Kraska, P., and L. Neuman. 2011. "Philosophical and Theoretical Foundations." In *Essential Criminal Justice and Criminology Research Methods*. Upper Saddle River, NJ: Prentice Hall.

Lemke, Thomas. 2002. "Foucault, Governmentality, and Critique." *Rethinking Marxism* 14, 3 (September).

Litowitz D.E. 1997. *Postmodern Philosophy and Law*. Lawrence, KS: University Press of Kansas.

___. 1998. "Internal versus External Perspectives on Law: Toward Mediation." *Florida State University Law Review* 26, 127 <law.fsu.edu/journals/lawreview/frames/261/litofram.html>.

Mill, John Stuart. 1906. *Utilitarianism*. Chicago, IL: University of Chicago Press.

___. 1989. "On Liberty." In Stefan Collini (ed.) *Mill, On Liberty and Other Writings*. Cambridge: Cambridge University Press.

Mills, C. Wright. 1959. *The Sociological Imagination*. London: Oxford University Press.

Murphy, Jeffrey G., and Jules L. Coleman. 1990. *Philosophy of Law: An Introduction to Jurisprudence*. Boulder, CO: Westview Press.

Pearce, Frank 2001 *The Radical Durkheim*, second edition. Toronto: Canadian Scholars Press.

Raphael, D. 2001. *Concepts of Justice*. Oxford: Oxford University Press.

Rawls, J. 1971/1999. *A Theory of Justice*. Cambridge MA: Harvard University Press.

Rose, Nikolas. 1999. *Governing the Soul: The Shaping of the Private Self*. London: Free Associations Books.

Rose, Nikolas, Pat O'Malley, and Mariana Valverde. 2006. "Governmentality." *Annual Review of Law and Social Science* 2.

Rose Nikolas, and Mariana Valverde. 1998. "Governed by Law?" *Social & Legal Studies* 7.

Schwartz, Richard L. 1992. "Internal and External Method in the Study of Law."

Law and Philosophy 11.

Tamanaha, Brian Z. 1996. "The Internal/External Distinction and the Notion of a 'Practice' in Legal Theory and Sociolegal Studies." *Law and Society Review* 30, 1

Valverde, Mariana. 2003. *Law's Dream of a Common Knowledge*. Princeton and Oxford: Princeton University Press.

Wellford, Charles. 2007. "Crime, Justice, and Criminology Education: The importance of Disciplinary Foundations." *Journal of Criminal Justice Education* 18.

Zizek, Slavoj. 2002a. *On Belief.* London: Routledge.

___. 2002b. *Welcome to the Desert of the Real.* London: Verso Books.

___. 2008. *In Defense of Lost Causes.* London: Verso Books.

___. 2009. *First as Tragedy, Then as Farce.* London: Verso Books.

PART I

INTERNAL APPROACHES

In the introductory chapter we asked the reader to think about justice on a spectrum. We urged the reader to consider justice through the lenses of the ways we study and problematize justice. We remind you that the chapters in this section have been selected because they share certain traits — they are studies of justice that occur from within accepted precepts of justice in the disciplines that are investigated. These precepts allow the authors of the studies to suggest that justice can be served when the system is modified to repair the errors that these scholars have uncovered. These are traits that allow them to be categorized as internal. We remind you that an internal perspective of justice examines the workings of justice from the perspective of the inside of the system and determines justice against normative and consensus-based standards. Each of the three chapters you are about to read is critical of some part of the criminal justice system, but they are critical from within. The three chapters that follow are written from the point of view of those who work within the system — the corrections worker, the lawyer and the journalist.

They seek to suggest interventions that will bring the system back to a just baseline. For instance, an inefficient corrections program should not be used if it is not achieving its goals of rehabilitation (see Chapter One by Weinrath, Murchison and Markesteyn), a Supreme Court that is usurping the role of the legislature in its decision making should be called upon to stop disrupting its place in the rule of law (see Chapter Two by Luther) and newspapers should be asked to curb their salacious coverage of youth crime to better reflect a type of journalism that is apprised of newsworthy stories and responsible coverage (see Chapter Three by Sampert and Froese). Each of the chapters that follow in this section asks us to return the system back to a baseline and suggests that the prescription would be in the name of justice. These approaches thus have a corrective tendency. The bounded and incremental nature of these approaches and their pleas to return the area studied to baseline belies the positivism we suggested in the introductory chapter. We call this an internal analytic and ask the reader to imagine that these are spaces occupied on a continuum at the furthest point from externalism, which we discuss in the next section, prior to Chapter Four.

CHAPTER ONE

MEASURING SUCCESS OF CORRECTIONS PROGRAMS

The Evaluation of the Minobimasdiziwin Prison Gang Intervention Program

Michael Weinrath, Melanie Janelle Murchison and Trevor Markesteyn

JUSTICE IN CORRECTIONS

For some, justice connotes punishing the bad, while, for others, it is offering help and assistance to offenders, particularly those historically disadvantaged through racial discrimination, class bias or both. Surveys of Canadians and citizens in other nations indicate that strong public support still exists for rehabilitation as a corrections goal, but punishment is also viewed as a viable objective (Roberts and Hough 2005). Correctional administrators find themselves right at the nexus of this punishment/rehabilitation dilemma. If their efforts to make institutions humane places end up giving them too "comfortable" an appearance, they are criticized for being "soft" on crime (Roberts 2005). On the other hand, even well-run rehabilitation programs often fall short of high success rates. Large-scale meta analyses and reviews of many rehabilitation programs still show that, on average, even good programs reduce reoffence rate by a modest 5 to 10 percent (MacKenzie 2006). Punishment may well be worthwhile for its own sake, but those who believe that greater use of custody reduces reoffence have little evidence to support those claims (MacKenzie 2006).

Alternatively, what can offenders reasonably expect from the corrections system? What is justice for offenders, what do they consider to be fair treatment? An intuitive reaction from some might be, "who cares what offenders think?" Yet others have argued that fair treatment by the justice system is critical to avoiding repeat crimes. According to Sherman's (1993) "defiance theory," the more unjust offenders consider their handling by justice agents, the more likely they are to remain "defiant," angry and motivated to continue to commit crimes. In a similar vein, Braithwaite (1989) has proposed that offenders should be held accountable by the community; however, they should also be welcomed back and respectfully "reintegrated" back into society to facilitate changing their behaviour. These authors seem to postulate that that the offender's perception of the justice they receive may be linked to their future recidivism.

Prison gang members are a group of considerable concern in Canadian federal and provincial correctional institutions, as well as in other jurisdictions (Gaes et al. 2002; Griffin and Hepburn 2006; Leger 2003). Prison gang members are identified as being more involved in institutional misconduct generally, including staff and inmate intimidation and assaults, and control of the institutional drug trade.

Manitoba is particularly troubled, with prison gangs involved in a large-scale riot at Headingley in 1996 (Hughes 1996) and a large riot at Stony Mountain in 2009 (*Winnipeg Free Press* 2009). In between these riots, serious gang-related assaults have occurred at the Winnipeg Remand Centre and Stony Mountain, including two homicides. Manitoba is known to possess overrepresented corrections populations of Aboriginals, even in comparison to its large Indigenous population (Grekul and LaBoucane-Benson 2008). The evidence of poverty and crime rates within these communities is well documented (Grekul and LaBoucane-Benson 2008). There is some evidence that Aboriginal prison gangs in the Prairie provinces originated in Manitoba, with federal penitentiary gangs in Alberta and Saskatchewan having been started by gang inmates transferred from the Stony Mountain institution in Manitoba. Transferred for causing problems, inmates from Manitoba gangs such as the Manitoba Warriors, Indian Posse and Native Syndicate began recruiting and formed similar gangs in Alberta and Saskatchewan (Grekul and LaBoucane-Benson 2008).

So, what can be done about prison gangs? Traditionally, correctional authorities utilize intelligence gathering, inmate transfer and isolation tactics to try to manage prison gang members (Grekul and LaBoucane-Benson 2008; Jones, Roper, Stys and Wilson 2004). Administrators can become knowledgeable of gang activities through informants, then can act by transferring problem gang members to other facilities and isolating gang inmates on special units or in segregation cells. However, correctional authorities are still left with the question of what to do with prison gang members when they are eventually placed back into the general population; justice officials remain concerned about what to do with gang members upon release at the end of sentence into the community. It is difficult to isolate inmates for their entire sentence, and, eventually, frequent transfers are not logistically possible or always effective. Morally and practically, however, correctional authorities still need to pursue their mandate of promoting and facilitating pro-social behaviour change, even with gang members.

This chapter provides preliminary results from an impact evaluation of Minobimasdiziwin, a prison gang program operated by Manitoba Correctional Services at the adult Headingley Correctional Centre and

Manitoba Youth Centre. The program seeks to facilitate individuals' leaving a gang and their successful reintegration into the community, avoiding further reoffence or achieving some measure of harm reduction in the commission of less serious offences (that is, less violent offences) or less frequent recidivism. Its delivery generally relies on the intervention being provided to a single gang at a time. This has been lauded as an appropriate strategy by some, as it builds on the positive (and alternative) dynamic of support and group commitment that the gang provides its members (Bracken, Deane and Morrissette 2009, 2007).

Prison Gangs and Corrections

Prison gangs are a large problem in correctional facilities because they promote predatory behaviour within a facility and a culture extremely negative towards staff and administration (Delisi 2004; Gaes et al. 2002; Cunningham and Sorenson 2007; Zaitzow and Houston 1999). Gangs seek dominance in the institutional drug trade, warring amongst themselves, resulting in serious injuries. In some senses, prison gangs represent the most negative features of the inmate subculture in that they undermine administration and promote illicit activities, undercutting efforts by prisoners to change their behaviour. Prison gang members are also referred to as criminal organization members because they come from community-based street gangs or biker gangs and they maintain their gang relationships and identity even when incarcerated.

Prison gangs are acknowledged as a significant challenge in Canada at both the provincial and national levels. In the 1990s, street gangs and criminal organizations increased in numbers and influence as they recruited within correctional facilities. In a national survey, Kelly and Caputo (2005) report that prisons gangs can serve as sources of recruits for street gangs. In a federal study, it was found that one in six federal prison admissions is affiliated with a gang or criminal organization (Nafekh and Stys 2004). Nafekh and Stys found that the majority of gang members were from Quebec, followed by the Prairies, Ontario, B.C. and the Maritimes. Gang members tended to be younger, more violent, involved in more assaultive behaviour and more often in possession of drugs than other corrections populations.

The Prairie provinces face particular challenges with Aboriginal prison gangs (Alberta Corrections 2003; Nafekh 2002; Grekul and Laboucane-Benson 2008; Weinrath, Swait and Markesteyn 1999). In Manitoba, Headingley Correctional Centre and Stony Mountain institution both report that approximately 30 to 35 percent of their inmate population has a gang affiliation, although not all members are Aboriginal. Nafekh (2002) found that, nationally, about 7 percent of all Aboriginal inmates were gang affiliates. In his study comparing under twenty-five Aboriginal gang members to other under twenty-five Aboriginal inmates, Nafekh (2002) found that prison gang members were more likely to live in a criminogenic area, have criminal associates and have little or no employment history. They were also more likely to be aggressive, hostile and hold negative attitudes towards law enforcement. Grekul and Laboucane-Benson (2008) found from their qualitative interviews with Aboriginal gangs that their genesis has roots in structural inequalities in Canadian society. Discrimination and ruptured families result, in some cases, in Aboriginal youth seeking out the gang to provide social support.

Gang Suppression Strategies

Justice for corrections officials and inmates who wish to be protected from predators involves suppression of troublesome inmates, which usually includes prison gangs. Correctional strategies to deal with prison gangs have focused on intelligence gathering, segregation and separation strategies such as housing gangs in separate units or high security units, isolation of incompatible gang members from each other, segregation of gang leaders and transfer of gang members to other institutions (Decker 2003; Ruddell, Decker and Egley 2006). In the large U.S. state prison system, a midwest state was able to designate one minimum security institution as "gang free," only housing inmates who had no gang affiliation (Rivera, Coweles and Dorman 2003). This strategy, regrettably, is more realistic in the U.S. because of their high incarceration rate; it is generally not feasible in Canada because of our smaller prison populations. In Manitoba, at the time this chapter was written, larger gangs such as the Manitoba Warriors and Afrikan Mafia are isolated in their own unit in the provincial Headingley Correctional Centre, while others are dispersed. Following a riot in 2009, Stony Mountain now uses the separation strategy for gangs such as the Manitoba Warriors, Hells Angels and Native Syndicate.

Gang Leaving Programs

In Ludlow, Massachusetts, in the early 1990s the local prison designed a program specifically for gang members that worked in stages to transition inmates out of gangs and into the general population (Toller and Tsagaris 1996). In the first phase, identified gang members are isolated and observed. They are expected to renounce gang membership. They then gradually earn more privileges and work their way out into population. Successful inmates are placed into a three-week, three-session-a-week cognitive skills program. Initial reports of this program were very positive: only 23 of 190 (9 percent) returned to segregation. However, aside from this early report, there is little in the way of other outcome data on this program (for example, institutional misconduct or recidivism). Toller and Tsagaris provide no descriptive data, nor is a comparison group, control group or quasi-experimental analysis offered.

Getting inmates to leave their gangs is also referred to as a "denouncing" strategy. Inmates are counselled upon entering the facility to leave the gang, and placed in segregation if they refuse. There is little in the way of data on the effectiveness of this approach. Denouncing is coupled with the general "zero tolerance" approach to gangs noted above and hence is expensive to implement and maintain due to limits on available institutional beds. There is no consensus on this as a viable strategy. Some correctional professionals feel that this approach is the only means to allow personal change and effectively deter gang activity. The other perspective is evident in Manitoba at Stony Mountain institution, as staff counsel current prison gang members to avoid illicit activities, but not to try to formally leave their gang until they are released from prison.

Treatment Programming for Gang Members

Justice for gang members, one assumes, is for them to be provided with opportunities to change their behaviour so that they can successfully leave the gang life behind. Case management of prison gang members, however, need not be unique: their needs can be assessed, they can be referred to programs, and plans for their release can be put in place. Program planning is likely still a higher priority for gang members because they generally have higher needs than other inmates and should benefit more from interventions aimed at criminogenic needs such as anger management, criminal thinking, pro-social relationships, educational/vocational training and employment.

While not unique in needs, case management can be more complicated for gang members because they often have more violent histories (and are higher risk) than other corrections populations and they may lack interest in programs. Maintaining current status in a prison gang always holds the potential of further involvement in negative activities within the institution. Moreover, one still has to deal with the issue of gang membership. How to successfully engage prison gang members in treatment while they are still affiliated with their criminal organization is a challenge. Correctional programs generally do not work as well within an institution, so how do criminal justice practitioners promote behaviour change, or encourage leaving the gang while inmates are active members of security threat groups?

Taking the view that prison gang inmates can be treated as high needs offenders, the Correctional Service of Canada has attempted to put them through the traditional case management process, and some programming has met with success (Di Placido et al. 2006). In a well-designed retrospective study, Di Placido and her colleagues matched forty treated gang members with equal numbers of non-treated gang members, treated non-gang members and non-treated non-gang members. The study used inmates from Canada's Prairie-based federal penitentiaries, and used mostly Aboriginal street gang members for its gang samples. Programming consisted of cognitive-behavioural programming in anger management, sex offender treatment and psychiatric rehabilitation. They were followed up after programming to assess institutional behaviour and then after release for reoffence. Declines were observed in institutional misconduct for the treated gang group. Results showed the treated non-gang group recidivated the least, followed by the treated gang group. The non-treated gang group did the worst.

Cognitive behavioural treatment (CBT) can be thought of as a mainstream approach to programming for offenders, and likely is Eurocentric in its view of Canadian society and the goals and objectives of a primarily white, male culture. For instance, it is highly unlikely that individuals who identify themselves as connected to Indigenous communities would conceive of cognition or behaviour as something individual (a European innovation) as opposed to collective (as in Aboriginal traditions, which emphasize the communal interest). How likely is it, then, that CBT is culturally sensitive to the needs and aspirations of Aboriginal offenders? Andrews and Bonta (2006), two proponents of CBT, argue that such treatment will work regardless of structural or individual level influences of gender and race, so long as the programs are sound in design and operation. They do not dispute that incorporating gender sensitive or culturally sensitive pieces might help, but insist that unless needs such as education, employment, peer influence, attitudes and addictions are targeted, additional socio-cultural features will not matter.

Given the high over-representation and recidivism of Aboriginal peoples in custody (Perreault 2009), some investigators argue that to be effective, gang treatment must take into account colonization and the historical problems encountered by Aboriginal peoples. Bracken and his colleagues (2009) observe that Aboriginal peoples are socially and economically marginalized as evidenced by their lower life expectancy, higher death rates through injury and suicide, lower average incomes and higher unemployment rates. Much of this is attributed to colonization, suppression of Aboriginals by the dominant group through institutional means such as treaties and the reserve system and active efforts to undermine or destroy indigenous culture by devices such as the residential school system (Hamilton and Sinclair 1991). The criminal justice system is another mechanism of suppression, and the over-representation of Aboriginals in the system has been well established for some time by various government inquiries (Hamilton and Sinclair 1991; RCAP 1996) and regularly reported, government-kept official statistics (Perreault 2009). For example, in 2007–2008 Aboriginal Canadians made up only 3 percent of the adult Canadian population, but comprised 22 percent of all admissions to custody. In Manitoba, Aboriginals make up 12 percent of the population and 66 to 69 percent of admissions to remand or sentenced custody. Thought of another way, an Aboriginal person is over five times as likely to be incarcerated as is a non-Aboriginal person.

To be effective, Bracken, Morrissette and Deane (2009) argue that treatment must take into account the effects of colonization, and they argue for the use of the gang dynamic to effect treatment. They report on a community-based program, Ogijiita Pimatiswin Kinamatiwin (OPK), that involves members of the same gang housed under one roof in Winnipeg's inner city. An ex-gang member runs the program. The impetus for this program came from senior gang members who wished to help some of their peers leave the gang life. Thus, the participants in OPK have a sense of collective belonging that links their past to their future — the connection to the gang persists, but illegal future behaviours are discouraged. Beginning in 2001, the program has provided carpentry training and referral to educational opportunities. By the end of 2007 the program had worked with fifty gang members. Bracken, Morrissette and Deane explain the program as follows:

> OPK seeks to work with gang members to manage the harmful effects of colonization. It works to address the issues of structure, culture and biography as these relate to the gang members wishing to desist. Participants in OPK must cognitively and emotionally come to terms with their position as colonized people within Canadian society. This intrapersonal and social transformation may be described as symbolic healing or decolonization. (Bracken et al. 2009: 69)

Among thirty-four participants between 2001 and 2006, there were no reconvictions for gang-related offences, although there were some arrests for parole violations, domestic violence and minor assaults (Deane, Bracken and Morrissette 2007). The authors do not provide more detailed statistics.

Using the gang dynamic in a supportive manner is certainly appealing in the abstract. Indeed, the notion of older gang members trying to help younger members leave the gang appears quite noble and empowering from a justice perspective. Yet the use of the gang dynamic, other than the OPK program, is not supported by other program outcomes. In the city of Winnipeg, one infamous example involves the Paa Pii Wak halfway house (*Winnipeg Free Press* 2009). Paa Pii Wak opened in 2003 and was originally intended to deliver culturally sensitive Aboriginal treatment and healing. One of the strengths of their programming was the inclusion of ex-gang members amongst staff. The program was abruptly shut down in 2009 after a police investigation revealed gang activity and drug dealing were occurring within the halfway house. Nine staff members and clients were arrested. Offenders and ex-offenders involved included high ranking members of the Manitoba Warriors, who had taken over the halfway house and restricted entry to non-gang members.

Klein and Maxon (cited in Bracken et al. 2009) acknowledge that gangs form an "oppositional culture" that allows them to justify their anti-social actions because of their "victim status" — that is, those who are disadvantaged by race, low socioeconomic status or weak family support. This is particularly troubling as some observers suggest that offenders generally do not fare well if treated within a group of similar individuals. Putting groups of offenders into the same treatment regime can have counter-productive effects (Arnold and Hughes 1999; Dishion, McCord and Poulin 1999; Mathys and Born 2009). Inmate groups have been found to reinforce negative ideas and behaviours, promoting misconduct.

In summary, very little strong research is available on the outcomes of prison gang strategies. There is a particular dearth of study on treatment interventions directed at prison gang inmates. Prison gang members appear treatable, but there is some question as to whether treating them as one entity is an effective method. The results of OPK are limited and the Paa Pii Wak debacle suggests that group treatment may not be an effective intervention and, in fact, can be counter-productive. We assess the Minobimasdiziwin prison gang program run at the provincial Headingley Correctional Centre (HCC) in Manitoba. Like OPK, this program is aimed at gang members who are treated as one gang group at a time. Unlike the OPK study, we utilize a research design incorporating matched controls and a substantial follow-up period.

PROGRAM DESCRIPTION: THE MINOBIMASDIZIWIN ("GOOD LIFE") PROGRAM

The Minobimasdiziwin program was created by Manitoba Corrections in response to the increased number of street gang members, the increase in gang-related crimes, the public profile of gangs, the increased presence of gang members within correctional centres in Manitoba and the security threat they pose within correctional institutions. The program was designed to complement the provincial Institutional Gang Management Strategy already in place in correctional centres. The Minobimasdiziwin program is part of a wider strategy to reduce the threat posed to society by street gang members. As an intervention program, it is an important piece in a continuum of prevention, intervention and suppression activities by the Manitoba government to address gang-related activity.

The Minobimasdiziwin program takes place over the course of seven weeks, Monday through Friday, every morning or afternoon for two hours. The objectives of the intervention program are to bring about a positive change in criminal attitudes over the duration of the program, enhance personal motivation and self-confidence in the ability to change, to establish links with external agency supports available to gang members in the community and reduce the likelihood of re-involvement with the criminal justice system after gang members' release from custody. This is accomplished by utilizing the combined resources and skills of trained, experienced corrections staff, community agencies and Aboriginal spiritual care providers and healers, all of whom follow a structured program design. The program combines the well-regarded criminogenic needs approach with traditional Aboriginal cultural teachings to provide an intervention to primarily Aboriginal gang groups.

The title *Minobimasdizwin*, literally translated from Ojibway, means the "good life." Originally called "the gang program" when it was first offered, it was a challenge getting voluntary participants and those who attended were often immediately defensive. Any perceived change in pro-criminal, pro-gang thinking could result in ridicule and the real threat of violence. Indeed, any program participant who revealed during a one-on-one session that they were intent on leaving the gang were advised not to renounce until they were out of custody. Happily, this did not continue and the program appeared to develop a good reputation amongst the inmates.

To date, seven sessions of Minobimasdiziwin have been run.

ASSESSING MINOBIMASDIZIWIN

Process Indicators

Our study incorporated features of both process and outcome evaluation (Rossi, Lipsey and Freeman 2004). The process portion assessed participant feedback: the program materials, the facilitator's performance and participant perceptions of self-change. Participant data were obtained by requesting program input from them at the end of the program using an anonymous (but supervised) self-administered paper and pencil questionnaire comprised of forty questions, measured on a five-point Likert scale. The scale response options (not at all, very little, somewhat, a fair amount or a great deal) were scored and, if required, inverted so that a higher score could always be interpreted as a positive reflection for ease of interpretation (coded to the positive).

In addition, two standardized measures of attitudinal change were administered to assess whether or not the program participants' anti-social feelings changed in a measurable way. Specifically, two measures of criminal attitudes and orientation, the Criminal Sentiments Scale–Modified (CSS–M) (Simourd 1997) and the Pride In Delinquency (PID) scale (Shields and Whitehall 1991), were administered on three occasions: pre-program, mid-program and post-program. The CSS–M is a three-point Likert-type scale that measures anti-social attitudes, values and beliefs directly related to criminal activity. It consists of forty-one items grouped into five sub-scales: attitudes towards the law (such as, "pretty well all laws deserve our respect"), courts (such as, "almost any jury can be fixed") and the police (such as, "the police are honest"), tolerance for law violations (such as, "a hungry man has the right to steal") and identification with criminals (such as, "people who have broken the law have the same sorts of ideas about life as me"). To score the CSS–M, each endorsement of an anti-social statement (or rejection of a pro-social one) yields two points, whereas rejection of an anti-social statement (or acceptance of a pro-social one) yields a score of zero. Undecided responses are scored as one. Thus, higher scores reflect the presence of greater criminal attitudes, values and beliefs.

The PID scale was used to complement the CSS–M as a measure of criminal attitudes. The PID is a ten-item self-report instrument scored on a 21-point Likert-type scale from −10 to +10. Negative numbers (−1 to −10) indicate the respondent would feel badly about committing the behaviour, and positive numbers (+1 to +10) mean that the subject would be proud of committing the behaviour. Scores of zero indicate the subject is undecided. Higher scores, therefore, indicate greater criminal attitudes.

Program Participants

Data for the program groups allowed for up to fifty-four respondents to assess process indicators such as satisfaction and attitude change. There were forty-three inmates available as a comparison group. The subject group averaged 24.2 years of age (sd = 3.3), Aboriginal gang members made up the bulk of the study group (82.7 percent), and they averaged fifteen prior convictions (sd = 9.2).

Controls

A matched control group of thirty-eight gang members not taking the Minobimasdiziwin program was constructed based on prior convictions, age and ethnicity. The comparison group was put in place to assess program effects on recidivism as rigorously as possible. Process measures such as facilitator assessment and pre-/post-attitudinal measures have their place in evaluation, but behavioural indicators are crucial to effective program assessment (Farrington 2006). The comparison group was also quite young, mostly Aboriginal and had a high number of prior convictions, essentially matching the test group.[1]

Recidivism

Recidivism outcomes were obtained by tracking participant repeat contact with the justice system after their re-entry into the community on the basis of new convictions and readmission to sentenced custody. Reoffence was also classified by severity and violence. Each gang member was primarily tracked using the Manitoba Corrections Offender Management System (COMS), a provincial automated file system that records each inmate admission and relevant background demographic data and legal information, such as new charges. Because COMS only counts admissions to Manitoba provincial custody, the RCMP criminal record check system (Canadian Police Information

Centre, or CPIC) was used to ensure crimes outside the province (or that did not involve custody) were counted.

Dropouts

Evaluations of programs are often hampered by large numbers of program dropouts. It is difficult to conclude that a program is effective if few participants complete it. Data gathered from "did not completes" are not included in the overall analyses, but dropping out is not considered a large problem in our study. The dropout rate of seven previously offered sessions averaged 33 percent (26/72), ranging from a high of 60 percent to a low of 14 percent. People did not complete for a variety of reasons, but it is important to note that most often offenders were obliged to quit because of an imposed change in institutional or legal status, that is, they were transferred, sentenced or released. In other words, very few dropped out because of a lack of program interest.

EFFECTIVENESS OF MINOBIMASDIZIWIN

Participant Feedback

The mean scores received from participants at the end of the seventh offering of the Minobimasdiziwin program are reported in Table 1. These results indicate the offenders, on average, perceived that the program facilitators did a very good job of presenting materials, that the participants understood the program material and that, most importantly, at the program's end they felt the material helped them understand why they get involved in crime and the cost of crime and taught them specific skills to reduce the probability of future criminal behaviour. Ratings over 4 on a 5-point scale reflect strong approval. The program average range of 4 to 4.3 is most acceptable. Scores indicate an obvious improvement from the start of the program (3.4) and generally strong performance in almost all groups. The participant evaluation results show that the Minobimasdiziwin program is positively perceived by those who complete it. The process evaluation results are particularly

Table 1: Participant Program Assessment by Program Group

	HCC	MYC	MYC	HCC	HCC	HCC	HCC	HCC	HCC	Total Avg.
	1	1	2	2	3	4	5	6	7	
Facilitator Performance	3.2	4	3.7	4.4	4.6	4.3	4.6	4.7	4.5	4.2
Program Materials	3.5	4	3.4	4.6	4.7	4.7	4.7	4.8	4.5	4.3
Participant Change	3.3	4.1	3.2	4.3	4.3	4.2	4.3	4.2	4.4	4
Overall Score	3.4	4	3.6	4.4	4.5	4.4	4.5	4.6	4.5	4.2

Notes: HCC= Headingley Correctional Centre; MYC= Manitoba Youth Centre; N=50

encouraging because cognitive-based programs are typically quite dry, requiring innovative teaching methods, activities, exercises and videos to hold participant attention and maximize responsiveness. The cognitive behavioral treatment strategies and the participation of Aboriginal spiritual care providers and other community resources seemed to engage the participants. From a justice perspective, clearly the prison gang participants involved felt the program helped them.

Attitudinal Change

The CSS–M scores for the program participants at three points in time are displayed in Figure 1. The results show that all of the program groups with the exception of the most recent young offender group reported a decrease in their criminal attitudes over time from pre- to post-program. The average pre-program CSS–M score across all groups (N = 54) was 52.3. At mid-program the average was 46.5, and at program's end it measured 40. The drop in criminal sentiments from pre- to post-program was statistically significant, whereas the decrease from start to mid-point and from mid-point to end were not. Figure 1 also displays the variation across program groups. As might be expected, the youth gang members' criminal sentiments pre-program scores were lower than adults', indicating anti-social attitudes are well entrenched as older gang members at HCC.

There were a couple of exceptions to otherwise quite remarkable overall positive results. For instance, the second time the program was offered at HCC the results showed an unexpected slight increase in criminal sentiments at the mid-point of the program, but that group did finish with a final score lower than the pre-program-assessed levels. The most recent running of the program at Manitoba Youth Centre (MYC), (identified as MYC2) had a

Figure 1: Change in Criminal Sentiment Scores of Gang Program

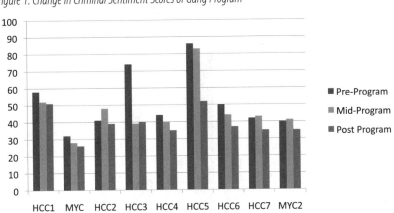

Note: N = 50

CSS–M that increased from 41 to 43 and to 46 by the end of the program. This was identified as a problematic group by program facilitators. First, all the participants were remand and quite anxious about their upcoming court cases, contributing to anxiety and perhaps a more negative view of the courts and the police (both these areas were scored exceptionally high during the post-testing). Finally, and perhaps most importantly, there was a mixing of gang members in the MYC2 program, which led to conflict and problems in running the group. This report, although anecdotal, is interesting when one considers the advice of Bracken, who believes in using a single gang dynamic to promote change. Thus, forming bonds with others in a program is likely more difficult for gang members, but with rival gangs it may well be impossible.

Figure 2 shows the self-reported PID scores across the program groups (N = 54). Again, it appears the intervention program had the desired effect of decreasing delinquent attitudes and beliefs. The average self-reported pre-program PID score was 125.9. At mid-program this score dropped to 119.1. When measured again at the end of the program it had decreased on average to 98.0. Statistically, the mean decrease from pre-program post-program was significant, as was the drop from mid-program to post-program. However, the decrease from start to mid-point was not significant. These findings are similar to the CSS–M, and suggest that the length of program is important. It takes a fair amount of time for lessons to be learned.

Once again the results varied depending on the group. Most notable are the very high PID scores of the participants who took the program in the spring of 2006 (represented by HCC5 in Figure 2). This program group was made up of only three individuals and thus they may represent an outlier. As Figure 2 shows, their PID scores were, on average, roughly three times

Figure 2: Change in Pride In Delinquency Scores of Gang Program

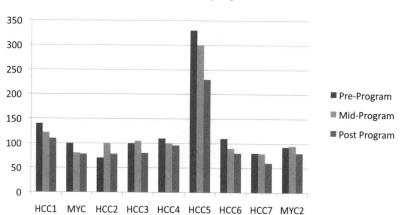

higher than any other group. Nonetheless, even these abnormally high scores dropped over the duration of the program.

Again, the PID overall positive results did not follow a uniformly consistent downward trend. Indeed, the two other groups for HCC and one group for MYC (represented by HCC2, HCC3 and MYC2 in the figures) actually expressed higher PID scores at mid-program. Their scores ultimately declined below pre-program levels, but this finding is perplexing. Could it be that a shorter-term program with gang members actually entrenches criminal pride? Facilitators noted that gang members will often rally their peers if their pro-gang attitudes and values are directly questioned. They have modified the program over time to emphasize the program's "good life" focus, downplaying the "gang intervention" part.

To put the decrease in criminal attitudes into perspective, the Minobimasdiziwin program graduates' scores on the PID and CSS–M were compared to those of other inmates reported in Simourd and Van de Ven (1999), which used a sample of 141 medium security inmates from a Correctional Service of Canada penitentiary in Ontario. The majority of the federal offenders were serving a term for a violent offence. Interestingly, the scores obtained post-Minobimasdiziwin program, when they were at their lowest, were still roughly double those reported by Simourd and Van de Ven. One possible explanation is that gang members have more entrenched criminal attitudes than some federal inmates. As indicated by the decrease in scores over the course of the program, and although inroads were made, the challenge of facilitating a replacement of pro-criminal attitudes, values and beliefs with more pro-community, pro-social attitudes, values and beliefs is significant. Given that entrenched attitudes are learned over a lifetime of surviving on the street and the fact that real change takes persistent effort over time, even a modest change in criminal attitudes is a significant outcome for a seven-week program.

Post-Release Reoffences

To contextualize our gang reoffence outcomes, we consider as a benchmark Manitoba Corrections' official two-year adult inmate recidivism rate of 67 percent. The Manitoba Corrections reported recidivism rate is calculated using COMS. About two-thirds of inmates released from Manitoba correctional facilities reoffend, and high-risk offenders reoffend at an even higher rate (Weinrath and Coles 2003). For youth coming out of secure custody, Manitoba Corrections reports that the rate hits 90 percent. Consequently we might expect our subject pool to engage in more frequent and serious reoffence.

We broke reconviction down by year, severity and recommitment type. First year post-release reoffence rates did not differ significantly between the treatment and control groups. About 28 percent of treatment cases reoffended, compared to 30 percent of the comparison group. By the second year, 76.8 percent of the program group had reoffended, compared to only 65.8 percent of the comparison group. These results are worse for the treatment group compared to the benchmark of 67 percent set by Manitoba Corrections. By the fifth year, 93 percent of the program group and 84 percent of the controls had reoffended. The differences are generally small and none of them were statistically significant.

Violence counts were lower but we observed the same pattern of small or trivial differences. A total of 28 percent of the treatment group were newly convicted for violence, compared to 29 percent of the comparison group. Reconviction for crimes against the person increased to 38 percent by the second year and 54 percent by the fifth year of treatment, not much different from the comparison group (37 percent and 53 percent year, respectively).

Readmissions were approximately 53 percent for both groups in the first year, while 68 percent of the treatment group were readmitted by the second year compared to only 63 percent of the controls. By the fifth year, however, 93 percent of the program subjects had been readmitted compared to a lower proportion (82 percent) of the controls. None of these differences were statistically significant. This suggests that even if there is an effect from Minobimasdiziwin, it does not persist into the second year and there is little evidence of any impact by year five.

The subject pool in Figure 3 includes both adult and young offender treatment and comparison groups, possibly confounding effects. We ran separate analyses for adults and youth, but did not observe any differences. Mean reoffence differences for new criminal events were generally similar.

Figure 3: Recidivism Yes/No Percentage for New Convictions, Readmission to Custody

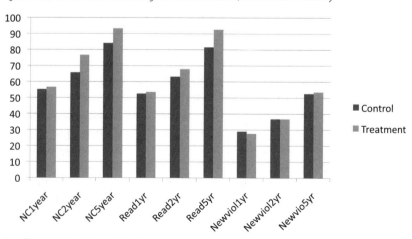

Note: Treatment N = 43; Controls N = 38

In summary, none of the differences between the treatment and comparison groups were statistically significant. Minobimasdiziwin participants were just as likely to reoffend as gang members who did not participate.

WHY CBT PROGRAMMING SEEMS TO FAIL

The Minobimasdiziwin program is perceived as a success by the gang participants. Using a mix of Aboriginal cultural teachings and cognitive skills training, the program received very favourable evaluations of facilitator performance and program content, and participants also reported that they felt the program had a good effect on them. The program also showed improvement in its administration over time, as participant impressions improved from the first few times the program was delivered. In addition, findings from two commonly used indices, the CSS–M and the PID, indicate that the Minobimasdiziwin program can effect short-term change in the anti-social values and attitudes of the gang members who complete it.

Despite positive perceptions of the program and the improvement in pro-social attitudes, the quantitative analysis of post-release outcomes displays relatively high recidivism rates for participants, which indicates that attending the program did not help gang members avoid future problems with the law. Even when contrasted with a matched control group who received no specialized training, the program appeared to make no difference in time to failure, severity of convictions or readmission to custody.

There are a number of potential explanations for program failure. It might be that the comparison group was not truly comparable, that something was perhaps not considered during the matching process. It is also a possibility that the program worked well within the institution, but the lure of the gang and a lack of proper follow-up on release attenuated Minobimasdiziwin effects. Inmates may have left prison with the best intentions but were not able to maintain their motivation when they encountered similar social circumstances and old gang mates. It may be that the program did not have much impact because it was operated in a correctional facility instead of the community, a perennial problem with correctional treatment (Andrews et al. 1990). Not only prison gang culture, but the inmate culture generally and the oppressive institutional routine may have impaired program efficacy. Finally (and more cynically), it may be that prison gang members are simply quite resistant to treatment, but they might go through the motions in a correctional centre program for something to do or to gain some credits towards early release. The preliminary results from OPK suggest that the community may be a more effective setting when working with gang members.

The difficulty with most of these explanations for the failure of Minobimasdiziwin failure is that we must consider that the Correctional Service of Canada (CSC) has managed some success with gang inmates using cognitive behavioural programming that was run in a penitentiary setting (Di Placido et al. 2006). While we do not have the data to do a direct comparison of inmate groups, their inmate gang participants are all serving more than two years, while Headingley Correctional Centre deals with provincial inmates serving less than two years, or remand inmates accused of crimes. It is difficult to accept that CSC benefited from dealing with low-risk inmates; if anything they were likely high-risk inmates. An important discrepancy to consider is the greater length of the CSC programs (six to eight months compared to Minobimasdiziwin's seven weeks). In addition, because provincial inmates are serving short sentences or on remand (which often is short term) they may not have the same amount of time to contemplate and invest in individual change.

The most salient distinction we observe, however, is the breakup of gang members into different program groups for CSC, while Manitoba Corrections attempted to deal with most gangs as single units. As the literature suggests, using offender peer groups for programming is fraught with peril. Isolating gang members on the same unit and then having them take a program together pits their treatment regime directly against their oppositional gang culture, a formidable task. The Winnipeg experience with the Paa Pii Wak halfway house is illustrative of the types of problems that can result. Even the OPK program we discussed earlier had gang members mix with other community members in their program, thereby exposing them to other, more pro-social perspectives on the world.

CONCLUSION

Our findings have implications for program evaluation research. Results reinforce the importance of long-term quantitative outcome measures. Scholars such as Farrington are quite correct when they insist that process indicators of program success must be viewed cautiously (Farrington 2006). Subjects may well demonstrate that they have learned program materials, developed skills and feel positive towards a program upon completion, but this may have a negligible relation to how they behave subsequently. Indeed, the Minobimasdiziwin evaluation was well designed; use of participant perceptions to improve programs is necessary and useful for program fine-tuning, while the use of pre-/post-psychometric scales to measure attitudinal changes is a strong design feature. Were one to simply use these process measures as markers for program success, however, they would quite clearly have been misleading in this case. The Minobimasdiziwin program might illustrate the classic difference between "what they say" and "what they do" and strongly supports the use of experimental design in program evaluation.

Managing inmate gangs in the prison presents formidable challenges. If a gang is confined to one unit to safeguard other inmates, this limits their opportunity to receive effective programming. There is not much opportunity for any gang members who wish to improve themselves or plan for release in such a setting. In a sense, the corrections system has given up on these inmates, and justice is limited to a punitive response. Isolation of gangs should be used as a last resort; otherwise dispersal and monitoring throughout a prison should be the preferred method. If justice for gang members is a chance to change, something should be provided, but a program should also have a reasonable chance of success. If justice to the public means providing opportunities for rehabilitation, then correctional administrators must work to find housing solutions for inmates and act on the best research to provide the most effective programming.[2]

Notes

1. T-tests and chi square contingency tables were run to ensure that the groups were comparable. Matching was generally very successful. There were no statistically significant differences observed.
2. As a consequence of the evaluation, Manitoba Corrections no longer operates the "Good Life" program and has looked at other types of programming for gang members.

References

Alberta Corrections. 2003. *Special Interest Offenders*. Edmonton: Alberta Solicitor General.

Andrews, D., and J. Bonta. 2006. *The Psychology of Criminal Conduct*, fourth edition. Cincinnati, OH: Anderson.

Andrews, D., I. Zinger, R. Hoge, J. Bonta, P. Gendreau, and F. Cullen. 1990. "Does Correctional Treatment Work? A Clinically Relevant and Psychologically Informed Meta-Analysis." *Criminology* 28.

Arnold, M., and J. Hughes. 1999. "First Do No Harm: Adverse Effects of Grouping Deviant Youth for Skills Training." *Journal of School Psychology* 37.

Bracken, D., L. Deane and L. Morrissette. 2007. "Desistance Within an Urban Aboriginal Gang." *Probation Journal* 54.

___. 2009. "Desistance and Social Marginalization: The Case of Canadian Aboriginal Offenders." *Theoretical Criminology* 13, 1.

Braithwaite, J. 1989. *Reintegrative Shaming*. New York, NY: Cambridge University Press.

Byrne, J., and D. Hummer. 2007. "Myths and Realities of Prison Violence: A Review of the Evidence." *Victims and Offenders* 2,

Bourgon, G., and B. Armstrong. 2005. "Transferring the Principles of Effective Treatment into a 'Real World' Prison Setting." *Criminal Justice and Behavior* 32.

Cunningham, M., and J. Sorensen. 2007. "Predictive Factors for Violent Misconduct in Close Custody." *Prison Journal* 87.

Decker, S. 2003. *Understanding Gangs and Gang Processes*. Richmond, KY: Eastern Kentucky University.

DeLisi, M, M. Berg, and A. Hochstetler. 2004. "Gang Members, Career Criminals and Prison Violence: Futher Specification of the Importation Model of Inmate Behavior." *Criminal Justice Studies* 17.

Di Placido, C., T. Simon, and T. Witte. 2006. "Treatment of Gang Members Can Reduce Recidivism and Institutional Misconduct." *Law and Human Behavior* 30.

Dishion, T., J. McCord, and F. Poulin. 1999. "When Interventions Harm: Peer Groups and Problem Behavior." *American Psychologist* 54.

Farrington, D. 2006. "Methodological Quality and Evaluation of Anti-Crime Programs." *Journal of Experimental Criminology* 2.

Leger, S. 2003. *Criminal Organizations: Identification and Management of Gangs and Criminal Organizations in CSC (Permanent Briefing Book)*. Ottawa, ON: Correctional Service of Canada.

Gaes G., S. Wallace, E. Gilman, J. Klein-Saffran, and S. Suppa. 2002. "The Influence of Prison Gang Affiliation on Violence and other Prison Misconduct." *Prison Journal* 82.

Grekul, J., and P. Laboucane-Benson. 2008. "Aboriginal Gangs and Their (Dis) Placement: Contextualizing Recruitment, Membership, and Status." *Canadian Journal of Criminology and Criminal Justice* 50.

Griffin, M., and J. Hepburn. 2006. "The Effect of Gang Affiliation on Violent Misconduct in the Early Years of Confinement." *Criminal Justice and Behavior* 33.

Hamilton, A., and M. Sinclair. 1991. *Report of the Aboriginal Justice Inquiry of Manitoba*. Winnipeg, MB: Government of Manitoba.

Hughes, E. 1996. *Report of the Independent Review of the Circumstances Surrounding the April 25–26, 1996 Riot at the Headingley Correctional Institution*. Winnipeg, MB: Manitoba Justice.

Jones, D., V. Roper, Y. Stys and C. Wilson. 2004. *Street Gangs: A Review of Theory, Interventions and Implications for Corrections*. Ottawa, ON: Correctional Service of Canada.

Kelly, K., and T. Caputo. 2005. "The Linkages Between Street Gangs and Organized Crime: The Canadian Experience." *Journal of Gang Research* 13.

MacKenzie, D. 2006. *What Works in Corrections*. New York, NY: Cambridge University Press.

Mathys C., and M. Born. 2009. "Intervention in Juvenile Delinquency: Danger of Iatrogenic Effects?" Children and Youth Services Review 31.

Nafekh, M. 2002. *An Examination of Youth and Gang Affiliation within the Federally Sentenced Aboriginal Population*. Ottawa: Correctional Service of Canada, Research Branch.

Nafekh M., and Y. Stys. 2004. *A Profile and Examination of Gang Affiliation Within the Federally Sentenced Offender Population*. No R-154 Research Branch, Ottawa: ON: Correctional Service of Canada.

Perreault, S. 2009. "The Incarceration of Aboriginal People in Adult Correctional Services." *Juristat* 29, 3 (July). Ottawa: Statistics Canada.

Rivera, B., E. Cowles, and L. Dorman. 2003. "An Exploratory Study of Institutional Change: Personal Control and Environmental Satisfaction in a Gang-Free Prison." *The Prison Journal* 83.

Roberts, J. 2005. *Literature Review on Public Opinion and Corrections: Recent Findings in Canada*. Ottawa, ON: Correctional Service of Canada.

Roberts, J., and M. Hough. 2005. "The State of the Prisons: Exploring Public Knowledge and Opinion." *The Howard Journal* 44.

Rossi, P., M. Lipsey, and H. Freeman. 2004. *Evaluation: A Systematic Approach*, seventh edition. Los Angeles: Sage.

Royal Commission on Aboriginal Peoples. 1996. Ottawa: Minister of Supply and Services.

Ruddell, R., S.H. Decker, and E.J. Arlen. 2006. "Gang Interventions in Jails." *Criminal Justice Review* 31.

Sherman, L. 1993. "Defiance, Deterrence, and Irrelevance: A Theory of the Criminal Sanction." *Journal of Research in Crime and Delinquency* 30.

Shields, I.W., and G.C. Whitehall. 1991. "The Pride in Delinquency Scale." Paper presented at the Eastern Ontario Correctional Psychologists' Winter Conference, Burritts Rapids, Canada.

Simourd, D. 1997. The Criminal Sentiments Scale – Modified and Pride in Delinquency Scale. Criminal Justice and Behaviour, 24, 1.

Simourd, D., and J. Van de Ven. 1999. "Assessment of Criminal Attitudes: Criterion-related Validity of the Criminal Sentiments Scale–Modified and Pride in Delinquency Scale." *Criminal Justice and Behaviour* 26.

Toller, W., and B. Tsagaris. 1996. "Managing Institutional Gangs — A Practical Approach Combining Security and Human Services." *Corrections Today* 58.

Vittori, J. 2007. "The Gang's All Here: The Globalization of Gang Activity." *Journal of Gang Research* 14.

Weinrath, M., M. Swait and T. Markesteyn. 1999. "A Comparison of Prison Gang Members and Non-Members in a Western Canadian Province." Paper presented at the annual meetings of the American Society of Criminology, Boston, MA.

Weinrath, M., and R. Coles. 2003. "Third Generation Prison Classification: The Manitoba Case." *Criminal Justice Studies* 16.

Winnipeg Free Press. 2009. "The Case Against Paa Pii Wak." At <winnipegfreepress. com/breaking news/the-case-against-Paa-Pii-Wak-39486767.html>.

Zaitzow, B., and J. Houston. 1999. "Prison Gangs: The North Carolina Experience." *Journal of Gang Research* 6.

CHAPTER TWO

EXTRA-LEGAL POLICE POWERS IN CANADA

The Rule of Law and the Enigma of Retroactive Decision Making

Glen Luther

> Certainly there can be no rational ground for asserting that a man can have a moral obligation to obey a legal rule that does not exist, or is kept secret from him, or that came into existence only after he acted, or was unintelligible, or was contradicted by another rule of the same system, or commanded the impossible, or changed every minute. (Fuller 1969: 39)

Canadian law is seen around the world as a generally fair and just system. This is in large part because Canadians believe strongly in the rule of law as admirably described above by Lon L. Fuller. Our law is in fact a combination of two kinds of law. There are statutes and regulations passed by legislatures, including the federal Parliament (statutory law). This is combined with the common law, which is law as interpreted by judges in their written decisions, which form the integral parts of our legal system. The judiciary, through its decisions, is tasked with interpreting statutory law. Yet as nations such as Canada have drafted constitutions, the judiciary has been required by those same documents to give content to rights (such as the right to be free from unreasonable search and seizure). It is the judicial discretion to interpret laws and give content to rights that gives rise to challenges by legal scholars and some judges in terms of the Court's legitimacy and its role in the apparatus of justice. What should a court's role be in this constitutional complex? Do the limits of justice itself require courts to restrain their own discretion? What do we as Canadians believe about the Court's ability to make law through its decisions? Canadian judges, of course, are appointed by our governments and are by their nature elites in that they are all senior lawyers and mostly male (though this is beginning to change). What then gives judges the right to make laws in a democratic country like Canada?

I am a criminal lawyer and law professor. I am interested, in particular, in police powers in Canada. The police, like other state actors, are bound by the laws of the land (what we lawyers refer to as the "rule of law," which denotes that the government is as bound by these rules as laypersons). When the police act, the legitimacy of their actions will, naturally, in a democracy like Canada, be governed by the rule of law and depend on whether or not they acted in accordance with the law. Indeed, the Supreme Court of Canada has recently confirmed that police action that is illegal will be, as a result, unconstitutional (*R. v. Grant* 2009: para. 54). Unfortunately, as I will attempt to show, the law in Canada concerning police powers is often judge-made law and, as such, police actions have often been brought to courts where accused persons and others have questioned how a police power could have been lawful when no express law authorized the police action. In other words, the actions of police are being validated *as lawful through after-the-fact judicial decision making.* This can be construed as court action that takes the place of the legislative role, leaving us to question whether justice in Canada is served when unelected officials effectively make law.

THE KNOWLTON/RUSSIAN PREMIER CASE

I will start with an example that, while occurring in 1971, is a current and important example given recent Canadian events surrounding both the Vancouver Winter Olympics of 2010 and the even more recent G8/G20 summit held in the summer of 2010 in Huntsville and Toronto. In 1971 the premier of the then U.S.S.R. was visiting Canada. While in Ottawa, the premier was assaulted, an incident that was widely broadcast on Canadian television. Several days later, the premier was to visit a well-known and centrally located hotel in Edmonton. The police in Edmonton, being concerned about the previous week's incident in Ottawa, decided to fence off a small part of downtown Edmonton surrounding the hotel. No law was passed by any government allowing this state action. Nonetheless, the police concerns were real (as evidenced by the Ottawa incident), and it was surely imperative that Canada's international guest be protected. It seemed a reasonable and suitably tailored measure to block off a one-block area of the city to protect this important guest. Certainly no one in government showed any concern with the police actions.

On the other hand, Mr. Knowlton, being an apparently ordinary and law-abiding Edmonton citizen, was concerned with the police decision and the fact that no law authorized blocking off the street. To Mr. Knowlton the fence the police had erected limited his right to walk on the public street. He said he wished to take photographs of the premier, and he decided he wanted to take his pictures from along the street the police had blocked. It appears he had no nefarious intent, and there was no evidence that he was intending to harm the premier in any way. The police, though, were insistent that Knowlton was not allowed on that particular street, and they arrested him and charged him with "wilfully obstructing a police officer in the execution of duty" as he had refused to listen when told he was not allowed to cross the barrier. The legal issue in Mr. Knowlton's case was thus whether the police officer was acting in the execution of duty when he instructed Mr. Knowlton not to cross the police-erected barricade.

As you think of this incident, consider the two sides of the case. The police argued that they had a duty to protect the premier of Russia and that their decision to erect the barrier was a reasonable way to do that. Mr. Knowlton argued that no law allowed the police to act as they did and, as a law-abiding and peaceful citizen, he was entitled to walk down a public street in a Canadian city. The case ended up in the Supreme Court of Canada, Canada's highest court (*R. v. Knowlton* 1974). It should be noted that it is unquestioned that the police have several legal duties that are in fact set out in statute form and passed by legislatures. Both the RCMP and city police forces are governed by police acts that, while varying in detail, generally describe those duties as requiring the police to act "for the preservation of peace, order and public safety, the enforcement of law and the prevention of crime" (*Alberta Police Act* c. 85. s. 26(1)). These general duties are perhaps non-controversial and necessary. How, though, do these general duties translate into a specific power to close a public street and to direct a citizen not to enter a certain area?

The Supreme Court of Canada had the final say and, to them, the common law authorized the police to act as they did. While the judges agreed that no statute or other written law specifically authorized the erection of the barrier, the police action was reasonable in the circumstances as being in accordance with their general duties to keep the peace, which here required that they protect the premier. The Court unanimously held that such an action was therefore justified in the circumstances. One way to read the decision is to say that the Court saw Mr. Knowlton's actions as quite unreasonable and thus his refusal to follow the police direction not to enter the restricted area was unlawful (also see *Ghani v. Jones* 1969).

Our Court relied upon an earlier English Court of Criminal Appeal decision, *R. v. Waterfield* (1963). That case spawned what has become known as "the Waterfield test" for the creation of police powers at common law (that is, judge-made police powers). The Supreme Court described the test in its decision in *Knowlton*:

> The police having interfered with the liberty of the appellant, or more precisely, with his right to circulate freely on a public street, the questions to be determined are, as formulated by the Court of Criminal Appeals in *Regina v. Waterfield and Another* [1964: 164 at 170] whether such conduct of the police falls within the general scope

of any duty imposed by statute or recognized at common law and whether such conduct, albeit within the general scope of such a duty, involved an unjustifiable use of powers associated with the duty.

The problem presented, though, is that the Court did not set out when the police could take such action, only that in the circumstances what the police did was, in their view, reasonable and justifiable. Would they have the same power if the premier had not been assaulted a week earlier in Ottawa? Would they be entitled to take the same action if the visitor was not of such political high standing but rather was an American movie star, for example? Such questions were neither posed nor answered.[1]

THE CHARTER AND ITS IMPACT

In 1982 Canada adopted the *Charter of Rights and Freedoms,* which enshrined the rights of Canadians in a supreme law and which includes the right not to be arbitrarily detained or imprisoned (Part 1 of the *Constitution Act, 1982.*). Therefore, Mr. Knowlton's argument appeared to have now been granted constitutional status. The Supreme Court made clear early in its interpretation that the Charter was and is intended to act as a check on state power and is not a grant of power to the state (see *Hunter v. Southam Inc.* [1984] 2 S.C.R. 145). The Charter did, however, mean that the lawfulness of police power would be an issue in many more cases than it was before the Charter's enactment. This was because now when the police acted unlawfully toward an accused person (and thereby breached their Charter rights), the accused could apply to the Court under s. 24 of the Charter for an "appropriate remedy," including the very powerful remedy set out specifically in sub-section 24(2) to exclude evidence where its admission into a criminal trial could bring the administration of justice into disrepute. This meant that in many cases the accused would be newly empowered to argue that the actions of the police were illegal and that the accused should be found not guilty because of that fact alone.[2]

For example, soon after the Charter came into effect, in *R. v. Dedman* (1985), the accused argued that he should be acquitted of impaired driving because the police stopped him in a checkstop for which the police had no statutory authority allowing cars to be stopped at random. On the other hand, the evidence before the Court was that Canadians believed in the need for impaired driving checkstops. Why then did Parliament not enact such a power before the Supreme Court was asked in the Dedman case to consider the question? It is significant to note that, by and large (at least prior to 1982), police powers to arrest and detain people were largely limited to situations where the police had formed a reasonable belief that a specific individual had committed an offence. Where the police have such a belief they may arrest that person and charge them with an offence (*Criminal Code*, 1985, s. 495). Where the police do not have such a belief the law had long assumed that the individual had the "right to be let alone." The Dedman case then raised the issue as to whether or not Mr. Dedman could be detained based on nothing other than the fact that he was driving a motor vehicle. At the time, the Crown argued that Dedman had stopped voluntarily when the officer waived him into the checkstop and therefore, on this argument, an issue of police powers did not arise. In essence, the Crown argued that since he stopped voluntarily (and no force was used by the officers) he had waived any right to complain about the lack of statutory basis for the stop of his car.

The Court swiftly rejected the Crown's argument when they sensibly said that any reasonable person in Dedman's place would have felt that they had no choice to stop for the police officer when waved over to the side of the road. Therefore, no true consent was present as such police action is by its nature "coercive" and the accused's actions were not truly voluntary.[3] He was therefore "detained" within the meaning of the Charter. But the Court did not end its analysis there. The Court instead decided, based on the Waterfield test, that the police should have the power to conduct impaired driving checkstops and that therefore the police officer's actions were authorized not by statute but rather by the common law. Therefore, the Supreme Court decided that there is a police power for checkstop, as it is within the general scope of police duties and was a justifiable use of police powers associated with those duties. The important legal/political issue, however, is who should have made the decision that the police should have such power?

Police Powers, Courts and Legislators

Legislators are, of course, the elected representatives of Canadians and are constitutionally empowered to make and change laws. Courts, on the other hand, are empowered to solve disputes based on those laws. Generally, when courts make law it is a controversial thing. It seems generally true to say that legislatures are the more legitimate and proper forum for making laws. They can discuss such changes, make proposals, invite submission, commission studies and so on, so that when the majority of the legislature decides to make a change of law, in theory at least, such change has engendered discussion and is the result of deliberation by the elected representatives of the people. It is also then subject to Charter scrutiny in the courts. It appears to some judges that legislators have sometimes shied away from making controversial decisions about policing and have been prepared to let the courts do the tough slogging when it comes to difficult police power issues. As I asked above, why did Parliament not enact such a power? Certainly after the Supreme Court's decision in *Dedman* there was no perceived need for it to do so, and it is significant that it has not done so. One problem, though, concerning the

Court's judge-made law is, and remains, that it is unclear what a checkstop is and how and where it should be conducted.

Parliament has been distinctly silent about the latter issues. Therefore, cases continue to arise in which the Court is faced with deciding whether a particular police action was authorized by the decision in *Dedman*.[4] An irony of the Waterfield test is that in that particular case the Court decided that the police did not have the power to do what they did. The Court was in fact clear that its role was not to create new powers but only to decide whether a particular action by a particular police officer was lawful. The common law develops based on particular fact patterns and, as such, is retroactive in its nature in that the Court approves or disapproves of an action after the fact. Not knowing in advance whether they have a power to do a certain action must be frustrating to officers, and very likely tends to encourage officers to push the limits of their powers with the thought that if their action is later to be found to be within the scope of their general duties and justifiable, they will have then established a new police power.

The Waterfield test continues to be applied by the Supreme Court to approve of police action retroactively and appears to create new police powers in common law. In several recent cases the Supreme Court has discussed the test and applied it to new situations. In *R. v. Godoy* (1999), for example, the Court announced that there would be a power to enter a home when it was the source of a hang-up 911 call. In *R. v. Kang-Brown* (2008), a divided Court seemingly approved the power to use sniffer dogs on reasonable suspicion to detect drugs in luggage and elsewhere.[5] In *R. v. Mann* (2004) the Court created a power to "investigatively detain" persons the police reasonably suspect have a connection to a "recent or on-going offence" where it is reasonably necessary in the circumstances, and in *R. v. Clayton* (2007) the Court upheld a blockade of a parking lot's exits where the officers had a report of several individuals possessing handguns in that lot. Again, while each of these decisions might on their own be seen as sensible under the circumstances, it is the scope of the resultant powers and their application to new and different fact patterns that is unclear. It remains controversial that it was the courts that created the power and not the legislatures.

The *Mann* and *Clayton* cases are two of the most controversial of the group of cases.[6] The judges themselves have disagreed over the scope of their power to make new laws. In *Mann*, for example, the judgment of the majority of the Court was written by Justice Frank Iaccobucci. He introduced the issues before the Court as follows:

> As stated earlier, the issues in this case require the Court to balance individual liberty rights and privacy interests with a societal interest in effective policing. Absent a law to the contrary, individuals are

free to do as they please. By contrast, the police (and more broadly, the state) may act only to the extent that they are empowered to do so by law. The vibrancy of a democracy is apparent by how wisely it navigates through those critical junctures where state action intersects with, and threatens to impinge upon, individual liberties.

Nowhere do these interests collide more frequently than in the area of criminal investigation. Charter rights do not exist in a vacuum; they are animated at virtually every stage of police action. Given their mandate to investigate crime and keep the peace, police officers must be empowered to respond quickly, effectively and flexibly to the diversity of encounters experienced daily on the front lines of policing. Despite there being no formal consensus about the existence of a police power to detain for investigative purposes, several commentators note its long-standing use in Canadian policing practice (Stribopoulos 2003).

At the same time, this Court must tread softly where complex legal developments are best left to the experience and expertise of legislators. As was noted in *Watkins v. Olafson* (1989, 760):

> Major changes requiring the development of subsidiary rules and procedures relevant to their implementation are better accomplished through legislative deliberation than by judicial decree. It is for that very reason that I do not believe it appropriate for this Court to recognize a general power of detention for investigative purposes. The Court cannot, however, shy away from the task where common law rules are required to be incrementally adapted to reflect societal change. Courts, as its custodians, share responsibility for ensuring that the common law reflects current and emerging societal needs and values.... Here, our duty is to lay down the common law governing police powers of investigative detention in the particular context of this case.

Many justices believe that Parliament is best suited to make new laws, but allow for incremental law making at the level of the judiciary. However, when a court decides that in a particular case the officers had a certain power to act as they did, from that time onward and without new legislation changing the law, the police will in fact have a new power, but one that will be uncertain in scope because it was made by a judge in a very particular context. Subsequent to *Mann*, the lower courts have been struggling to discover the limits on this new power and are often disagreeing with one another on those limits.[7] Note that in Fuller's description of the rule of law given at the beginning of this chapter, the suggestion is that individuals need to know what the law is in advance. In this area, though, that is not occurring.

Even judges and law professors often disagree with each other about what a certain judgment means.

In *Clayton*, as a further example, the judges of the Supreme Court disagreed among themselves as to what their decision would mean in the future. That case involved handguns. What if the report to the police was about knives or what if the offence involved was not a violent offence but a property offence? What about a bank robbery involving a note and no weapon — are the police able to set up a roadblock? What if the report, rather than suggesting a particular parking lot, involved a whole neighbourhood? Would the Court approve of roadblocks in such circumstances? Interestingly, in a recent high-profile case involving a military officer in Ontario subsequently charged with several violent sexual assaults, the police reportedly set up a roadblock on a rural road for the sole purpose of stopping all vehicles to check the tires of each vehicle that travelled on the road as apparently distinctive tire tracks were left at one of the crime scenes (Blatchford 2010). Such police action is apparently carried out in reliance on the *Clayton* decision's power to set up roadblocks.

Again, in *Clayton*, the majority of the Court saw themselves as only approving of the particular police action at issue. Justice Rosalie Abella said about the scope of the power she had recognized:

> The determination will focus on the nature of the situation, including the seriousness of the offence, as well as on the information known to the police about the suspect or the crime, and the extent to which the detention was reasonably responsive or tailored to these circumstances, including its geographic and temporal scope. This means balancing the seriousness of the risk to public or individual safety with the liberty interests of members of the public to determine whether, given the extent of the risk, the nature of the stop is no more intrusive of liberty interests than is reasonably necessary to address the risk.

Such generalized language, especially the use of the word "reasonable," prevents an accurate assessment by the police of when they can use the power that was decided existed in *Clayton*. When is an offence "serious," when is the information sufficient, how large can the geographical and temporal scope be and when is a stop reasonably necessary?

Note another attribute of this area is that once the Supreme Court decides an issue it effectively becomes non-reviewable. When Parliament passes a new law, on the other hand, parliamentarians know that law may be challenged in court as not being in accordance with the Constitution and, therefore, courts always have the power to review legislation for constitutionality. This would seem to have a deterrent effect on Parliament. With the Court there is no review mechanism, although it is, of course, possible for Parliament to change the law again, but even then there remains the possibility for review in court. As such, the Court's decisions are in effect final and non-reviewable (except by the Court itself). The possibility of a change of legislation caused by a Supreme Court decision and the ongoing reaction of Parliament and courts to each other's decision have been labelled as the "dialogue" between the courts and legislatures (Hogg and Thornton 2001: 107).

In almost all occasions where the Court has employed the Waterfield test to create a new police power, it has rued the fact that the issue had not been dealt with by statute. Yet, in the face of a perceived failure of such parliamentary action, the Court has, for the most part, seen it as its obligation to clarify what police power exists and what police powers the courts are prepared to create and recognize. In *Dedman*, as we have seen, the Court created the power to conduct checkstops to combat impaired driving. There, Justice Dickson, in dissent, complained that this was not the Court's job but rather was a job that should be left to Parliament (*R v. Dedman* 1985, para. 24).

The Supreme Court's actions seem a bit blinkered in that it is clear that the area of arrest is largely statutory, and one wonders why the Court has never suggested that the failure to legislate should be seen as an intentional omission on the part of the legislators (which would bar action by the Court). Further, where the Court has found gaps but has not created powers at common law, especially in the area of search and seizure, Parliament has often responded by enacting statutory powers (see Fairburn 2008).[8] As well, there is now broad statutory power for courts to grant so-called general warrants. That is, there is expressly a power in an issuing court to authorize the police in a given situation to "do any thing" specified in the warrant (see Coughlan 2003). To suggest, therefore, that there is no legislative action in areas of search and seizure and in arrest and detention seems disingenuous.

There is no question that there is a substantial body of legislation in force that authorizes arrests and detentions. Yet the Supreme Court has continued to create powers at almost every turn. Recently, it appears that some members of the Court have recognized that more caution is required in this regard. For example, in *Kang-Brown*, Justice Louis LeBel, who spoke for four of the nine justices, lamented that the Court had moved away from its steadfast guardianship of the civil liberties of the accused in favour of generating new police powers.

The majority, however, seemed prepared to create new police powers. They were led by Justice Ian Binnie saying the Court had "crossed the Rubicon," by which he apparently meant that the Court should now feel its responsibility to further declare and refine police powers when it thinks it appropriate to do so (*R v. Kang-Brown* 2008 para. 22). Interestingly, Justice Binnie based his position largely on a belief that the litigants were entitled to know that a court was prepared to make law when necessary. This is quite ironic as a justification. The argument seemingly rests on the notion that there ought to be more certainty in the law, and that it should be knowable in advance. By their very nature, however, new common law powers are known to exist only after the fact, and it is the possibility of their creation that can be argued renders the law uncertain.

It appears that the Court has lost sight of what it was attempting to do in devising the Waterfield test. The current attitude seems to conflate the two branches of Waterfield into a single question that asks, "Did the police need this power to carry out their general duties?" If so, the answer seems to be that "they shall have it." This is the point made by Justice Lebel, in his dissent in *R v. Orbanski*, when he said:

> The adoption of a rule limiting *Charter* rights on the basis of what amounts to a utilitarian argument in favour of meeting the needs of police investigations through the development of common law police powers would tend to give a potentially uncontrollable scope to the doctrine developed in the *Waterfield-Dedman* line of cases, which — and we sometimes forget such details — the court that created it took care not to apply on the facts before it (*R. v. Waterfield* 1963). The doctrine would now be encapsulated in the principle that what the police need, the police get, by judicial fiat if all else fails or if the legislature finds the adoption of legislation to be unnecessary or unwarranted. The courts would limit *Charter* rights to the full extent necessary to achieve the purpose of meeting the needs of the police. The creation of and justification for the limit would arise out of an initiative of the courts. In the context of cases such as those we are considering here, this kind of judicial intervention would pre-empt any serious *Charter* review of the limits, as the limits would arise out of initiatives of the courts themselves. (*R v. Orbanski* 2005: para. 81)

It seems that such a formulation is not a "test" at all, but simply a method by which police powers will forever be extended and declared with little attention being paid to the inherent value of statutory construction and parliamentary responsibility and equally for the fundamental freedoms at stake. It is the latter that the Charter was surely designed to limit, and yet the Court's continued willingness to expand police powers seems the most distinctive feature of the Charter era.

The actions of the provincial, city and police authorities surrounding the security issues at the Vancouver 2010 Olympic Games are instructive here. As Pue and Diab (2010) argue, the gaps in police powers that surround such security issues are real, at least in the sense that the police often act in our society with apparent state and public support, but without a statutory or even common law mandate to do so. Further, it appears that some police forces have realized that it matters not what actual powers they have as long of there is the public perception that they have such powers, at least at the time of such events. Consider, for example, the Vancouver City bylaw that prohibited protest signs throughout the games. Such a bylaw is almost certainly contrary to the Charter right to freedom of speech (and one presumes will eventually be found unconstitutional), but as long as no court holds it to be so until well after the games are over, the prohibition's aim will have been achieved despite the fact that no eventual convictions will be registered in court. Further, after the G20 summit, the Toronto police apologized for over-stating their statutory power to control the perimeter of the fences surrounding the downtown meeting site (*Globe and Mail* 2010). Yet, such an acknowledgment only came about after the event was completed when it no longer would have any effect on the actions of the authorities or the protesters present at the event. It appears that neither the Ontario legislature nor the federal Parliament was willing to provide police with the powers they needed to control the barrier, so the police simply made up a power. Oddly, of course, we may find that the courts eventually and retroactively provide the very power the police concocted at the time.

SHOULD COURTS CREATE POLICE POWERS?

As I have shown, police powers created at common law raise important issues about our fundamental belief in the rule of law as a cornerstone of a modern democracy. While it is the courts that create the common law, it is in fact the unwillingness of our governments to concentrate on creating fair, comprehensive and just laws that govern what steps our police can take in carrying out their duties that has caused a problem. As it is, it is the gap between parliamentary willingness to do the job at hand and the sensitivity of the courts to criticism that they are overly protective of individual rights that leaves us with incomplete and unwritten laws granting police vague and easily justifiable powers that present a real challenge to a fair and just system. One hopes that in the future the courts will be less willing to create police powers at common law. That responsibility ought to be squarely placed on our governments, for it is they who should be prepared to take on the difficult responsibility of setting out when and how police should act. They are, after all, the ones who the electorate holds to account. The decisions of the legislators may also be scrutinized by the guardian of our civil liberties, the judiciary. Ultimately, is justice not better served when we hold fast to the checks and balances inherent in the rule of law? If courts are charged with after-the-fact approval of police powers, have we not destabilized the presumption that there is one rule that applies for all Canadians (that is, since the police are acting on the basis of law that approves its conduct that may become "made" at trial)? How can there be procedural justice when the police and citizens must guess as to the scope of state power, and when the judiciary mistakes itself for the elected official? The creation of police powers by courts destabilizes the procedures of justice that we take for granted in Canada, and it strips our Constitution of protections we thought were meaningful. How justice is practised can then have a powerful effect on issues of substance — our liberty and what we expect from our police and our judges.

Notes

1. Before the *Charter of Rights and Freedoms*, infra, was enacted, the Supreme Court of Canada relied upon *Waterfield* on several occasions to authorize police actions. See for example: *R. v. Stenning*, [1970] S.C.R. 631, *Poupart v. Lafortune*, [1974] S.C.R. 175, *Lyons v. R*, [1984] 2 S.C.R. 633, and *Reference re: Judicature Act* (Alberta), s. 27(1), [1984] 2 S.C.R. 697.

2. This is, of course, an oversimplification. While the exclusion of evidence will in some cases not result in the automatic acquittal of the accused as there may be other evidence of guilt, in most of the cases involving illegal detentions, the exclusion of the evidence, found as a result of the illegality will mean that there is no remaining evidence to prove the accused's guilt.

3. The issue of waiver of Charter rights has been oft discussed by the Supreme Court of Canada. The latest decision is that in: *R. v. Woods*, 2005 SCC 42. The related issue concerning when an accused was detained in the meaning of the Charter has engendered much case law. If an accused is not "detained" by the police the interaction has been held not to raise Charter concerns. See most recently: *Grant*, above, *R. v. Suberu* 2009 SCC 33, *R. v. Nesbeth*, 2008 ONCA 596, *R. v. Reddy*, 2010 BCCA 11 and *R. v. Davidson*, 2010 ONSC 1508.

4. See, for example, *R. v. Mellenthin*, [1992] 3 S.C.R. 615, *R. v. Ladouceur*, [1990] 1 S.C.R. 1257, *R. v. Hufsky*, [1988] 1 S.C.R. 621 and *R. v. Nolet*, 2010 SCC 24.

5. In *Kang-Brown* the Court was strongly divided and it is unclear exactly what the Court held. Four of the judges certainly were of the view that a new power should be enacted. A fifth judge also agreed generally with the powers creation although the nature of the power he recognized is considerably different from that created by the other four. See also: *R. v. A.M.*, 2008 SCC 19.

6. See also: *R. v. Orbanski; R. v. Elias*, 2005 SCC 37, where the Court created the power to conduct road side sobriety tests at common law as part of the "operability" of the impaired driving legislative scheme. The Court there further held that the common law acted as a "reasonable limit" on the right to counsel under the Charter.

7. See: *R. v. Yeh*, 2009 SKCA 112, *Reddy*, above and *Nesbeth*, above.

8. In the article, Fairburn traces how ss. 184.2, 487.01, 492.2, 492.1, 487.05, and 487.092 were all enacted in response to court decisions in which police were found not to have had the power to do what they had done.

References

Alberta Police Act, S.A. 1971, c. 85.

Blatchford, C. 2010. "The Case Against the Colonel: 'Lingerie Break-Ins' and a 'Treasure Trove' of Photo Evidence." *Globe and Mail*, February 10.

Charter of Rights and Freedoms, Part 1 of the *Constitution Act, 1982*, being Schedule B to the *Canada Act 1982* (U.K.), 1982, c. 11.

Coughlan, S. 2003. "General Warrants at the Crossroads: Limit or Licence?" 10 C.R. (6th) 269.

Criminal Code, R.S.C. 1985, c. C-46

Fairburn, M. 2008. "Twenty-Five Years in Search of a Reasonable Approach." 40 SCLR 55.

Fuller, Lon. L. 1969. *The Morality of Law*, revised ed. London: Yale University Press.

Ghani v. Jones, [1969] 3 All ER 1700 (C.A.).

Globe and Mail. 2010. "Police Admit No Five-Metre Rule Existed on Security Fence Law." June 29.

Hogg, P., and A. Thornton. 2001 "The *Charter* Dialogue between Courts and Legislature." In Paul Howe and Peter H. Russell (eds.), *Judicial Power and Canadian Democracy*. Montreal and Kingston, ON: McGill-Queen's University Press.

Hunter v. Southam Inc., [1984] 2 S.C.R. 145).

Lyons v. R, [1984] 2 S.C.R. 633.

Poupart v. Lafortune, [1974] S.C.R. 175.

Pue, W., and R. Diab. 2010. "The Gap in Canadian Police Powers: Canada Needs 'Public Order Policing' Legislation." *Windsor Review of Legal and Social Issues* 28, 87.

R. v. A.M., 2008 SCC 19.

R. v. Clayton, 2007 SCC 32).

R. v. Davidson, 2010 ONSC 1508.

R. v. Dedman, [1985] 2 S.C.R. 2.

R. v. Godoy, [1999] 1 S.C.R. 311.

R. v. Grant, 2009 SCC 32.

R. v. Hufsky, [1988] 1 S.C.R. 621.

R. v. Kang-Brown, 2008 SCC 18, [2008] 1 S.C.R. 456.

R. v. Knowlton, [1974] S.C.R. 443.

R. v. Ladouceur, [1990] 1 S.C.R. 1257.

R. v. Mann, 2004 SCC 52.

R. v. Mellenthin, [1992] 3 S.C.R. 615.

R. v. Nesbeth, 2008 ONCA 596.

R. v. Nolet, 2010 SCC 24.

R. v. Orbanski; *R. v. Elias*, 2005 SCC 37.

R. v. Reddy, 2010 BCCA 11.

R. v. Salituro, [1991] 3 S.C.R. 654.

R. v. Stenning, [1970] S.C.R. 631.

R. v. Suberu 2009 SCC 33.

R. v. Waterfield, ([1963] 3 All ER 659 (C.C.A.).

R. v. Woods, 2005 SCC 42.

R. v. Yeh, 2009 SKCA 112.

Reference re: Judicature Act (Alberta), s. 27(1), [1984] 2 S.C.R. 697.

Stribopoulos, J. 2003. "A Failed Experiment? Investigative Detention: Ten Years Later." *Alberta Law Review* 41: 335.

Young, A. 1991. "All Along the Watchtower: Arbitrary Detention and the Police Function." *Osgoode Hall Law Journal* 29: 329.

Watkins v. Olafson, [1989] 2 S.C.R. 750.

CHAPTER THREE

PUNKS, FIREBUGS AND THE LAUGHING GIRL

Youth Crime Coverage in the *Winnipeg Sun*

Shannon Sampert and Robert Froese

Crime is the perfect news story. It contains all the fundamental elements of news worthiness, with obvious heroes and villains, timeliness, conflict, drama and an ultimate resolution that comes with either an arrest or a trial (Hackett and Gruneau 2000: 35). Moreover, crime stories are in ready supply and easily accessible to media outlets struggling to maintain newsroom budgets in an era of falling circulation rates and diminishing television audiences. In Winnipeg, the Winnipeg Police Service employs a media relations team that provides the media with a daily supply of media releases regarding reported crimes and arrests. However, as numerous studies (see, for example, Surette 1998; Chermak 1995; McCormick 1995) have indicated, the gatekeeping role of the police in providing information to the mainstream media about crime results in coverage of crime that is distinctly framed from a legalistic or police perspective. Moreover, the type of coverage afforded to crime often ignores its underlying factors.

This chapter examines the *Winnipeg Sun*'s coverage of crime and, more specifically, its coverage of juvenile crime in the month of May 2008. We will first outline the methodology used in the study and provide a context of the newspaper market in which the *Sun* is located. We then explore the tabloid tradition and history and its ideological underpinnings. We move onto an overview of youth crime and the legislative responses in Canada and provide an analysis of the news stories found in May, focusing on three main stories that deal with car thefts, arson crimes and the death of a Winnipeg taxi cab driver by a group of kids on a joy ride. Our findings suggest that the *Sun* employs a crime control model to youth justice that supports the police and denounces alternative forms of punishment. Moreover, the *Sun* plays a key role in blaming specific actors within the legal system, particularly the judiciary and politicians, for failing to address the issue of youth crime. By doing so, the newspaper reveals its neo-conservative ideological stance, which is supported by and supports that of traditional tabloid readership.[1]

METHODOLOGY

Using content analysis, we investigated the agenda-setting and framing functions of the *Winnipeg Sun* in the articulation of crime stories, editorials, columns and letters to the editor. We employed a 50 percent rule for inclusion in the analysis. That is, at least half of the story had to be specifically about crime in order to be included. The rationale for focusing on the month of May is three-fold. First, it represents an average month in the staffing of newspapers and police departments — it is neither during summer vacations nor during other holidays. Second, it is not a period in which great demands are made on the household budget or when there is heavy alcohol use such as the Christmas and New Year time period. Statistics Canada points to a correlation between alcohol use and crime. There is also a correlation between poverty and crime, particularly property crimes. Finally, May is not (usually) a month in which cars are left running because of low temperatures, which is common in the winter months and a precursor for vehicle thefts (Dauvergne 2008).

Content analysis is a quantitative approach that involves the systematic counting of media texts in order to provide an understanding of their "symbolic content" (Neuman 2000: 293). Inherent in this analysis is an understanding of the role of the media in agenda setting and framing issues. Agenda-setting theories suggest that more attention paid to an issue by the media will result in the public viewing that issue as important. More recently, Stuart Soroka determined that in Canada, agendas are set by different groups depending on the issue type. When the issue is about unemployment, the agenda is set by the public. When the issue is in reference to policy ideas such as the debt, the agenda is set by the government. When the issue is in reference to the sensational, the media set the agenda in providing salience to the issue (Soroka 2002: 18). Thus, in the coverage of crime, particularly sensational crime, it is often the media who determine the salience of the issue by focusing time and attention to particular stories (and, in the process, ignoring other stories).

Framing is another way in which the media influence how an issue is understood. In framing, our attention is directed "to a limited set of attributes" (Nesbitt-Larking 2007: 335). As Tuchman puts it, framing provides us with a "window on the world and the perspective it gives us" (in Nesbitt-Larking 2007: 335). Framing occurs in the type of news story used to discuss crime and who is considered a source of information. By understanding the type of story, we determine whether the information is relatively unfiltered by opinion, as would be the case in a simple news story, or if the story is heavily mediated by opinion, as would be the case of newspaper columns, letters to the editor and editorials. We argue that the *Winnipeg Sun*'s crime coverage relies heavily on mediated editorial format that frames the stories as part of the social construction of crime to amplify public outrage and create panic. Further, in relying on the police as a main source of information, the *Winnipeg Sun* naturally frames crime stories from a law-and-order perspective. Thus, media elites, in this case the columnists and the editorial writers for the *Winnipeg Sun*, advance a particular agenda on crime. In the case we will assess, youth crime is defined as an issue of importance to its news consumers.

FEAR MONGERING AND EXCOMMUNICATION: THE CREATION OF A MORAL PANIC IN THE *WINNIPEG SUN*

Soroka's analysis of the agenda-setting function of the media, particularly sensational events, dovetails somewhat with our understanding of how a moral panic is manufactured. Stan Cohen's groundbreaking work regarding the social construction of crime suggests that a "condition, episode, person or group of persons, emerges to become defined as a threat to societal values and interests" (in Feeley and Simon 2007: 41–42). When this occurs, the media respond with stereotypical news coverage, relying on experts who provide policy responses. As Feeley and Simon argue, "policy entrepreneurs have learned not only how to mobilize and amplify moral outrage in order to generate moral panics, but also how to create the conditions that gave rise to it in the first place" (2007: 43). Feeley and Simon agree that the creation of a moral panic for a policy "problem" requires "elite interest, state interest, and mass media… to work in concert to construct and to diagnose social problems, and then to prescribe solutions for them" (2007: 44).

Crime stories do more than just titillate and entertain readers. As Katz (2010: 232) outlines, they also perform as a ritual moral exercise. For Katz, the coverage of crime in the media allows the reader to reflect on the moral tale being offered. Reading the morning paper "induces the reader into a perspective useful for taking a stand on existential moral dilemmas" (Katz 2010: 235). Ruth Klinkhammer and David Taras take this further by suggesting that coverage of high profile court cases provide society with the opportunity to perform "rituals of degradation" and "ultimate acts of excommunication" (2001: 579). Because our legal system has defined boundaries and rules, deviations from those rules create societal outrage. People then "come together to express their outrage over the offense and to bear witness against the offender" and in doing so "develop a tighter bound of solidarity than existed earlier" (Erikson in Klinkhammer and Taras 2001: 576–77).

In the coverage of crime and, more specifically, youth crime in the *Winnipeg Sun*, society bears witness to the failings of the judicial system in supporting police who must deal with repeat young offenders. To do this, the *Sun* relies on what Glassner calls the "narrative techniques of fear mongering," using repetition of misinformation to support its perspective (Glassner 2004: 820). Another common narrative of fear mongering is taking isolated incidents and turning them into trends. Finally, fear mongering relies on the narrative technique of "misdirection" (Glassner 2004: 822) — one that shifts the focus away from specific culpable groups and places it on others.

The creation of the moral panic through fear mongering and excommunication occurs in the context of the *Winnipeg Sun* as a tabloid newspaper. Owned by the Sun Media chain, a subsidiary of Quebecor (Quebecor Inc. 2010), the *Sun* is one of a chain that publishes in Edmonton, Calgary, Ottawa and Toronto. The *Winnipeg Sun* began publishing in 1980 but today struggles to compete against the *Winnipeg Free Press*, a broadsheet that dominates the newspaper market in Winnipeg. In an average week, the *Free Press* publishes and circulates about 100,000 more newspapers than the *Sun*'s approximately 27,000 copies (Canadian Newspaper Association 2010: 15). The *Sun* replicates the style of journalism found in other tabloids, catering to a mostly working class audience with a "populist emphasis on the injustices done to the 'average'" reader (Shattuc in Debrix 2003: 152). Thus the choice of the *Sun* as a newspaper to study provides a window into the agenda-setting and framing of crime by a populist newspaper.

Tabloid-style newspapers have been around since the seventeenth century and style themselves after the oral traditions found in folk tales and used by the town crier (Shattuc 1997: 14). In the tabloid,

> reality must be described and truth must be revealed in a flashy, surprising, gripping, shocking, often moralizing, and sometimes anxiety-spreading manner. The reality of tabloid realism is a sensational one. But the tabloid narrative must also be made accessible to a large [number] of people. It must use images and languages that can be readily understood and easily recognized by the vast majority. (Debrix 2003: 152)

Tabloids, in maintaining accessibility to their working class demographic, rely on short sentences, with blunt words and large graphics (Forsyth 2006: 84).

What is particularly interesting about the tabloid format is its ideological underpinnings. While much has been done to examine the right-wing stance of tabloid papers in the United Kingdom, particularly in relation to the popular Rupert Murdoch-owned *Sun* tabloid, less has been written about Canada's situation. Analyses of media stories about crime have focused on the national papers (such as the *Globe and Mail* or *National Post*) or local broadsheets such as the *Toronto Star*. Quebecor-owned *Sun* papers have been largely ignored. One reason may be because their readership is low when compared to other papers in the same market base. Another reason may be that *Sun* papers are viewed as less important or "too common." Similarly, research on radio, particularly in the 1960s and 1970s, was viewed as unimportant by academic researchers because they saw it as marginal and technologically inferior to television (Hilmes 2002). However, examining the rhetorical style of the *Winnipeg Sun* is important because it does provide an understanding of the construction of crime among a specific demographic: the Winnipeg working class. Indeed, as a tabloid narrative, the *Winnipeg Sun* narrative relies on "images and languages that can be readily understood and easily recognized by the vast majority" (Debrix 2003: 152).

The rhetoric of the *Winnipeg Sun* can be viewed as "authoritarian populism." This rhetoric appeals to "competition, possessive individualism, and a them-against-us ideology." Politically conservative, the language and format privilege a "heterosexual, male, white, conservative, capitalist world view" (Hall in Shattuc 1997: 21). Moreover, tabloid texts must cater to audiences who "insist on reading stories that somehow are about them, are related to their own life work environment or cultural practices. Tabloid literature must be based on a reality-like context, something that the public has had a chance to experience" (Debrix 2003: 152).

YOUTH CRIME

Concerns about how governments control youth crime are nothing new. Controlling children and their deviant behaviour has been under discussion for centuries, with the term "juvenile delinquent" first coming into use in the eighteenth century (Smandych 2001: 11). Canada implemented its *Juvenile Delinquents Act* in 1908. In 1984, the federal Parliament passed the *Young Offenders Act* (YOA). Then, in 2003, the current *Youth Criminal Justice Act* (YCJA) came into force. The YOA was viewed by many as too soft on crime; however, under the YOA, use of courts and custody for youth had risen, and by early years of the millennium, "Canada had one of the lowest rates of youth diversion and one of the highest rates of youth custody in the world" (Bala et al. 2009: 132). The implementation of the YCJA was viewed as a political compromise that could address public concerns regarding high profile violent young offenders and the rates of incarceration for those committing non-violent offences (Bala et al. 2009: 133).

The legislative responses to youth crime in Canada are reflective of competing models of youth justice, each of which contains specific philosophical principles and responses to youth crime. The "welfare model" focuses on the needs of the youth, admonishing the police and the courts to assist and aid the young offender. The "justice model" focuses on criminal repression and "emphasizes youth procedural rights and proportional sentencing" (Corrado et al. 2010: 400). A "crime control model," like the justice model, also focuses on repression of crime but emphasizes "the protection of the public through incapacitation of young offenders and custodial sentences" (Corrado et al. 2010: 400). Deterrence is viewed as an important component of the crime control model. The crime control model's main tenet is that the state and the courts are responsible for maintaining order (Reid-McNiven 2001: 137). A "corporatist model," formulated in the 1980s, moved toward broader discretion for those working with young offenders, and it "embodies a decreased reliance on the formal criminal procedures central to the justice model" (Corrado et al. 2010: 400). A final model amalgamates the previous models under what is called a "modified justice model" and it calls for procedural fairness, the protection of society and holding young people accountable for their crimes (Corrado et al. 2010: 400). There is evidence of components of all these models in the YCJA. However, as we will show, there is a clear bias towards the justice and crime control models in the *Winnipeg Sun*'s treatment of youth crime.

Youth Crime in the Winnipeg Sun

Crime was a dominant story in the *Winnipeg Sun* in May 2008. For example, the *Sun*'s front page (which is only graphics with very limited text) featured photographs of police on five days and stories about crime on twenty-one days in May 2008 (out of a potential thirty-one days). In total, the *Winnipeg Sun* ran 337 stories in May that dealt with crime. Of the 337 items on crime, the vast majority were new stories, while 24 were written by columnists, 6 were signed editorials and there were 55 letters to the editor. Put into perspective, the *Winnipeg Free Press* published 185 items on crime including 3 columns, 3 editorials and 11 letters to the editor. It is important to remember that the *Free Press* has considerably larger column spaces than the *Sun*, indicating an even heavier proportional emphasis on crime at the *Sun*. News stories dealing with youth criminals also dominated the coverage in the *Winnipeg Sun*. In stories in which the age of the criminal is made known, almost a third dealt with young offenders (44 stories or 28.6 percent). Thus, from an agenda setting perspective, it becomes clear that the *Sun* spent a great deal of time covering crime in Winnipeg, potentially increasing its salience as a policy issue in the eyes of its readers. While we cannot make the connection between the level of the *Sun*'s attention to crime stories and Winnipeggers' interest in crime, based on the number of letters to the editor that appeared in response to crime stories, it is clear that these stories certainly resonate with many of its readers.

From a framing perspective, the *Sun* relied on the police officers as the first source quoted in more than a third of the stories that had a source (44 percent, or 93 stories). This is significant because the first source on a story

Table 1: Type of Story by Newspaper

	News Story	Letter to the Editor	Editorial	Column	Crime Stats
Winnipeg Sun	226	55	6	19	31
Winnipeg Free Press	168	11	3	3	0

provides the framework for our understanding of the story. The police were the main interpreters of the story in a plurality of the stories. The next most prevalent sources were the Crown prosecutors and the defence attorneys, who were quoted in slightly more than 7 percent of the stories each. As a result, the dominant frame of the stories in the *Sun* is one of law and order and, more specifically, a law-and-order frame that relies on crime control with a focus on protection within a judicial setting. Indeed, alternative sources such as the John Howard Society or community organizations that work with young people were not provided.

What is quite interesting is that the *Sun* clearly plays favourites in its analysis of crime. In its coverage, the *Sun*'s tone toward the police was positive, while its tone toward the justice system was quite negative.[2] In the 187 articles in which the police were identified, the *Sun*'s handling of the story was positive 26.7 percent of the time, neutral 64.7 percent and negative in just 8 percent of the stories (another 0.5 percent were considered mixed). On the other hand, in the 180 stories in which the justice system was mentioned (including coverage of trials, comments from judges and lawyers or from individuals within the justice system), 5.6 percent were positive, 38.3 percent were negative, and 51.7 percent were neutral (another 4.4 percent were considered mixed). This suggests then that the *Sun* separated the police from the machinations of the justice system, considering police actions to be relatively positive compared to the justice system. This would appear to be somewhat supportive of a crime control model, which is impatient with alternative forms of sentencing. Indeed, as articulated in the *Sun*, the current response to youth crime was viewed as revolving door justice that puts ordinary citizens and the police at risk.

Punks, Firebugs and the "Laughing Girl"
An example of this framing can be found in the May 9, 2008, coverage of a seventeen-year-old car thief who had been fitted with a GPSS anklet to track his whereabouts. Winnipeg police revealed the youth had removed the anklet. This story received extensive coverage in the *Sun*. The initial news story appeared on page four under the graphic header "Local Law & Order," a header that is regularly repeated within the *Sun*. The story described the seventeen-year-old in the first sentence as a "serial car thief." The decision to call him a serial car thief rather than a repeat offender appears deliberate because it is not in the normal lexicon to use the term "serial" when referring to a criminal unless it is in reference to a serial killer. In that same paragraph, the story detailed the youth's attempt to attack a police officer when he was arrested. Continuing in the story, reporter Chris Kitching quoted police and the police union as saying "the allegations are further proof car thieves don't care about court conditions or the well being of police or the public." Later, the reporter suggested that the police union "has repeatedly called for court

judges to keep the worst offenders in custody and federal politicians to make auto theft a standalone offence carrying serious punishment. The 'revolving door' situation is frustrating for police" (Kitching 2008b: 4).

On the next page, Tom Brodbeck's column had the headline, "Change that law: Hard-core teen car thieves need at least 10 years in boot camp." Beside the column, the *Sun* published a cartoon that depicted two young men, one who is wearing a ball and chain with the ball labelled "GPSS anklet." He is holding a screwdriver in his hand and scowling. The second young man, with his baseball cap worn backwards, is kneeling down examining the anklet and asks the question, "GPSS?" to which the other youth replies, "Greasy punk security system." Brodbeck's column echoed this framing — one that sets the police outside of the judicial system — suggesting police are in danger: "We've already had several cops hit by car thieves in stolen vehicles in recent months." Brodbeck depicts police as powerless in dealing with these types of criminals and surmised that it is the law that is at fault, writing, "we need to change the Youth Criminal Justice Act." He continued by arguing that, "at the end of the day, if our elected officials can't — or won't — pass laws to keep our communities safe, we're in deep trouble" (Brodbeck 2008: 5). For both Kitching and Brodbeck the problem was not the police, who themselves are placed in danger, but the politicians in Ottawa, who are failing to "fix" the YCJA, which both reporters argue is not working.

An editorial that appeared on that same day criticizes "lax youth laws and lenient courts" for the problem of car thefts by teens. The editorial then lauded the Winnipeg police's strategy of "singling out the worst chronic car thieves for intensive observation... [as] the best local control remedy" (Feuer 2008: 10). On the same page, a letter to the editor, deemed the "Letter of the Day," called car thieves "sociopaths" and "psychos" and suggested that the criminal justice system is a "farce," while at the same time worrying about the safety of police officers who these thieves may "purposefully attempt to maim or murder" (Higham 2008: 10).

These examples illustrate further the dichotomy employed by the *Sun* that differentiates between the working class hero, the police officer, and the elites — in this case, Ottawa politicians and judges. The police are depicted as being at the mercy of the deviant criminal; the elites are depicted as willfully ignoring an issue of public safety. The working class hero is one of us and we are then by extension all at risk — something Brodbeck underscored when he suggested that the next victim of these crimes could be a child (2008: 5). There were also strong neo-conservative underpinnings to the discussions about the youth crime. Brodbeck suggested that bad parenting may be in part to blame for the seventeen-year-old punk's bad behaviour. Additionally, the editorial's headline, entitled "All it takes is mom and dad," quoted a Washington DC police officer who stated that in taking care of the problem of youth crime "it doesn't take a village... it takes Mom and Dad" (Feuer 2008: 10). This line of thinking individualizes the issue of youth crime.

The alarmist language found in these news items is also troubling. For example, Brodbeck made the declaration that "if our elected officials can't — or won't — pass laws to keep our communities safe, we're in deep trouble" (2008: 5). Brodbeck claimed the "city of 650,000 is at severe risk" because of car thieves. A letter to the editor suggested that there has been an epidemic of car thieves running down police officers. In reality, all of these claims are simply not true. Indeed, the crime statistics printed by the *Sun* on the same page as the Kitching story showed that car thefts were down in Winnipeg by 26 percent and attempted car thefts had dropped by 46 percent. Despite this, the story was framed to play to a sense of panic and outrage at the impotence of politicians to protect the ordinary citizen and the police.

On May 31, 2008, Laurie Mustard's column described car thefts as "vehicular terrorism." Mustard stressed that these car thieves are murdering law-abiding citizens and questions why Winnipeggers aren't "mad as hell, standing by the thousands outside the Legislative Building demanding immediate action to remove these Death Lottery lowlifes from the street" 2008: 6). He went further:

> Screw these monsters' rights. Create a special interim law, within the law, empowering our police and justice system to remove these highly dangerous potential killers from the streets until something makes them understand that vehicular terrorism will no longer be tolerated. And they don't get out till they do understand. Freedom is a privilege. I'm truly sorry that some children's lives are a horror story of abuse, neglect, negative programming and so on. Sorry that for some, love is a movie thing. But when those reasons are used as excuses and rationalization for life-threatening terrorist acts on city streets — targeting the lives of innocent, law-abiding people, it's safety first, compassion later.

Class plays a role in this fear mongering. In his column, Brodbeck pointed to addictions, abuse and poor community support as potential reasons for this type of crime (2008: 5). The subsequent editorial, however, went even further, suggesting that while affluent teens may resort to playing video games like *Grand Theft Auto*, "their counterparts from poorer parts of town do the real thing" (Feuer 2008: 10).

This hyperbolic language suggests that none of us are safe from criminals and that instant incarceration without the benefit of basic human rights is the only recourse. In this case of teenage car theft, the *Sun* performed ritual acts of degradation in its depiction of youth crime and, in doing so, created an environment of fear. Schissel points out that this type of rhetoric "draws on public fears and stereotypes to make a point" (2001: 97). Moreover, the images of poorer communities, contending with abuse and addictions, "play on an already existing racialized bias in the community and use these biases to create anxiety in the reader" (Schissel 2001: 98).

The racialized bias is also evident in an arson story in the May 8, 2008, issue of the *Sun*. The story was highlighted on the front page with the headline "Firebugs 'normal'" and found on page three with the headline "Firebug kids 'wild': North End resident says arsons 'normal around here'" (Kitching 2008a: 3). In other words, the North End is viewed as a place where anarchy is the norm. The "firebugs" are young boys, aged five to nine, who are too young to be charged and thus have "been turned over to their parents or guardians." The use of the term "parents or guardian," rather than the more concise collective "family," is a subtle suggestion that the home life of these children is unstable, again invoking neo-conservative sentiments that it is poor parental supervision that is responsible for youth crime. Indeed, these kids are deemed to be running "wild," a subtle retelling of the stereotype for Aboriginal people, who dominate the demographic in the Winnipeg's North End.

A follow-up editorial on May 11, 2008, reported that the "firebugs… have parents and guardians who likely couldn't care less about these damages, dangerous and near-death situations" (Romaniuk 2008: 11). The public moralizing continued, particularly when there was a suggestion that the lack of recreational facilities in the North End exacerbates the situation: "what's equally disturbing is the willingness of misguided social watchdogs to blame their actions on a supposed shortage of recreational points which they claim would keep more kids and youths out of trouble." As Ross Romaniuk wrote: "It's not up to us to dig into public and community coffers to put those young hands into sports and positive recreational pursuits, rather than matches. It's up to the parents to carry the ball in keeping kids from becoming fire-starting punks, at our peril" (2008: 11). A letter to the editor published on May 12, 2008, supported this idea. Comparing the firebugs to "terrorists," letter writer Dan McDonald suggested that the parents should be charged because "kids that age shouldn't be running around and should be at home locked inside a yard with a huge fence or maybe an armed guard to keep them there too. No joke either, these parents stink so where's Family Services each time!" (2008: 8). The public excommunication in this case is aimed at the families and the province, who have failed to keep children safe.

Couple this story with another that ran on May 12, 2008. The headline read: "Fear on the streets: Cops urge caution after savage North End attacks" (Horbal 2008: 3). The article outlined a series of random attacks on individuals walking in the city's North End by culprits described as "aboriginal in appearance." The word "savage" can again be viewed as a subtle metaphor for out-of-control Aboriginals, with the North End becoming shorthand for the deeply ingrained stereotypes of Aboriginal people — that they are wild savages, untamable and uncontrollable. Moreover, Winnipeg's North End serves as a physical site for public excommunication. It is shunned by the rest of the city, a place in which "good" people do not live with a clear separation between "us" and "them."

Not only was the coverage of crime in the *Sun* racialized, it was also at times deeply gendered. The final example is that of the "laughing girl" coverage. On March 29, 2008 Antonio Lanzellotti's taxi was hit by a stolen car. Lanzellotti was killed. The fourteen-year-old male driver of the car was charged with manslaughter and a passenger in the car, a sixteen-year-old girl with no previous criminal record, was charged with possession of goods obtained by crime. Winnipeg police released details of their video interview with the sixteen-year-old girl that showed her giggling and joking during the interview. This earned her the title "laughing girl," which was used consistently by the *Sun* in its follow-up articles.

First, the sixteen-year-old became a stand-in for all individuals charged under the YCJA. Because she made the statement that Lanzellotti "had to die sometime," her demeanor was viewed as characteristic of youth criminals "thumbing their noses at the rest of us" and as "mouthy teens… [who] defy authority, and laugh at the Act" while "thousands more will suffer" (Rutherford 2008: 10). Rutherford's editorial did cite the girl's defence lawyer, who had made it clear that the girl was remorseful and may have been trying to put on a brave face during the police interview. However, this perspective was roundly denounced in the editorial and, despite the fact that the sixteen-year-old had no criminal record, she was depicted as a hard-core criminal.

This depiction resonated with *Sun* readers. In a letter to the editor printed the next day, the sixteen-year-old was described as having no regret or remorse and, further, that she and the boy, who had taken off his police-monitored ankle bracelet, were "not fit to live in a civilized society. They need to be removed until such time they can demonstrate decent behaviour" (Gilmore 2008: 10). The public ostracizing of the "laughing girl" is complete, with the editorial pages and the *Sun* readers joining in their condemnation of her socially unacceptable conduct.

More importantly, the "laughing girl" raised the spectre of girls behaving badly, which continued in the *Sun* with a news article written on May 16, 2008. The story began: "In yet another case of girls gone wild, two young girls are accused of setting a new house on fire and wreaking havoc on another this month, city police say" (Kitching 2008d: 14). Police Constable Blair Good indicated that the arrest of the two girls "reflects a rise in violent and other crimes allegedly committed by females" (Kitching 2008d: 14). In reality, it is certainly true that rates of incarceration for women have increased dramatically, particularly for racialized women, but as Snider suggests, "moral panics about violent girls, female stalkers, and homicidal mothers sell newspapers and magazines" and exist as a type of backlash against feminism (2006: 335). The "laughing girl" served as an example of the moral panic that girls no longer behave along gendered lines, but instead are just as violent as boys.

The fear mongering narrative is obvious in the coverage of youth crime in Winnipeg. First, the *Sun* uses repetition (Glassner 2004: 820) to show that crime and, more specifically, violent crimes by youth are out of control in Winnipeg, despite the fact that, according to Statistics Canada, youth crime rates remain stable (Taylor-Butts and Bressan 2006). Moreover, auto thefts are not considered violent crimes and, as previously indicated, the number of auto thefts in Winnipeg also declined in 2008. However, readers of the *Winnipeg Sun* would not be left with that impression. Indeed, the numerous letters to the editor printed in May 2008 point to a fear of increased lawlessness among youth, particularly those who live in the North End. Additionally, the *Sun* takes isolated incidents and turns them into trends, something Glassner considers a common narrative technique of fear mongers (2004: 820). For example, the unfortunate death of Antonio Lanzellotti, killed when hit by a stolen vehicle, became a trend that columnists, editorialists and letter writers wrote about with great concern. Finally, fear mongering relies on the narrative technique of "misdirection" (Glassner 2004: 822). By focusing only on youth crime and the failure of parents to properly control their children, the *Sun* avoids discussions about improving living standards for those who live within the North End and, in particular, Aboriginal people who live in poverty. Additionally, this fear mongering is coupled with what Katz called "ritual moral exercises" and the "ritual acts of excommunication." The racialized area of the North End becomes an area that is demonized as unsafe, rife with savages and full of terrorist acts. It is pitted against the rest of Winnipeg as a place to avoid, and the *Winnipeg Sun* acts as an avenue through which the "common man" can view and comment on the carnage left by out-of-control youth aided and abetted by a too-soft judicial system. The police serve as the lone moral arbiter, the one consistent safeguard against potential anarchy and, in the *Sun*, the police are viewed as heroes.

It becomes clear from the way it covers crime in the city that the *Winnipeg Sun* views itself as the champion for its readers, who feel unsafe in their city. The *Sun* and its columnists are strong supporters of the police and a crime control model that would see more youth placed in jail. Its depiction of crime in the North End is inherently racialized and class-based, and the depiction of juvenile offenders is hyperbolic and dramatic. Discussions about policy directions and responses to crime are quite negative, with politicians presented as being incapable of responding to crime, particularly youth crime.

Why is this important? While any discussion of the effect of the newspaper coverage in the *Sun* on how Winnipeggers think about crime would be methodologically specious, it becomes clear from examining the letters to the editor that many agree with the *Sun*'s depiction of youth crime. The letters speak of the public's frustration with the government and the judiciary, who they view as failing in their attempts to protect their property and keep them safe. Moreover, those whose letters appear in the *Sun* feel that the Winnipeg Police Service is doing the best it can in a system that favours the criminal, particularly the juvenile criminal. Thus, for a segment of people living in Winnipeg, the way crime is represented in the *Sun* mirrors their reality and unites them in a public square that gives them opportunity to excommunicate and denounce lawbreakers and those soft on crime.

In the context of theorizing justice, the *Sun*'s coverage of crime and, in particular, youth crime relies on a type of populism that creates a simple dichotomy of good versus evil. The crime control model, which pushes for increased incarceration as a way of deterring crime, is viewed as the only solution in a city in which citizens and their working heroes, the police, are seen as being under attack. Policy directions are then discussed within this narrow paradigm without an understanding or appreciation of the nuances regarding why crime occurs. Moreover, the shaming or excommunication of those who offend provides a way of uniting *Sun* readers through public moralizing on a common goal. In this neo-conservative utopian vision put forth by *Sun* columnists, the family takes care of its own so the state does not have to.

Notes

1. The authors would like to thank the anonymous reviewers for their feedback. As well, we would like to thank the Canadian Centre for Policy Alternatives for its SSHRC CURA funding and the University of Winnipeg for its research grant.
2. All stories were coded to determine the tone toward the criminal, the justice system, the victim, the community and the police, and the coder was asked to determine if the tone was positive, negative, neutral or mixed. For example, a positive story about the police would be one that described officers as working class heroes. A negative story about the criminal would be one that described him or her as a punk. A story that was considered to be mixed contained both positive and negative attributes, and a story that was neutral did not make any normative evaluation.

References

Bala, Nicholas, Peter J. Carrington and Julian V. Roberts. 2009. "Evaluating the *Youth Criminal Justice Act* after Five Years: A Qualified Success." *Canadian Journal of Criminology and Criminal Justice* 51, 2.

Brodbeck, Tom. 2008. "Change That Law." *Winnipeg Sun*. May 9.

Canadian Newspaper Association. 2010. *Circulation Data Report, 2009*. At <cna-acj. ca/en/system/files/2009CirculationDataReport_3.pdf>.

Chermak, Steven M. 1995. "Crime in News Media: A Refined Understanding of How Crimes Become News." In Gregg Barak (ed.), *Media, Process, and the Social Construction of Crime: Studies in Newsmaking Criminology.* New York: Garland Publishing.

Corrado, Raymond, Karla Gronsdahl, David MacAlister and Irwin M. Cohen. 2010. "Youth Justice in Canada: Theoretical Perspectives of Youth Probation Officers." *Canadian Journal of Criminology and Criminal Justice* 52, 4.

Dauvergne, Mia. 2008. *Canadian Crime Statistics, 2007.* Ottawa, Statistics Canada. At <statcan.gc.ca/pub/85-002-x/2008007/article/10658-eng.htm>.

Debrix, François. 2003. "Tabloid Realism and the Revival of American Security Culture." *Geopolitics* 8, 3 (Autumn).

Feeley, Malcom, and Jonathon Simon. 2007. "Folk Devils and Moral Panics: An Appreciation from North America." In David Downs, Paul Rock, Christine Chinken and Conor Gearty (eds.), *Crime, Social Control and Human Rights to States of Denial.* Portland: Willan Publishing: 39–52.

Feuer, Ed. 2008. "All It Takes Is Mom and Dad." *Winnipeg Sun* 09 May: 10.

Forsyth, James. 2006. "New Kid on the Block." *Foreign Policy* September/October.

Gilmore, Cathy. 2008 "Lock Kids Up." *Winnipeg Sun* 02 May: 10.

Glassner, Barry. 2004. "Narrative Techniques of Fear Mongering." *Social Research* 71, 4 (Winter).

Hackett, Robert A., and Richard Gruneau. 2000. *The Missing News: Filters and Blind Spots in Canada's Press.* Ottawa: Garamond Press.

Hall, Stuart, Chas Critcher, Tony Jefferson, John Clarket and Brian Roberts. 2010. "The Social Production of News." In Chris Greer (ed.), *Crime and Media: A Reader.* London: Routledge.

Higham, Gord. 2008. "Three Strikes Please." *Winnipeg Sun* 09 May.

Hilmes, Michele. 2002. "Rethinking Radio." In Michele Hilmes and Jason Loviglio (eds.), *Radio Reader: Essays in the Cultural History of Radio.* New York: Routledge.

Horbal, Julie. 2008. "Fear on the Streets: Cops Urge Caution After Savage North End Attacks." *Winnipeg Sun* 12 May: 2.

Katz, Jack. 2010. "What Makes 'Crime' News?" In Chris Greer (ed.), *Crime and Media: A Reader.* London: Routledge.

Kitching, Chris. 2008a. "Firebug Kids 'Wild'." *Winnipeg Sun* 08 May.

___. 2008b. "Local Law and Order: They Run Wild, You Pay." *Winnipeg Sun* 09 May.

___. 2008c. "Thief Breaks In, Takes Vehicle, then Crashes Into Building." *Winnipeg Sun.* 14 May.

___. 2008d. "Girls Accused of House Arson." *Winnipeg Sun* 16 May.

Klinkhammer, Ruth, and David Taras. 2001. "Mercy or Murder? Media Coverage of the Robert Latimer Supreme Court Decision." *Saskatchewan Law Review* 64, 2.

McCormick, Chris. 1995. *Constructing Danger: The Mis/Representation of Crime in the News.* Halifax: Fernwood Publishing.

McDonald, Dan. 2008. "Parents Stink." *Winnipeg Sun* 12 May.

Mustard, Laurie. 2008. "Bright Side: It's Street Terrorisim." *Winnipeg Sun* 31 May.

Nesbitt-Larking, Paul. 2007. *Politics, Society, and the Media,* second edition. Peterborough: Broadview Press.

Neuman, W. Lawrence. 2000. *Social Research Methods: Qualitative and Quantitative Approaches,* fourth edition. Toronto: Allyn and Bacon.

Quebecor Inc. 2010. At <quebecor.com/NewspapersWeeklies/Dailies.aspx>

Reid-MacNevin, Sharon. 2001. "Toward a Theoretical Understanding of Canadian Juvenile Justice Policy." In Russell C. Smandych (ed.), *Youth Justice: History, Legislation, and Reform.* Toronto: Harcourt.

Romaniuk, Ross. 2008. "Carry the Ball, Don't Drop It." *Winnipeg Sun* 11 May.

Rutherford, Paul. 2008. "Thumbing Their Noses." *Winnipeg Sun* 01 May.

Soroka, Stuart. 2002. *Agenda-Setting Dynamics in Canada.* Vancouver: University of British Columbia Press.

Schissel, Bernard. 2001. "Youth Crime, Moral Panics, and the News: The Conspiracy Against the Marginalized in Canada." In Russell C. Smandych (ed.), *Youth Justice: History, Legislation, and Reform.* Toronto: Harcourt.

Shattuc, Jane M. 1997. *The Talking Cure: TV Talk Shows and Women.* London: Routledge.

Smandych, Russell C. 2001. "Accounting for Changes in Canadian Youth Justice: From the Invention to the Disappearance of Childhood." In Russell C. Smandych (ed.), *Youth Justice: History, Legislation, and Reform.* Toronto: Harcourt.

Snider, Laureen. 2006. "Making Change in Neo-Liberal Times." In Gillian Balfour and Elizabeth Comack (eds.), *Criminalizing Women: Gender and (In)Justice in Neo-Liberal Times.* Halifax: Fernwood Publishing.

Surette, Ray. 1998. *Media, Crime and Criminal Justice* second edition. Belmont: Wadsworth Publishing.

Taylor-Butts, Andrea, and Angela Bressan. 2006. *Youth Crime in Canada, 2006.* Ottawa, Statistics Canada. <statcan.gc.ca/pub/85-002-x/2008003/article/10566-eng.htm>.

PART II

EXTERNAL APPROACHES

At the furthest end of the spectrum from the internal approaches, we can find external approaches to problematizing justice. Here we see examinations of justice systems from above — the authors engaging in these studies use the vantage point of a bird's eye view to analyze practices of justice. The systems can be reflected upon from this more abstract place, and the distance allows the researcher to reflect and unpack the power structures of justice that they study. These researchers seek to understand the means by which justice is distributed and potentially redistributed.

Largely, externalists will be reluctant to prescribe a policy suggestion following their studies, preferring instead to describe, unpack or deconstruct the relational nature of the justice interactions they interrogate. The idea of description as an analytic is not banal though. The relational nature of power in the justice system can be very complex and nuanced, and the description of these relational dynamics from an external position can reveal novel ways of thinking about justice. Thus an external study of the Aboriginal laws that are enforced in Canada can demonstrate the surprising ways in which law disguised as amelioration can further marginalize the already oppressed (see Chapter Four by Patzer).

An external analytic can call for a new method or way of thinking about justice when, for instance, it asks us to consider that justice can be considered to be simultaneously intangible, but thought about from a critical realist perspective (as Datta suggests in Chapter Five). The external approach can allow us to study the ways in which governments are both complicit in and condone corporate malfeasance, and it allows us to reconsider the nature of criminalization and criminality in Canada (see Chapter Six by Bittle). An external account can ask us to re-examine laws that were passed to aid the plight of new and scared mothers, but which have been reconstituted as a means of criminalizing those same populations in surprising ways (see Chapter Seven by Kramar). In each case, the chapters that follow do not recognize a baseline of justice. They do not suggest that policy changes could return us to a just state. They indeed might reject baselines entirely, and instead suggest that it is the lens that exposes the problematic of justice that is the worthwhile objective.

The chapters that follow, then, encourage the study of systems of justice more broadly and endeavour to unpack the justice interactions and the relational power dynamics that persist in those systems or in the term justice itself. The authors of these studies do not ask us to assume the place of a player inside the system. They ask us to consider the justice relations and their distributive nature, and they reveal the ironies and, in some cases, absurdities that are achieved within the current governing order. Yet, even in these external approaches, largely devoid of policy deliverables, we see affinities with prospective change. For instance, Bittle, Kramar and Patzer implicitly recognize that current systems of governance in their respective fields are inadequate. We would be guessing that this dissatisfaction would lead them to suggest alternate approaches. Perhaps they would resist this temptation and say simply that they would be happy to unpack and analyze future iterations of redistributed justice in their respective fields. To do so would further move their work towards the furthest reaches of externalism. It is this flirtation with prospective change that suggests a third category that we suggest in the next section — perspectives which bridge the divide.

CHAPTER FOUR

LEGITIMATE CONCERNS
Aboriginal Rights and the Limits of Canadian Justice
Jeremy Patzer

THE *AB-ORIGINAL* CRISIS OF LEGITIMACY

Aboriginal rights disputes make for a substantive research area that is well suited for a discussion of the most fundamental notions and controversies surrounding law and justice. They are the residue of an infamous past, conjuring ghosts that haunt Canadian history, politics and law. Whether the issues are discussed aloud or not, challenging notions are always at play: sovereignty, legitimacy and making things "right" in a present that follows a history of seemingly irreparable harms.

An examination of the contours of Aboriginal rights and title case history reveals a complicated and compromising evolution for the Supreme Court of Canada. No longer able to rely on antiquated and unpalatable justifications for Aboriginal dispossession, the late twentieth century Court opened itself up to entertaining claims of rights and title that had not been previously extinguished by treaty. An unspoken crisis arises, however, in its unwillingness to question the Crown's acquisition of sovereignty, despite the fact that Aboriginal rights and title are meant to be based in the *unceded* practices and lands of prior occupants. There is thus a tension that concerns not only the legitimacy of the Crown's assumption of sovereignty over Aboriginal peoples, but also the legitimacy of the courts to determine justice at this site of conflict.

But the law depends on the negation of the layperson's "naïve intuitions of fairness" (Bourdieu 1987: 817), while simultaneously suggesting that it enjoys a privileged relation to justice. This it does with the mobilization of hermetic forms of expert knowledge that are meant to distinguish it from the raw instrumentality of violence or domination. The most recent development in Aboriginal rights and title jurisprudence — the cultural rights approach — does precisely this. It asserts that the answers to questions concerning Aboriginal rights — their nature, their limits and whether or not they exist for the claimant — inhere culturally within the Aboriginal claimants themselves. In this way the judiciary is able to avoid fundamental questions concerning the Crown's acquisition of sovereignty, as well as the fact that the onus is on the prior occupants to prove rights or title as against the colonizers.[1]

LAW AND ITS PRACTICE

In seeking to answer fundamental questions about law and the juridical field, one must be mindful not to invent histories that render the advent of law inevitable and the idealized notions of its purposes self-evident. The kind of history that Michel Foucault (1977) calls "effective" opposes the search for pure origins and preordained culminations. Pierre Bourdieu (1987: 833) also insists that "nothing is less 'natural' than the 'need for the law'" — in other words, than the idea of appealing to the services of a professional after the moment of injustice. Much of the work of the law, though, is oriented toward convincing us otherwise. Bourdieu's description of the confrontation staged by law — the trial, or legal proceeding — invokes the image of actors possessing a certain technical competence that act, by proxy, for lay people external to the legal field. And since legal expertise sees the law as grounded purely in its own internal dynamic, it has evolved a process of rationalization and erudition that promotes a social division between the lay person and the legal professional. Such a process of rationalization thereby contributes to the separation of judgments based on legal thought and the "naïve intuitions of fairness" often held by the lay client (Bourdieu 1987: 817). The result is that the system of juridical norms seems, to all involved, totally independent of, rather than essential to, the power relations that such a system sustains and legitimizes. In this way the juridical field carves out broad sectors of social life in which legal expertise — not possessed by the lay person — is seen as necessary to achieving certain social objectives.

But what of justice and truth? Even though the juridical field often seeks to neutralize the standard of fairness, truth or justice put forth by the lay person, this does not mean that it has no need whatsoever for these ideals. On the contrary, the particular social power wielded by the juridical is dependent not only on the separation of professional from laity, but also on the ability to intimate a transcendental basis to its expertise when necessary. Bourdieu (1987) discusses a number of legitimating customs that are geared toward this: the principled interpretation of venerated legal texts, a rhetoric of autonomy, neutrality and universality, coupled with a near infinite elasticity in judicial interpretation. A strongly hierarchical court structure then ensures a final, authoritative decision in order to avoid the awkward appearance of multiple and competing normative frameworks. Legal scholars thus "have an easy time convincing themselves that the law provides its own foundation, that it is based on a fundamental norm, a 'norm of norms'" (Bourdieu 1987: 819). It is in such a manner that the trial is constructed "as an ordered progression toward truth" (Bourdieu 1987: 830).

One might wonder, however, if justice and truth need to be treated in such a cynical way. To a certain extent, yes. The assumption that universalizing frameworks such as justice, truth, natural law and a universal faculty of reason have some sort of real and independent existence can be problematic, especially when hermetic fields of expertise claim an exclusive knowledge of them in an effort to wield a particular type of social power. The later philosophy of Jacques Derrida, however, is particular in that he is eminently mindful of this, yet he still manages to allow justice to exist "in its own peculiar way." It is "not a positive idea or a blueprint for a state of affairs. It does not have any particular essence. But it is not purely situational or pragmatic. As inspiration, as force, as desire, it does exist for all of us" (Valverde 1999: 657).

For Derrida, if such a purity as justice actually exists, it embraces *singularity*, not universality: the irreducible and complex singularity of the situation that calls for justice, and the irreducible alterity we encounter in our engagements with "the Other." The problem with law, however, is that its very possibility lies in its universalization, that it operates as rule and regularity (Derrida 1992). Therefore, despite its intimations of a transcendental normative basis, law neither is justice, nor does it guarantee justice. In effect, the two suffer from substantial irreconcilabilities. No coded rule can serve as an absolute guarantee of justice. Rather, the only guarantee that consistently following a rule can offer is that justice is *not* being done all of the time. Thus, a judge's decision based in the law must impossibly be "both regulated and without regulation" in order to be just: "it must conserve the law and also destroy it or suspend it enough to have to reinvent it in each case, rejustify it, at least reinvent it in the reaffirmation and the new and free confirmation of its principle" (Derrida 1992: 23).

Yet, juridical practice does mobilize the image of justice to fortify its own particular brand of social power. There is a misleading reasoning to the law — sometimes with an almost actuarial quality — that wants to affirm that its ritual practices do in fact mete out justice. Valverde (1999: 658) talks about a "violent logic of abstract equivalence" and restitution in criminal law. As she observes, two years in prison for a robbery is a form of abstract exchange that reveals the vengeance underlying criminal law; yet, to take from Valverde again, one of the most interesting questions for criminologists should be "how a robbery could be equal to two years" (1995: 339). There is nothing inscribed in the heavens that reveals such an equivalency to be "true," mathematically or morally. Law is thus "the element of calculation" of a justice that is incalculable (Derrida 1992: 16), and our longing to conceive of the way we practise justice through law as somehow fundamentally grounded is what Derrida often termed *logocentric*. Logocentric ways of thinking "exhibit a longing for presence, for a constitutive reason (*logos*) and for an order of concepts claimed to exist in themselves, complete, self-referring and proper" (Douzinas, Warrington and McVeigh 1991: 10).

Much of this chapter is premised on the assertion that, at least implicitly, the law has an awareness of its own irreconcilabilities with justice. This is why Douzinas's above description of logocentrism as a longing is so apt. Interestingly enough, Derrida dealt with the subject of justice extensively in *Specters of Marx* (1994), a book in which he also introduced the notion of "spectrality" in order to problematize the distinction between the real and the unreal, life and death. In keeping with Derrida's theme of the spectre, one could say that law and its practice are haunted by the question of justice. Thus, although we can allow for justice to exist in its own peculiar way, it does not exist in the way that the law would maintain. Perhaps we have to allow that justice exists, then, precisely because it haunts us and the law. Why else would the law insist on keeping the discourse of justice and truth in its repertoire? That which haunts also legitimates. The law, while being insistent that justice is afoot, can actually feel upon itself the gaze of ghosts of illegitimacy. In fact, haunting can be the cause of such an insistence.

THE DETERMINATION OF ABORIGINAL RIGHTS AND TITLE

The legal struggles by Aboriginal peoples with Canada revolve around both rights and title. Individual activities such as fishing would fall under the categories of rights, whereas having exclusive access to a particular territory, in which an Aboriginal group can do almost any activity, would be termed Aboriginal title. While distinct, the legal history of the two are inextricably intertwined, as it was not until the late twentieth century that the Supreme Court of Canada (SCC) conceptually distinguished between specific practices as rights and larger assertions of title to land — thereby allowing specific rights to exist independent of claims to title (McNeil 1997).

Moreover, treaty rights are legally distinct from Aboriginal rights. For those First Nations who have signed treaties with the Crown, their rights embodied in those treaties are regulated and constitutionally guaranteed in statute through the *Indian Act* and the *Constitution Act, 1982*. Aboriginal rights, on the other hand, stem from a body of case law that exists at the problematic limits of treaty rights. They are meant to be the embodiment of justice at a site of conflict that can arise either with those Aboriginal groups who dispute the interpretation or infringement of their treaty rights, or with those Aboriginal groups who do not have any treaty rights recognized in statute to begin with.

St. Catherine's Milling and Lumber v. The Queen(1888)

One of the earliest and most fundamental cases concerning Aboriginal rights and title in Canada, *St. Catherine's Milling and Lumber v. The Queen* (1888) represents an enduring form of justice meted out to Aboriginal groups: that of discerning the intent of the sovereign in legal texts. With the dispute being between the Province of Ontario on one side and the Dominion of Canada and the St. Catherine's Milling and Lumber Company on the other, it is also a dispute of great historical consequence to Aboriginal Canadians that took place entirely between non-Aboriginal actors. The nature of what was then known as "Indian title" is at the heart of the issue precisely because it would determine what happened to title over the land through the *Constitution Act, 1867* and an 1873 treaty with an Ojibway group. The dispute arose when the Dominion awarded a licence to the lumber company to log in an area of land ceded by the Ojibway group in the treaty. The Province and the Dominion both felt that they had gained jurisdiction over the land when the treaty extinguished the Indian title. Canada's claim to the lands ceded by treaty, interestingly enough, was based on an argument that Indian title was akin to a full and absolute title. Ontario's claim to the lands, on the other hand, was premised on an assumption that the Indian title was merely a burden of usage on the radical, underlying title that had long been possessed by the Crown, thereby meaning that the *Constitution Act, 1867*, even though passed prior to the treaty, had passed the lands in question down to the Province. The case escalated to the SCC, and then beyond to the Judicial Committee of the Privy Council (JCPC) in London — a body that still had ultimate authority over the Canadian judiciary at that point in history. An interpretation of an eighteenth century king's intent embodied in the *Royal Proclamation of 1763*, which was the original decree that offered protections for lands declared as reserved for Indians, helped to resolve the issue. Ultimately, the JCPC found in favour of the Province of Ontario, stating that "the tenure of the Indians was a personal and usufructuary right dependent upon the goodwill of the Crown" (*St. Catherine's Milling* 1888: 46). These few words would be of monumental importance to Aboriginal groups, for, reduced to more of a right of use and existing only at the pleasure of the Crown, the nature of the title that they could legally pursue in Canada would thereafter be "drastically circumscribed" (Kulchyski 1994: 22).

In re Southern Rhodesia (1919)
Given the jurisdiction the JCPC had over numerous British colonies, it heard another influential case in 1919 concerning Aboriginal title that would later circulate throughout Commonwealth jurisprudence — this time in Southern Rhodesia. *In re Southern Rhodesia* (1919), like the *St. Catherine's Milling* case, actually revolved around a dispute between two bodies other than the indigenous inhabitants of the land in question. The Legislative Council of Southern Rhodesia claimed that title to as yet unalienated lands resided in the Crown, while the British South Africa Company, which had conquered the territory of Southern Rhodesia on behalf of the Crown, claimed title to these lands. Legal representatives intervened on behalf of the indigenous inhabitants of the region, however, to argue that they still had title to the land. Unlike *St. Catherine's Milling*, the *In re Southern Rhodesia* decision posed

a particularly vexing problem for the JCPC in that no express intention of the Crown could be found to indicate who had title over the lands in question. Its displeasure at this is tangible in the decision. In the end, the JCPC agreed that ultimate title still resided with the Crown. While this is perhaps not surprising, the decision handed down by the committee in this case has still become somewhat notorious in Aboriginal rights scholarship. Much of this is due to the overtly evolutionist and racist tone adopted by the lords in their decision:

> The estimation of the rights of aboriginal tribes is always inherently difficult. Some tribes are so low in the scale of social organization that their usages and conceptions of rights and duties are not to be reconciled with the institutions or the legal ideas of civilized society. Such a gulf cannot be bridged. It would be idle to impute to such people some shadow of the rights known to our law and then to transmute it into the substance of transferable rights of property as we know them. In the present case it would make each and every person by a fictional inheritance a landed proprietor "richer than all his tribe." On the other hand, there are indigenous peoples whose legal conceptions, though differently developed, are hardly less precise than our own. When once they have been studied and understood they are no less enforceable than rights arising under English law. Between the two there is a wide tract of much ethnological interest, but the position of the natives of Southern Rhodesia within it is very uncertain; clearly they approximate rather to the lower than to the higher limit. (1919: 233–34)

Naturally, representatives for the Indigenous peoples were insistent that rights translatable to private property had existed prior to colonization. But the JCPC arrived at a judgment that presented a no-win situation for the indigenous inhabitants with the following two bleak possibilities: if the Natives were located on the lower end of the scale of social organization previously mentioned, then they did not have any rights that could be conceived of as title under English law. On the other hand, if they were indeed as high on the scale of social organization as they had insisted, then "the maintenance of their rights was fatally inconsistent with white settlement of the country" such that this only proved "that the aboriginal system gave place to another prescribed by the Order in Council" (1919: 234). In essence, the Crown, in exercising jurisdiction over the territory in its regular activities, proved an extinguishment of title through conquest precisely because the purported "advanced nature" of the old indigenous order would not have permitted it. The council therefore found that the old state of things, whatever its exact nature, as it was before 1893, has passed away and another and, as their Lordships do not doubt, a better has been established in lieu of it. Whoever now owns the unalienated lands, the natives do not. (1919: 235)

Calder v. Attorney-General of British Columbia(1973)

By the time of *Calder v. Attorney-General of British Columbia* (1973), the Supreme Court of Canada was the highest court in the land. The Nisga'a Tribal Council and its four constituent First Nations bands brought an action against the Attorney General of British Columbia to claim a declaration that their title over their lands had never been lawfully extinguished. Indeed, "there was no treaty, no agreement with the Nisga'a surrendering their title and no explicit federal or provincial legislation that said their title was extinguished" (Kulchyski 1994: 61). The opinions of the SCC for and against the Nisga'a were evenly split, until Justice Pigeon found against them due to a technicality. The Nisga'a therefore lost their suit, but the written decision still contained a judgment of great import for Aboriginal groups with whom the Crown had not signed a treaty.

In effect, from the *Calder* case on, things would change significantly for Aboriginal rights and title. In complete agreement with the lower courts, the justices writing the decision found that the protections promised by the king in the *Royal Proclamation of 1763* did not apply to the Nisga'a. The pivotal moment in the decision, however, comes when Justice Judson states that there is no doubt that, in the *St. Catherine's Milling* case, the JCPC found that the *Royal Proclamation of 1763* was the source of "Indian title," but that he does not "take these reasons to mean that the Proclamation was the exclusive source of Indian title" (*Calder v. B.C.* 1973: 322). Its other source, then, arises simply from the common law's ability to recognize their prior occupation. In the end, six of the seven justices were in agreement on the fact that Aboriginal title could exist purely at common law. In stating this, the *Calder* decision created a new concept of Aboriginal title, essentially allowing Aboriginal groups who had not ceded their sovereignty in the form of a treaty to argue that they should have some form of continuing title over their own land. This, of course, was a development that would bring with it myriad questions concerning the practical operation and effects of this new source of title.

The Constitution Act, 1982 and R. v. Sparrow (1990)

To add to the uncertainty and anticipation, a critical statutory change following the *Calder* decision came with the repatriation of the Constitution in 1982. Section 35 of the *Constitution Act, 1982* affirmed the existence and recognition of three categories of Aboriginal peoples in Canada — the Indian, Inuit and Métis — as well as their "existing Aboriginal and treaty rights" (Canada 1982). Therefore, whatever tidal shift was being marked by the *Calder* decision and any future decisions would have the additional robustness of constitutional legitimacy. The unanimous SCC decision in *R. v. Sparrow* (1990) then provided a number of judicial interpretations and assertions arising out of the new dynamic of having a pre-existing legal doctrine of Aboriginal title elevated to constitutional status. The SCC interpreted the enactment of the *Constitution Act, 1982* as putting a greater burden of proof on those who would claim that Aboriginal rights or title had been extinguished by sovereign intent or exercise of jurisdiction. Governmental control or regulations were deemed insufficient proof that a right had been extinguished. It also recognized the *Constitution Act, 1982* as a fulcrum point in history after which Aboriginal rights were constitutionally protected, such that they could no longer be extinguished. Rather, from 1982 on, Aboriginal rights could only be infringed with careful justification. In addition, any intent to extinguish (prior to the *Constitution Act, 1982*) or infringe (after the *Constitution Act, 1982*) Aboriginal rights had to be "clear and plain" (*R. v. Sparrow* 1990: 1076).

However, in taking its cue from the wording of the *Constitution Act, 1982*, one of the most pivotal changes signalled by the *Sparrow* case was the very fact that the Court had begun speaking about Aboriginal rights in the sense of specific practices, since Reginald Sparrow had been charged with fishing with a drift net longer than was allowed under his band's food fishing licence. For the Court, the only loose ends left after *Calder* and *Sparrow* were the determination of what would count as an Aboriginal right, and for those who had not ceded title through treaty, what the nature of common law Aboriginal title would be. As I will explain below, using the courts to claim an Aboriginal right or claim title over a certain territory would not mean the automatic establishment of a regime akin to the treaty rights that existed for many Aboriginal groups under the *Indian Act*. On the contrary, the SCC saw itself as opening up a new territory of rights and title jurisprudence, one that heralded the advent of the "specific right" and saw the nature of Aboriginal rights and title as indelibly linked to the cultural identity of Aboriginal peoples.

ABORIGINAL CULTURE AND RIGHTS

In *R. v. Van der Peet* (1996), the SCC came up with a test, stating that "to be an Aboriginal right an activity must be an element of a practice, custom or tradition integral to the distinctive culture of the Aboriginal group claiming the right" (1996: 310). For the SCC, however, such aspects of Aboriginal society can only come from their pre-contact nature. Aboriginal rights therefore consist of those practices, customs and traditions that have continuity with those that existed prior to contact with European society. While the SCC maintains that Aboriginal rights can still exist in modern form, critics are recognizing the sources of indeterminacy, portions of arbitrariness and hair-splitting specificities that in fact offer the courts an unspoken, yet wide margin of discretion over their recognition. What qualifies as "integral," "distinctive" and in "continuity" with pre-contact tradition is largely in the eye of the beholder. Concerning specificity, the *Van der Peet* decision maintains that Aboriginal rights cannot be bundled together and also delimits rights recognition by historical community. Ultimately, this means that Aboriginal rights must be gained on a practice-by-practice and region-by-region basis.[2]

As for the definition of the content of Aboriginal title, the SCC decision in *Delgamuukw v. British Columbia* (1997) gives Aboriginal groups who have never ceded their land to the Crown the potential to regain the exclusive use and occupation of territory for a variety of purposes, including activities that are not derived from their pre-contact ancestors. The *Delgamuukw* decision tries to make clear that Aboriginal title can compete on an equal footing with full private ownership, but is in its own category situated somewhere between full title and a right of use. This is because the Crown is still seen as possessing a radical, underlying title to the land and because of several other restrictions particular to Aboriginal title: it is held communally, it can only be alienated to the Crown and, still with a certain form of cultural limitation, is limited to practices that are not "irreconcilable with the nature of the group's attachment to that land" (*Delgamuukw v. British Columbia* 1997: 1083). Where the line is drawn between permissible non-traditional practices and "irreconcilable" practices is another area of indeterminacy and contradiction, however, for the *Delgamuukw* decision itself refers to a group's attachment and special relationship to the land as being defined by past activities and uses (see Borrows 1999).

There is thus both a certain continuity, and discontinuity, between the early case law and this newest approach to Aboriginal rights. In basic terms, both periods have seen some recourse to questions of cultural difference as a basis for the standing of Aboriginal peoples before the law. The new cultural rights approach established by the *Van der Peet* test, however, harbours an ideal of Aboriginality often romanticized in late modernity. Whereas British colonial courts would once typically favour a colonized people's claim to distinct rights by virtue of the "advancement" of their social organization prior to contact, such groups must now demonstrate the opposite: "simple subsistence economies, comparatively simple technologies, rudimentary social organization, in other words, those qualities that make them 'distinct' from the dominant society" (Niezen 2003: 7). The worries over the cultural rights approach are made all the more acute by the fact that such romanticized images of indigeneity are far from ideal for Aboriginal groups seeking redress through the law. It is an idealized standard against which they can readily be found wanting. Failure to live up to an image of authentic and idealized difference can work to the detriment of an Aboriginal group, and

Bruce Miller's (1998) observations as an expert anthropological witness have been of a societal backlash against the use of cultural notions such as the sacred in American and Canadian courts. Rather than "spiritual heirs," Aboriginal claimants are apt to be construed as "culturally contaminated, corrupted descendants of their putatively spiritual ancestors" (Miller 1998: 89). Aboriginal Canadians are thus held accountable to an exotic vision of difference, and, when it concerns rights and title, it is a vision elected and handed down by the judiciary. This is why rights are apt to be anchored in a time that is immemorial, in a place sacred and rustic in its ancient traditions and in practices that are quaint and primitive. Any departure from this ideal constitutes a strategic risk for Aboriginal rights claimants.

Astonishingly, the SCC has also largely avoided discussing Aboriginal self-government in the wake of *Delgamuukw*, despite the fact that having title over territory would seem to require it (McNeil 1997, 1998, 2009). Indeed, as will be discussed below, a fundamental problem with the cultural rights approach as a whole is that it represents an avoidance of a larger, more critical discussion of autonomy, self-determination and sovereignty, instead choosing to discuss Aboriginal rights and title in terms dictated by depoliticized cultural formulae.

LOGOCENTRISM AND INHERITANCE

In all the different practices of justice outlined above, the onus on the judiciary was to arrive at a principled method of determining justice — even if this sometimes meant inventing completely new formulae. Elegant logics parsed out with multiple premises that mobilize a complex mixture of precedent, statute and principle serve to subdue potential cynicism concerning the judgments. Such misleading logic disguises the near infinite flexibility and the "proportion of arbitrariness" in the operation of the law, and thus distinguishes it from overt practices of violence and domination (Bourdieu 1987: 826).

In this context, while much of the academic debate concerning the *In re Southern Rhodesia* decision ends with the "scale of social organization" passage and a condemnation of its exceedingly Eurocentric approach to land tenure, one of its most striking and unappreciated aspects is the very conundrum the JCPC was facing in its practical task of finding justice. The committee's decision, and the arguments contained therein, do not end with this infamous paragraph. No statute or agreement existed that spelled out who was meant to have title to the lands in question, and representatives for the Indigenous peoples were insistent that rights translatable to private property had existed prior to colonization. The highest court in the British Commonwealth was therefore cornered into an unspoken crisis of legitimacy, being obliged to dispense justice through an as of yet unascertained, but legally principled, method. In the end, it came up with the method outlined above — a creative twist of logic that rendered the extinguishment of native title inescapable in any eventuality.

But this can also work in the opposite direction. Such an unspoken crisis of legitimacy was renewed once more with *Calder*. However, readily called into question by the late twentieth century, Eurocentric evolutionist discourses such as seen in *In re Southern Rhodesia* would become more difficult to mobilize and justify in relation to determinations of justice. In addition, as Brian Slattery (2005) explains, historical explanations such as *terra nullius* — the idea that Aboriginal lands were legally considered unoccupied and could therefore be appropriated through simple occupation — had less jurisprudential currency than most believe and represent a fairly inaccurate retelling of Commonwealth legal history. Indeed, the very existence of treaties and the legal concept of extinguishment of title betray the fact that Aboriginal occupation of the land was seen as having juridical dimensions. And the judiciary, for its part, always seeks to present a principled means of determining justice — even in the wake of colonization, an almost unmanageable legal problem. In the *St. Catherine's Milling* (1888) decision, invoking the will of the sovereign of a more "civilized" society embodies an implicit appeal to what should simply be considered right in the order of things — this was the sufficiently "principled" method of determining justice at that time. The JCPC, for *In re Southern Rhodesia* (1919), found a way to infer, and even make inevitable, the sovereign's intent to extinguish the title of a colonized people. But what happens when that order of things — that source of legitimacy — is no longer justifiable? For the *Calder* case in the late twentieth century, then, the Supreme Court's decision achieved a careful and strategic management of justice by creating an additional source of Aboriginal title in Canada — one that preserved the legitimacy of past jurisprudence, all the while creatively negotiating a new justice to come.

There is always an urgent desire that there be an absolute and foundational grounding for what we do in the name of metaphysical ideals, and law is far from immune to this exigency. This explains the critical importance of a judicial posturing that demonstrates interpretative strategies and the rhetoric of universality: it implies that the decision to be made pre-exists the act of deciding (Asch and Bell 1997). Justice dictates, judges follow. Juridical expertise in its constant and unflinching exercise suggests presence — the presence of justice through an attachment to a fundamental grounding. This is akin to what Jacques Derrida terms metaphysics — a "metaphysics of presence" that not only suggests that justice exists, but that it is also touched, accessed and at work in the law. In spite of so many things — dissenting opinions, inconsistent case law or result-oriented decisions in highly politicized situations — judicial discourse projects a transcendentalization of norms in order to intimate the presence of justice. But the vast and complex edifice of legal expertise still butts up against its own limits from time to time, encountering the ghost of its own illegitimacy. This is representative of the instability and irreconcilability between law and justice, but also of the inevitable politics of memory and inheritance that haunt our attempts at justice:

> If I am getting ready to speak at length about ghosts, inheritance, and generations, generations of ghosts, which is to say about certain *others* who are not present, nor presently living, either to us, in us, or outside us, it is in the name of *justice*. Of justice where it is not yet, not yet *there*, where it is no longer, let us understand where it is no longer *present*, and where it will never be, no more than the law, reducible to laws or rights.... No justice — let us not say no law and once again we are not speaking here of laws — seems possible or thinkable without the principle of some *responsibility*, beyond all living present, within that which disjoins the living present, before the ghosts of those who are not yet born or who are already dead, be they victims of wars, political or other kinds of violence, nationalist, racist, colonialist, sexist, or other kinds of exterminations, victims of the oppressions of capitalist imperialism or any of the forms of totalitarianism. (Derrida 1994: xviii; emphasis in original)

In her study of German post-unification trials for human rights violations in the former East Germany, Christiane Wilke (2010) finds the courts haunted by ghosts from their own failed trials of Nazi perpetrators. In such profoundly compromising situations, sometimes "the institutions that are asked to 'settle accounts' with a haunting past are themselves unsettled by the spectral presence of injustices they had either committed or failed to address" (Wilke 2010: 74). In Canada, surely the courts have been haunted at times by the ghosts of past failures to address the injustices of colonialism. In over a century of Aboriginal rights and title jurisprudence in Canada, every decision concerning the rights of colonized peoples has carried with it a weighty jurisprudential inheritance of precedents and legal principles — much of it serving to limit the justice that could be made available to Aboriginal peoples. This is why Derrida's concept of inheritance is inextricably entwined with an injunction on responsibility: one must "filter, sift, criticize" that which is handed down, nothing is to be taken for granted (Derrida 1994: 18).

In essence, much of Canada's jurisprudential history up until the late twentieth century seemed to amount to two somewhat incongruent conclusions: Aboriginal peoples' rights to and possession of their land does have juridical dimensions, yet all of this is for naught should the Crown act otherwise. The former conclusion is attested to by the early royal charters and patents examined by Slattery (2005) and an entire history of treaty-making, while the latter is illustrated with a history of title "extinguishment" as a post-hoc legal justification for the colonization of those lands unceded by treaty. Thus, in that late twentieth century moment when the judiciary was poised to make a change to Aboriginal rights and title, perhaps it was faced with generations of ghosts from a jurisprudential history of which no one could be proud. In discussing the interpretation and significance of the still somewhat new *Constitution Act, 1982*, the *Sparrow* decision cites an essay by Noel Lyon on the same topic. The lines quoted, however, have less to do with the practical application of section 35 than with offering moral exculpation to the courts for such a sad legal history: "Section 35 calls for a just settlement for aboriginal peoples. It renounces the old rules of the game under which the Crown established courts of law and denied those courts the authority to question sovereign claims made by the Crown" (Lyon 1988: 100). Although the *Sparrow* decision's quote of Lyon stops there, Lyon (1988: 100) goes on to claim that "those courts were bound to legitimize every sovereign act of suppression of aboriginal cultures." This claim about the moral impotence of the courts prior to the *Constitution Act, 1982* is an interesting one. It would seem invalidated by the fact that the *Calder* decision chose to recognize a form of Aboriginal title at common law nine years prior to it, and even more so by the fact that the *Calder* decision rooted itself in early nineteenth century decisions authored largely by Chief Justice John Marshall of the Supreme Court of the United States — making that country the first jurisdiction to recognize a common law doctrine of Aboriginal title, some 150 years in advance of *Calder*. Parallel to this, the 1990 *Sparrow* decision's affirmation of the "clear and plain" rule concerning the extinguishment of Aboriginal rights and title was taken from the 1941 case of *United States v. Santa Fe Pacific Railroad*.

THE QUESTIONS NOT ASKED

There is a larger question of inheritance, however. It is a questioning of inheritance that continues to be particularly unsettling for the courts for if *Calder*, the *Constitution Act, 1982* and *Sparrow* announced the need for a new direction in Aboriginal rights and title jurisprudence, the direction chosen in the recent cultural rights decisions can be seen as an attempt to obscure those infamies of Canadian justice that have been preserved. Much of this stems from the fact that *the legitimacy of the courts and Canadian law over unceded rights and title is rooted in the questionable legitimacy of the Crown's sovereignty*. One of the greatest overriding questions, then, has been how the SCC might choose to filter, sift through and criticize what is ultimately its own questionable inheritance: being the arbiter of justice at this site of conflict.

What it has chosen, however, is to cover up rather than to question, with the strategic management of justiciability — that is, the subtle limiting of that which can be questioned and determined by juridical practices of justice. The justness of certain things cannot be decided by the courts; certain questions simply cannot be entertained. Indeed, there is a brief assertion in many of the recent cases that describes Aboriginal rights as the means "to reconcile the existence of pre-existing Aboriginal societies with the sovereignty of the Crown" (*R. v. Van der Peet* 1996: 315). What remains immobile, then — that which never changes in this equation — is the assumption that the Crown has ultimate sovereignty. How this came to be is not questioned. In this sense, Aboriginal rights and title jurisprudence is akin to a mountain of misleading and rationalizing logic piled atop a small core of colonial instrumentality. It is the *grundnorm*, or foundational rule, that forms the basis of this controversial body of law. But it is also unjustifiable, and so must remain unquestioned behind the eminently principled and complex workings of the legal practice of justice. A silence is therefore "walled up in the violent structure of the founding act" (Derrida 1992: 14).

Thus, with its own legitimacy rooted in the same illicit inheritance of colonization, the courts maintain a certain blind spot in their search for justice: the unquestioned, paramount sovereignty of the Crown. In turn, this perversion acts as both the condition of possibility and the cause of certain other aspects of contemporary Aboriginal rights and title jurisprudence — namely, an inverted burden of proof in the process of justice, and the very idea that the possibilities and limits of justice could or should be "culturally" located within Aboriginality itself.

Indeed, for a legal system that purports to base Aboriginal rights and title in prior occupation, Kent McNeil (2001: 324) points to the unanswerable question of "why the onus is on Aboriginal peoples to prove their own title as against the European colonizers when we all know that they were here occupying lands when the newcomers arrived." The cultural rights approach shelters Crown legitimacy by putting the burden of proof on Aboriginal claimants, entertaining each dispute as an open question, as something that may or may not be a right, or a right that may or may not exist. And although earlier case law, such as *In re Southern Rhodesia*, did much the same thing, current jurisprudence does so under the guise of protecting cultural difference and mobilizing a much more positive and endearing image of Aboriginality.[3] But in a post-1982 context, what the SCC has done is revived the era of extinguishment in a cloaked fashion. Where statutes and past precedents have made it such that Aboriginal rights and title are now constitutionally entrenched and can no longer be extinguished, the cultural rights approach simply brings extinguishment in through the back door by creating uncertainty over the initial existence of title or rights.

Michael Asch has noticed the dubious silence on certain issues, as well as the distracting culture talk. For him, "the Court has moved to rely on culture to determine the content of Aboriginal rights in order to avoid exploration in another area: political relations. The Court is determined not to confront the issue of how legitimate sovereignty was acquired by the Crown" (Asch 2000: 133). Others have noticed similar avoidances too. In considering the point in legal history after the *Sparrow* case, Chris Andersen (2005) stresses that the SCC had the option of protecting Aboriginal autonomy, but, with the *Van der Peet* decision, it clearly opted to protect some form of Aboriginal difference instead. John Borrows (1999: 558) asks, pointedly, "How can lands possessed by Aboriginal peoples for centuries be undermined by another nation's assertion of sovereignty? What alchemy transmutes the basis of Aboriginal possession into the golden bedrock of Crown title?" That alchemy is simply the inherent elasticity in judicial interpretation, for while there is nothing inherent to these political disputes that would make it inevitable that their resolution be framed as a cultural issue, the law is always able to conjure any number of purportedly self-evident premises that are meant to suggest otherwise. Thus, with the subtle revival of a theme from *In re Southern Rhodesia*, the deciding opinion in *Van der Peet* (1996: 320) modifies the basis of Aboriginal rights stated in *Calder*, previously taken from nineteenth century American jurisprudence, by stating that they "arise from the prior occupation of land, but they also arise from the prior social organization and distinctive cultures of aboriginal peoples on that land."

Some might be surprised at such a critique simply because the changes brought about through *Calder*, the *Constitution Act, 1982* and *Sparrow* marked a vast improvement over past case law. Indeed, some might consider Aboriginal title as fairly robust, and its burden of proof in Canada has thus far proven to be less onerous than in jurisdictions such as Australia (see Young 2008). But too many assumptions are naturalized in those conclusions; the burden of critique must be reversed. The point is that, in the wake of the usurpation of sovereignty, self-determination and territory, over time legal practices of justice had difficulty reconciling on even their own terms, the misleading veneer of the cultural rights approach, which serves to naturalize a resolution that would otherwise be an affront to what Bourdieu (1987: 817) terms "naïve intuitions of fairness." If one speaks the language of the law, there is a subtext replete with unquestioned, yet entirely problematic, principles. For the courts, there is no questioning the fact that the Crown has absolute sovereignty (with which Aboriginal rights must be reconciled). Their actions also suggest that there can exist a justice that remedies the removal of sovereignty from formerly independent, politically sourced peoples, without giving that sovereignty back — one needs only the correct legal formula and the aid of the law in order to arrive at it. Lastly, while the Crown will never again take rights or land away from Aboriginal peoples, "justice" may simply tell them that they do not have, in the first place, title to the land upon which they find themselves or the right to continue with a practice or activity.

CONCLUSION: HAUNTING JUSTICE

According to Christiane Wilke, haunting can be indicative of deeper injustices that defy resolution within a trial. Ghosts "are about a possibility of justice: they are reminders of a need for justice and can point to the impossibility of justice within the constraints of the law or a courtroom" (Wilke 2010: 77). Aboriginal rights and title law is haunted by its ghosts. Unlike Dickens' character Ebenezer Scrooge, however, the law never fully arrives at a cathartic and transforming moment of epiphany and redemption. Its haunting only aggravates its neuroses and its insistence that justice can be found through continued half measures. To be sure, "seeing the ghosts is not the same as doing justice to them" (Wilke 2010: 90).

Since 1973, Aboriginal rights and title jurisprudence has carried the hopes of justice as a revolutionary purity, a moment of legal epiphany that would bring about some form of undoing of the colonial travesty. After the positive developments for Aboriginal people in *Calder*, the *Constitution Act, 1982* and the *Sparrow* decision, the Canadian judiciary was standing on the edge of a precipice at which Aboriginal rights and title seemed poised to become an almost post-legal question — the moment of a triumphant coup for Aboriginal autonomy (see Anderson 2005). Instead, the Supreme Court of Canada maintained that rights and title are to be deduced from and bound to the courts' view of Aboriginal cultural difference. Its turn to the cultural rights approach has without a doubt reined in Aboriginal rights at a point when they had gained the most momentum. But a more fundamental strategic necessity is this: at a moment in history when Aboriginal people in Canada thought that the law might question its own self-identity, its own inheritance, that it might somehow be experiencing a period of epiphany and redemptive transformation, what we rather encounter is an elaborate new jurisprudence that continues to avoid confrontation with the question of the Crown's acquisition of sovereignty.

So much of the law's energies can be seen as centred on disguising the (not so) secret disparity between justice and itself. There is a gap between what justice is meant to be and what the law does. Yet, the fact of the matter is that we have fields of expertise — regimes of practical human activity — that purport to meet the needs and demands of justice. Every day, we apparently calculate, locate and apply justice. In this situation, the law has avoided entertaining one of the most important questions of justice in the wake of colonization, but it nevertheless continues to intimate that its expertise leads to justice.

Notes

1. This research was supported by the Social Sciences and Humanities Research Council of Canada.
2. The "region by region" claim is especially true for those groups that are spread out over a larger territory, such as with the Métis.
3. Although, interestingly enough, the *In re Southern Rhodesia* decision's evolutionist scale of social organization made its way into early Aboriginal title case law in Canada (cf. *Hamlet of Baker Lake et al. v. Minister of Indian Affairs and Northern Development et al.* 1980). This then found its way into the land claims negotiations process, with Indian and Northern Affairs Canada (INAC 2003: 8) stating that an Aboriginal group must demonstrate that it "is and was an organized society" in order to qualify for entry into negotiations with the federal government.

References

Andersen, Chris. 2005. "Residual Tensions of Empire: Contemporary Métis Communities and the Canadian Judicial Imagination." In Michael Murphy (ed.), *Reconfiguring Aboriginal-State Relations. Canada: The State of the Federation 2003*. Montreal, Kingston: McGill-Queen's University Press.

Asch, Michael. 2000. "The Judicial Conceptualization of Culture after Delgamuukw and Van der Peet." *Review of constitutional studies/Revue d'études constitutionnelles* 5, 2.

Asch, Michael, and Catherine Bell. 1997. "Challenging Assumptions: The Impact of Precedent in Aboriginal Rights Litigation." In Michael Asch (ed.), *Aboriginal and Treaty Rights in Canada*. Vancouver: University of British Columbia Press.

Borrows, John. 1999. "Sovereignty's Alchemy: An Analysis of Delgamuukw v. British Columbia." *Osgoode Hall Law Journal* 37, 3.

Bourdieu, Pierre. 1987. "The Force of Law: Toward a Sociology of the Juridical Field." *The Hastings Law Journal* 38, 5.

Calder v. Attorney-General of British Columbia. 1973. S.C.R. 313.

Canada. 1982. "Constitution Act, 1982." In <*laws.justice.gc.ca/eng/Const/Const_index. html*>.

Delgamuukw v. British Columbia. 1997. 3 S.C.R. 1010.

Derrida, Jacques. 1992. "Force of Law: The 'Mystical Foundation of Authority.'" In Drucilla Cornell, Michel Rosenfeld, and David Gray Carlson (eds.), *Deconstruction and the Possibility of Justice*. New York: Routledge.

___. 1994. *Specters of Marx: The State of the Debt, the Work of Mourning, and the New International*. New York: Routledge.

Douzinas, Costas, Ronnie Warrington and Shaun McVeigh. 1991. *Postmodern Jurisprudence: The Law of Text in the Texts of Law*. New York: Routledge.

Foucault, Michel. 1977. "Nietzsche, Genealogy, History." In Donald F. Bouchard (ed.), *Language, Counter-Memory, Practice: Selected Essays and Interviews*. Ithaca: Cornell University Press.

Hamlet of Baker Lake et al. v. Minister of Indian Affairs and Northern Development et al. 1980. 107 D.L.R. (3d) 513.

In re Southern Rhodesia. 1919. A.C. 210 (P.C.).

INAC. 2003. *Resolving Aboriginal Claims: A Practical Guide to Canadian Experiences*. Ottawa:

Minister of Indian Affairs and Northern Development.

Kulchyski, Peter. 1994. *Unjust Relations: Aboriginal Rights in Canadian Courts*. Toronto: Oxford University Press.

Lyon, Noel. 1988. "An Essay on Constitutional Interpretation." *Osgoode Hall Law Journal* 26, 1.

McNeil, Kent. 1997. "Aboriginal Title and Aboriginal Rights: What's the Connection?" *Alberta Law Review* 36, 1.

___. 1998. "Aboriginal Rights in Canada: From Title to Land to Territorial Sovereignty." *Tulsa Journal of Comparative and International Law* 5, 2.

___. 2001. "Aboriginal Rights in Transition: Reassessing Aboriginal Title and Governance." *American Review of Canadian Studies* 31, 1/2.

___. 2009. "Judicial Treatment of Indigenous Land Rights in the Common Law World." In Benjamin J. Richardson, Shin Imai and Kent McNeil (eds.), *Indigenous Peoples and the Law: Comparative and Critical Perspectives*. Portland: Hart Publishing.

Miller, Bruce G. 1998. "Culture as Cultural Defense: An American Indian Sacred Site in Court." *American Indian Quarterly* 22, 1/2.

Niezen, Ronald. 2003. "Culture and the Judiciary: The Meaning of the Culture Concept as a Source of Aboriginal Rights in Canada." *Canadian Journal of Law and Society* 18, 2.

R. v. Sparrow. 1990. 1 S.C.R. 1075.

R. v. Van der Peet. 1996. 137 D.L.R. (4th).

Slattery, Brian. 2005. "Paper Empires: The Legal Dimensions of French and English Ventures in North America." In John McLaren, A.R. Buck, and Nancy E. Wright (eds.), *Despotic Dominion: Property Rights in British Settler Societies*. Vancouver: University of British Columbia Press.

St. Catherine's Milling and Lumber v. The Queen. 1888. 14 A.C. 46 (P.C.).

United States v. Santa Fe Pacific R. Co., 1941. 314 U.S. 339

Valverde, Mariana. 1995. "Deconstructive Marxism." *Labour/Le Travail* 36.

___. 1999. "Derrida's Justice and Foucault's Freedom: Ethics, History, and Social Movements." *Law & Social Inquiry* 24, 3.

Wilke, Christiane. 2010. "Enter Ghost: Haunted Courts and Haunting Judgments in Transitional Justice." *Law and Critique* 21, 1.

Young, Simon. 2008. *The Trouble with Tradition: Native Title and Cultural Change*. Annandale, New South Wales: Federation Press.

NB: SCR = Supreme Court Reports
    DLR = Dominion Law Reports
    AC/PC = Appeal Cases/Privy Council (i.e., JCPC)
    US = United States Reports

CHAPTER FIVE

FOUCAULT'S STRUGGLE FOR JUSTICE

Bourgeois versus Popular Conceptions

Ronjon Paul Datta

> As we gather together in solidarity to express a feeling of mass injustice, we must not lose sight of what brought us together. We write so that all people who feel wronged by the corporate forces of the world can know that we are your allies. (New York City General Assembly, September 29, 2011, Occupy Wall Street)

TWO COMPETING APPROACHES TO JUSTICE IN FOUCAULT

In this chapter, I approach the problem of theorizing justice by drawing on two different approaches to justice found in the works of the French social analyst Michel Foucault (1926–1984), counted among the most significant resources in critical social analysis today.[1] I highlight a tension in Foucault's work between what will be called here an "internalist" approach (that is, his "nominalism") and an attenuated "externalist" approach, similar to some contemporary forms of realist methodology. I attend especially to a critical inspection of Foucault's theoretical reasoning and its consequences for theorizing justice. I also aim to demonstrate something about how to engage in critical and creative theoretical reasoning and why paying attention to the fundamental assumptions of a theoretical system is important. Fundamental assumptions substantially affect one's reasoning through the research process as a whole (methodology), and the more substantive components of theorizing in the social sciences about what kinds of questions one should ask and how we recognize whether or not a concept or a theoretical model is adequate to the issue at hand (Datta, Frauley and Pearce 2010: 244).

One major legacy of critical social science has been to convincingly argue that we always bring some preconceptions to the research process. This also means that social science needs to reflect upon theoretical work itself (Lopez 2003; Pearce 2001). One can, however, be proactive about this and consider what kind of conceptions to bring to one's research. Moreover, we cannot simply say that "theories" and "concepts" are, strictly speaking, tools that we pick up to do something or perspectives, because the concepts we have available to us both constrain and enable what we can do with them (Pearce 2001: 7). That we may have need of a concept or theory as a tool already assumes that we have a worthwhile project. This worth presupposes that the research is intellectually justifiable, justifications that are precisely theoretical in nature.

As it concerns theories as "perspectives," this too already presupposes that what we wish to look at is already defined. But definitions and the worth of research programs are always theoretically dependent — the world does not simply tell us what is important. Moreover, this kind of critical theoretical reflection is indispensable since if we cannot be clear about what we are talking about or examining when it comes to terms like "justice," it will be difficult for us to be able to understand what we are trying to get at. So, when it comes to thinking about justice, examining the concepts, rationales, analyses and explanations found in existing theoretical works provides a way for social scientists to think through the analytical and explanatory power and logical coherence of theoretical systems in which terms like "justice" do their work. Given how influential and important Foucault's work has been in the social sciences and humanities, especially when it comes to analyzing the emergence of modern political formations, it is a reasonable choice for reflecting on justice.[2]

FOUCAULT'S THEMATICS: AN OVERVIEW

Foucault is not a thinker easily defined and located in one discipline or another; he refused such identifications (Foucault 1972: 17). His writings address, in a very distinct and careful way, questions about how modern Western people have come to be concerned with madness and reason, criminality and sexuality, normality and abnormality, pleasure and perversity, art and governing. In doing so, he disturbs the self-evidence of how we experience, think about and judge ourselves and others as "reasonable" or as "normal" and how this in turn shapes what we see as a "problem." Foucault's main books like *The History of Madness* (2006c), *The Birth of the Clinic* (1975), *The Order of Things* (1994a), *Discipline and Punish* (1979) and *The History of Sexuality* (1994b) are primarily preoccupied with tracing the historical transformations and shifts of these experiences that orient our contemporary existence. He addresses how we develop and judge amongst proposed policy solutions and how domination and exclusion are exercised in the imposition of solutions to problems. In the process, he analyzed the generation of what counts as a serious social problem in the first place (Foucault 2003d: 60; 2003b: 181, 190–91; 1996: 408). He challenges many fundamental assumptions about the allegedly humanitarian features of Western civilization. He shows how relying on science and reason to solve our problems and free humanity rather traps us in different forms of mute, subtle and masked dominations pervasive in daily life (Foucault 1979; 1994b). He also drew attention to how the ostensible drive to gain the truth about human beings has made people subordinate to various systems of authoritative knowledge production that he called "discourses," deemed to be true, that justify various exercises of power, public policies, laws, regulations, domination and social exclusion, all too frequently to the advantage of those well-placed in a societal hierarchy.

His work suggests that a concern with justice and the resurgence of interest in social justice (see, for example, Brodie 2007; Fraser 2005) is peculiar, perhaps even out of step with what is actually happening. (This is a position closely linked to his internalist account.) He also inherits, from Friedrich Nietzsche, an iconoclastic critical sensibility about calling into question the dominant values perpetuated in social institutions and practices: it is possible to abolish and transform the dominant values in a society that serve to justify the dominance of groups like legal experts. In short, Foucault was an astute critical social analyst who attempted to diagnose the contingent ways in which our contemporary world enables and constrains people in Western civilization, making us what we are, and sought to account for how such a world has come to be so. His work refuses the limitations of the present and subjects it to relentless criticism in order to show how the ways we think and act that constitute our existence can be made otherwise.

Foucault's work provides a unique case for considering the theoretical merits and advantages of an externalist analytic when it comes to theorizing justice. This is because his own writings and interventions on justice themselves at times use an internalist approach and at others an externalist one. His externalist approach suggests that being too committed to an internalist approach that, by focusing on the specialized discourses and institutions of law, risks repeating the errors and illusions of bourgeois justice precisely by missing the bigger picture that laws, justice and state administration always occur within, are affected by and affect a complex totality of social relations (see, for example, Hunt 1993). Foucault's externalist approach suggests that the analysis of the administration of state law and justice must not obscure or ignore the political contexts and conflicts traversing class divided societies. Following from his externalist/realist approach, popular justice is theorized by Foucault as a value-system for making and enforcing decisions that are not mediated by, nor dependent on, the formal apparatuses of state law and justice with its rules, experts, courts and monopoly on violence (see, for example, Fitzpatrick 1992; Norrie 1996). In this regard, I will be arguing for a qualified externalist approach, based on Foucault's own reasoning, not least since it provides a way of avoiding the conflation of law with justice, a risk one runs when adopting an internalist approach.

My basic thesis is that Foucault's concept of justice as articulated in "On Popular Justice" (Foucault 1980), even though underdeveloped, is sociologically realist and externalist and refers to the immanent (existing but not necessarily practised) potential of people to mobilize the terms justice/injustice to indict and punish dominant classes who benefit from inequalities existing in societies. Furthermore, popular justice needs to be elaborated through accessible democratic political practices lest it devolve into the ideological form of bourgeois court justice.

A BRIEF INTRODUCTION TO METATHEORY, SOCIOLOGICAL REALISM AND FOUCAULT'S NOMINALISM

Metatheory is the branch of social science research concerned with the basic sets of assumptions that wittingly and unwittingly inform and guide any account of what is happening in the social world and how and why it is happening. Crucially, it requires offering justifications for why people should engage in some research projects, like thinking about justice, at all. Metatheory has three branches. The first is epistemology. It aims to address how people can gain valid knowledge about the world. The second is ontology. Ontology addresses questions concerning the nature of the world and the being of things. The third branch concerns normative, value-oriented issues (or an "axiology") about the nature of "the good" and problems about what one ought and ought not do. Metatheory also requires reflecting on theorizing and the links between methodology, substantive research and the social world. After all, if one can't figure out something of the nature of what one aims to investigate and how to gain some reasonable knowledge of it, it would be very difficult to do any reasonable research at all. Thus, basic metatheoretical assumptions in a theory inherently affect how one will be able to think about an issue like justice including how one is to go about doing research pertinent to the question of justice. Realism and nominalism are two types of metatheory in social analysis rather at odds with each other as concerns their respective theoretical and methodological commitments and assumptions.

Sociological Realism

Sociological realism is one strain of metatheory, and its roots go back to the classical tradition of sociology and social theory (Woodiwiss 2005; Frisby and Sayer 1986). Several basic tenets are crucial to sociological realism (Pearce and Woodiwiss 2001; see Woodiwiss 2005: 31–54). The first is that the social world is taken to exist independently of our knowledge or awareness of it. For example, one need not understand or even be aware of labour market forces and the workings of contract law to be an employee. The second tenet is the position that the world consists of matter for if it weren't accessible through our senses, there would be no reason to think that anything exists outside of our minds, and we would hence be unable to explain how people learn anything. These first two tenets imply that while knowledge changes and develops (we have the ability to learn from research; erroneous understandings can be corrected; knowledge is said to be "transitive"), the reality known does not change in the same way. That is, our knowledge of reality does not change or affect the real causal powers at work in the world, and hence social reality is said to be "intransitive" in relation to changes in knowledge (Bhaskar 1986). Realist ontology also implies that in order to accept that we actually do have valid (but provisional) knowledge (for example, physics and chemistry) we must hold that it is the structure of reality itself that makes this possible, not least since we as humans are part of the reality we aim to know.

Knowledge claims about the nature and workings of reality are held in check by realist metatheory, and researchers are reminded that there is a reality to be wrong about. Or, put differently, while there may be no one right answer, there are wrong ones. Moreover, since research is itself a social activity that takes place in particular historical contexts, it will inevitably be limited by existing beliefs and understandings. Realist epistemology also means that theories precede, but must not determine, research results. Researchers and theorists, after all, are born into and are socialized in specific social and historical circumstances, and hence some preconceptions are inevitably brought to the research process and affect how people come to understand research findings. But to rely on one's preconceptions, even if based on a widely accepted theory, means committing the error of theoreticism, merely using empirical data to illustrate a thesis decided in advance of empirical investigations.

There is one further component of this realism that is important, namely that it has a "stratified" or "differentiated" nature — there are different levels of the same reality (Frauley and Pearce 2007). The three levels are: the real, the actual and the empirical. The empirical is taken to be a subset of the actual, and the actual a subset of the real. The empirical is what people experience of the material world through their senses, the cognition of which depends on the linguistic resources available for describing it. The empirical can only apprehend a part of what can actually be experienced. In turn, what actually exists and happens is only a part of what could actually exist or be produced by real causal forces and mechanisms. For example, the taste of my turkey and Swiss cheese sandwich constitutes the empirical; each bite is different given the composition of the sandwich. The actual is the event of me eating that particular sandwich. At the level of the real, the restaurant that actually produced the sandwich that I in part experience with each bite and chew could have produced a range of other sandwiches that I could have actually ordered. This further implies that it is impossible for me to empirically experience all of the possibilities simultaneously. But, one can still conceptualize the real conditions (that are only partially actualized in any event) that make for a variety of possibilities about what sandwiches could be ordered and enjoyed (or not, as the case may be). This combination of what I actually ordered and could have ordered is the result of real components (chefs, ingredients, accounting, customer demand, my preferences and so on) such that it is possible for me to enjoy one of many items on the menu. Hence, what actually happens and what we can empirically apprehend through our senses does not exhaust what else could actually happen (that is, become an actual event). Realist metatheory thus makes it possible to think of alternative viable ways of configuring social life.

Foucault's Nominalism

While Foucault avoided labels for his work, "nominalism" is one he accepted (Foucault 2003d: 59; 2008: 317–18; Veyne 2010: 10; Datta 2007). In contrast to realism, nominalism as a metatheoretical position conventionally means affirming that only individual, singular things exist and that they cannot be grouped together on the basis of an underlying foundation. The names we give to things and the ways we group things are only social conventions of human language and systems and do not correspond to any more basic or natural qualities (Rajchman 1985: 74). In this view, every criminal or deviant is different. That judges or psychologists call them "criminal" or "deviant" is just a matter of a convenient shared habit. Thus, just because we call a group of offenders "deviants" does not mean that they all share a fundamental underlying real source for their criminal actions (for example, a deviant soul or personality defect).

Contemporary nominalists argue that "it is better to start off with detailed practices, details of what was done and what was said, and then make the intellectual effort to make explicit the 'discourse' [that is, the classificatory system] surrounding them" (Veyne 2010: 10). For Foucault, the things and kinds of people that we think about come into existence (are actually constituted) by our practices of naming them as such. This being so, Foucault's nominalism means rejecting that social reality exists independently of our knowledge of it (for example, classifying some as "mad" or "perverts," sharing a fundamental, real common feature that our classifications then accurately capture). This is why Foucault's nominalism involves a rejection of a realist approach. So, a nominalist approach to justice would reject any notion that justice could be a real, trans-historical thing that could be used to judge a state of affairs. Foucault's research focus is on the conventions and institutional conditions of labelling, naming and classifying and, crucially, the power relations in a society that make it possible for authoritative persons, like teachers for instance, to do so.

In his research practice, Foucault took highly authoritative classificatory systems, as found in scholarly books, manuals, policy documents, maps and technical drawings, as his main object of historical investigation. Foucault systematically engaged in looking at systems of naming, examining how "systems of thought" (or discourses) attempt to render an orderly and ostensibly truthful account of the world (Foucault 1994a; Foucault 1972). He examined the human sciences (such as psychology, sociology and criminology), impeccably analyzing and describing their contours and their historical, conceptual and institutional conditions of existence and production. He was the first to show how "Man/humanity" got named as an object of scientific knowledge in early nineteenth century Western societies, becoming a potential site of intervention and transformation to be guided precisely by a scientific approach to humanity (Foucault 1994a). This scientific approach was used to attempt to better both individual and collective life. For Foucault, research know-how generates the raw information to be transformed by the social sciences into systematic, scientific understandings of humanity and by policymakers in a variety of institutions (such as private enterprise, state institutions and schools) into policy techniques in the attempt to generate more effective, efficient and economical ways of improving performance (Datta 2007).

The production of knowledge of the social world, like schemes for identifying and classifying the good and the bad within a population, and the policy programs developed on this knowledge base as a means for improving performance, were also shown by Foucault to depend on a variety of small-scale but pervasive relations of domination that he called "power" (Foucault 1979; Foucault 1994b). In this respect, power relations are a pre-condition of the human sciences. Moreover, drawing on Foucault's work on the use of "police" (Foucault 2003b) as a technique for surveying and gaining knowledge of all facets of social life so as to render it more orderly and productive, a range of social analysts (see, for example, Donzelot 1979) have shown how "the social" was constituted by the power-knowledge techniques invented by police (see Brodie 2007: 96). The consequences of a nominalist approach provides a basis for rejecting realism because if gaining knowledge of the object (epistemology) and the existence of the object (ontology) are really one and the same process (that is, for Foucault, discursive practices subtended by power relations), the realist distinction between a social reality existing externally to and independently of knowledge is nonsensical. This is why, in stark contrast to sociological realism, major Foucauldian social analysts argue that "we do not try to characterize how social life *really* was and why" (Rose and Miller 1992: 177). A broader realist-externalist approach is thus dismissed by nominalist metatheory.

FOUCAULT'S DISPLACEMENT OF JUSTICE BY DEVELOPMENT AND SECURITY

The implications of a Foucauldian nominalist approach can be demonstrated by attending to his historical analyses of the emergence of modern government between the early sixteenth century and the early nineteenth century, when "liberalism" became influential (Foucault 2006b; 2008; Dupont and Pearce 2001). Crucially, a Foucauldian nominalist approach to justice can leave aside the question of law and power (Hunt 1993: 267).[3] In medieval monarchal rule, all transgressions of law were deemed an affront to the sovereign, which in turn justified revenge on the bodies of criminals. Modern rule depends on a very different sensibility (Foucault 1979). Modern governmental rule and power is characteristically productive and facilitative, targeting and aiming to shape what individuals and populations do. Focusing on individuals' bodily capacities is called "discipline" and targeting the life of populations in order to normalize them is termed "biopolitics" (Foucault 1994b: 139). Foucault shows in striking detail how the scientific search for what was normal came to inform policies for dealing with deviant and so-called abnormal persons and groups (Ewald 1990). (Thinking about terms like "standard deviation" and "normal curve" in quantitative analysis might be helpful here.) Such policies go far beyond a medieval sovereign's seeking to avenge a transgression of a command and instead enter into the diffuse terrain of administrative agencies, experts and the population itself.

Justice, Foucault points out, is basically a feudal-medieval, monarchical-religious concept and value closely tied to the royal way of thinking about rule (Foucault 1994b). For monarchism, a command-form of law and violence was the means through which to achieve a desired "state of justice" (Foucault 2006b: 109). In the medieval world, justice could be said to have been achieved if and when all persons willingly and lovingly served their superiors just as they willingly loved and served God — in doing so they became virtuous (Foucault 2006b). Social order was thought about in static terms, the aim of which was to emulate the divinely appointed and eternal order of the kingdom of heaven. The political texts and discourses of the late medieval world show that a concern for justice was a central value, suggesting that a modern concern with justice is rather anachronistic.

This medieval outlook on social order and coordination began to change with the sixteenth century emergence of a new political mentality concerned with how best to govern and hence not with either the state of justice or the problem of rulers securing their rule over a territory. Foucault calls this new outlook "governmentality." Governmentality is a system of political thought concerned with knowing what can be developed in the life of a population, attending to its individualized and collective elements within a secured territory — one that is secured both internally from rebellion and immorality and externally from other states. State governing, "the political form of government" (Foucault 2006b: 89), is a way of exercising power by finding out about, intervening in and shaping what people are doing by facilitating some actions deemed desirable by government officials and placing obstacles to others. This is why Foucault formulates government as "the conduct of conducts" and states that "to govern, in this sense, is to structure the possible field of action of others" (Foucault 2003c: 137–38). Let's take the example of aiming to reduce air pollution in a large city. Instead of attaching penalties, fines or imprisonment for driving a car with high emissions, a governmentalist approach simply raises the parking rates in a downtown core such that the cost of driving downtown, instead of taking public transit, for instance, becomes prohibitive. People then are more likely to do the right thing (from the point of view of an environmentalist public policy) even while freely acting in their own financial interests (saving a few dollars on the trip). There is then no need for a broad campaign of environmental justice or for lessons about a new "green" moral code to achieve the desired result.

The governmental concern with the future and development is derived from an old model of how Christian pastors are supposed to care for their congregation; it requires caring for each individual and the whole, all in the interest of future salvation. But, instead of a focus on salvation in the next world, with government there emerges a concerned for the well being of the population, supervised by the state, as the preferred path to security and future prosperity. The centrality of police is crucial to this process because it is a practice of gaining knowledge of everything that is happening in a society with the aim of improving its best parts (Foucault 2003b). Governmentality introduces a decidedly historical framework of perpetuating the development and betterment of populations. So, in contrast to medieval concerns and aims of seeking to mirror the timeless kingdom of heaven and state of justice guided by the hand of God, government has a different set of aims centred on the population. Significantly, the justification of government lies in the value of its goals (Foucault 2006b: 96). Intervening in the social world by gaining detailed knowledge of it (that is, police knowledge) was thus justified by recourse to arguments about a better future, requiring a focus on security deemed necessary to sustaining the ongoing project of criticizing, reforming and improving government and continuing to develop and improve the life of the population. The concern with governing economically and efficiently replaced the earlier value of the just kingdom with the value of a dynamic, growing economy.

Instead of teaching people religious or moral values, governing, especially as understood in liberalism, relies on economic markets to reward good behaviour and punish bad behaviour (that is, we are dealing with the marketization of morals). The classical form of moral reasoning focused on the broader communal consequences of one's actions. In modern governmentality, consequences are made to have financial costs. So, if you make immoral or bad choices, you will become poorer ("sin taxes" on tobacco and alcohol are a good example of this); make the right choices and your wealth will grow. The reverse is sometimes also argued to be the case: if you are poor, it is because you are immoral, lack motivation or are lazy. Moreover, it is believed that economic growth and capital accumulation, facilitated by economical and efficient government, seeks to optimize the conditions for making good choices. This, in turn, maximizes the utility for all and thus generates societal outcomes that come closest to achieving the greatest good and happiness for the greatest number (see Steiner 2010). That, in short, is how modern government is rationalized and justified in expert discourses. The emphasis on government and the development of optimal conditions for growth provides a new, distinctively modern value system for the whole of society. In short, the value of justice has been replaced by economic development.

Security also emerges as an important value and goal because it is taken to be the condition necessary for good government. Security, as a fundamental concern of government, is about "the future-oriented management of risks" (Valverde 2007: 172) and why security "deals in series of possible and probable events" (Gordon 1991: 20; see also Osborne 1996: 201). This gives us some indication as to why contemporary policing involves identifying "at-risk youths" and involvement in preventative measures (Zedner 2006; 2007). Security, in short, is about protecting desirable paths of efficient economic development (Datta 2011).

To follow Foucault's reasoning then, the older concern with justice is no longer a useful reference point for understanding the world and no longer corresponds to the modern political organization of social life. This perhaps explains in part the difficulty that we have today in generating a consensus about what justice means.

FOUCAULT: "ON POPULAR JUSTICE"

In an interview with anonymous French Maoist Marxists in 1971 (Foucault 1980), Foucault takes an approach to theorizing justice quite different from his nominalism while retaining a commitment to understanding present society via historical analysis. Foucault, in this period, was very concerned with contemporary politics and struggles (Macey 1993). Important here is his key role in the Groupe d'informations sur les prisons (GIP). GIP publicized the plight of prisoners by facilitating the circulation of statements made by prisoners themselves about the conditions of prison life (Macey 1993: 257ff.; Foucault 1979: 30).

The topic of discussion was "the project of June 1971, to set up a people's court to judge the police" (Foucault 1980: 1). Foucault focused on contrasting "bourgeois justice" with "popular justice." In bourgeois justice, justice is restricted to the workings of the existing judicial system, its discourses and practices. Bourgeois justice claims to offer an impartial and universal sense of what is just and court procedures are claimed to be the sole basis of justice as pronounced by judges, backed by the coercive power of the state when it comes to enforcing judicial decisions. In this regard, bourgeois justice itself can be said to be limited by being beholden to an internalist approach, referring only to its own workings.

Foucault rejects the idea of setting up a "people's court" largely modelled after that of existing bourgeois courts and contrasted it with "acts of justice by the people" (Foucault 1980: 1). He rejected the proposals of his Maoist interlocutors because,

> the forms of the state apparatus that we inherit from the bourgeois apparatus cannot in any way serve as a model for the new forms of organization. The court, dragging along with it the ideology of bourgeois justice and those forms of relations between judge and judged, between judge and the parties to the action, between judge and litigant, which typify bourgeois justice, seems to me to have played a very significant role in the domination of the bourgeoisie. When we talk about courts we're talking about a place where the struggle between the contending forces is willy-nilly suspended: where in every case the decision arrived at is not the outcome of this struggle but of the intervention of an authority which necessarily stands above and is foreign to the contending forces, an authority which is in a position of neutrality between them and consequently can and must in every case decide which party to the dispute has justice on its side. The court implies, therefore, that there are categories which are common to the parties present (penal categories such as theft, fraud; moral categories such as honesty and dishonesty) and that the parties to the dispute agree to submit to them. (Foucault 1980: 27)

The court form, then, should not be treated as "the natural expression of popular justice; but rather that its historical function is to ensnare it, to control it and to strangle it, by re-inscribing it within institutions which are typical of state apparatus" (Foucault 1980: 1). The basic elements of the court are: "(i) a 'third element' [arbiter/judge]; (ii) reference to an idea, a form, a universal rule of justice; (iii) decisions with the power of enforcement" (1980: 11). Foucault's interlocutors insisted that a people's court would not produce the type of distortions that Foucault argued were part and parcel of bourgeois justice. Foucault points to examples from the French Revolution in which Parisian workers conducted executions of opponents of the French Revolution: "The September [1792] executions were at one and the same time an act of war against internal enemies, a political act against the manipulations of those in power, and an act of vengeance against the oppressive classes" (Foucault 1980: 1). In making his argument, he analyzes the effects of a people's court that was established to find out who was really guilty or innocent and procedures for investigation "to establish the 'truth' or to find out what was 'just'" (1980: 2). This, however, amounted to a depoliticization of an active, ongoing struggle between social classes. For Foucault, the court form in that instance was a "deformation" of popular justice (1980: 2). He then generates an analysis to challenge the idea that a people's court could be a neutral institution. Indeed, in the case of the French Revolution, courts so constituted stood between the ascendant bourgeoisie who were in power and the common people (1980: 3).

Adding to his class analysis of how courts obscure politics and conflict, Foucault then outlines the history of the French legal system:

> In the Middle Ages there was a change from the court of arbitration (to which cases of dispute were taken by mutual consent, to conclude some dispute or private battle, and which is in no way a permanent repository of power) to a set of stable, well defined institutions, which had the authority to intervene and which were based on political power (or at any rate were under its control). (Foucault 1980: 4)

This change emerged as a consequence of the "financialisation of the judicial system" (1980: 4), which transformed it into a means for generating revenue by using "fines, confiscations" and the like — the judicial system became "profitable" for judges (1980: 4). Accompanying the financialization of the judicial system was "the increasing link between the judicial system and the armed force[s]," which made it possible to use the military to back the judicial "power of constraint" (1980: 5). This combination became powerful enough that "when, during the fourteenth century the feudal lords were faced with the great peasant and urban revolts, they sought the support of a centralised power, army and taxation system" (1980: 5). This is the birthplace of the modern state judicial apparatus. This is why Foucault thinks it is necessary to avoid forming a people's court because "the act of popular justice" has exactly targeted this centralization of powers that depends on the court form to depoliticize struggles (1980: 6). In contrast, class struggles have continually led disenfranchised and marginalized groups to challenge the power of the courts. This is also why "each time the bourgeoisie wished to subject a popular uprising to the constraint of a state apparatus, a court has been set up: a table, a chairman, magistrates, confronting the two opponents" (1980: 7).

A central component of bourgeois court practice is how it sets itself up as the authority on truth, justice and impartiality, making itself the sole arbiter between two opposed parties of what is just and unjust, combined with the "authority to enforce their decision" (8). Courts thus obscure the extent to which competing senses of justice are at stake, imposing a false consensus about what counts as justice on competing groups bringing their respective claims. Foucault articulates a key point about popular justice as follows:

> In the case of popular justice you do not have three elements, you have the masses and their enemies. Furthermore, the masses when they perceive somebody to be an enemy, when they decide to punish this enemy — or re-educate him — do not rely on an abstract universal idea of justice, they rely only on their own experience, that of the injuries they have suffered, that of the way in which they have been wronged, in which they have been oppressed; and finally, their decision is not an authoritative one, that is, they are not backed up by a state apparatus which has the power to enforce their decisions, they purely and simply carry them out. (Foucault 1980: 8–9)

With this statement, Foucault unambiguously distinguishes between justice as constituted in court proceedings and popular justice, which is external to it, with its own powers and criteria of justice; there is a clear distinction between the law of courts and what is taken to count as justice by the people.

Foucault stresses the importance of examining the repressive and broader societal effects of the state legal apparatus. As he puts it,

> The penal system has had the function of introducing a certain number of contradictions among the masses, and one major contradiction, namely the following: to create a mutual antagonism between the proletarianised common people [the working class] and the non-proletarianised common people [a potentially criminal underclass for instance].[4] (Foucault 1980: 14)

This was made possible by the combination of a "complex system of courts-police-prison" (1980: 14).

The role of this system was "to force people to accept their status as proletarians and the conditions for the exploitation of the proletariat" (1980: 14). The historical evidence on this point is clear: "From the end of the Middle Ages up until the eighteenth century, all the laws against beggars, vagabonds and the idle, all the police organisations designed to catch them, forced them — and this was of course their role — to accept at the particular place where they were, the conditions imposed on them, which were extremely bad" (15).

The bourgeois system also constituted a division among the populace between moral proletarians and non-workers, in which the latter are objectified as

> marginal, dangerous, immoral, a menace to society as a whole, the dregs of the population, trash, the "mob." For the bourgeoisie it is a

matter of imposing on the proletariat, by means of penal legislation, of prisons, but also newspapers, of "literature," certain allegedly universal moral categories, which function as an ideological barrier between them and the non-proletarianised people. (Foucault 1980: 15)

Foucault notes that schooling does much the same (1980: 20). These divisions made mass, armed uprisings, the "main danger against which it [the bourgeoisie] had to be protected," less likely (1980: 16). Sending non-proletarians into the army or police force, off to the colonies or to prison were ways that the non-proletarians were further divided. This had the added benefit of generating further differences between the army and the proletariat, useful for when the army was needed to suppress armed uprisings (1980: 17).

The judicial system also valorized "ideas about what is just and unjust, about theft, property, crime and criminals" that in turn provided an ideological commonality between the proletariat and the bourgeoisie as distinct from the "plebs" or dangerous classes (1980: 23). This in turn generated a broader moral consensus across class divisions that masked significant concrete inequalities and differences of interests between the bourgeoisie and the proletariat. In short, the judicial system constituted divisions among the working class from which the bourgeoisie gained the benefit of increased security.

Foucault then points toward the kind of just punishment enacted by popular justice. He contends that there is a kind of egalitarian symmetry between popular justice and bourgeois domination "by which the class enemy is repaid" for the "suffering" (1980: 28–29) experienced by the working class. Finally, for popular justice to work, Foucault argues that it must take a kind of democratic parliamentary form in which representatives of the people directly engage in political debate and struggle, thus providing a context in which the people can supervise their own administration of justice without reliance on an allegedly neutral third party (1980: 29).

FOUCAULT'S REALISM

In contrast to his nominalism, Foucault's analysis of popular justice implies that discourses cannot be the sole object of analysis even though he draws on historical records and documents about people's practices. The difference is that Foucault does not epistemologically or ontologically privilege the expert discourses of those concerned with government or law. Legal discursive practices (as pertains to court trials for instance) are analyzed and then explained in relation to other social forces (such as class conflict) and practices external to legal administration. These other forces substantially affect legal practices and the bureaucratized justice of the courts. In turn, laws and the courts indirectly affect and transform the class structure of French society, creating divisions among the working class, an effect advantageous to the maintenance of bourgeois dominance. Most pertinently, it is these latter effects, generated by the interaction of the legal structure with the class, political and societal structures, that are the object of indictment in manifestations of popular justice. Thus, in contrast to the conceptions of criminal justice, it is not only a guilty act that can be unjust and criminal, but major dimensions of societal organization, or even the entire societal hierarchy.

"On Popular Justice" has several realist components pertinent to theorizing justice in externalist terms. For example, Foucault focuses on the basic constituent elements of bourgeois justice, the material arrangement of court space, the practices involved (such as aural investigations to get at the truth of the matter and the guilt or innocence of parties), the power to punish and the real effects of decisions and punishment in constituting divisions amongst the people. Foucault theorizes courts as real, enduring structures that produce these effects, regardless of the reasons or interests in setting them up and regardless of the kinds of individuals involved (for example, revolutionaries or bourgeois jurists). The effects are independent of people's intentions or knowledge of the workings of courts, laws, justice, punishment and truth — this is a realist position. For instance, once a court is set up, it will, of structural necessity, produce the effects of appearing to be, and imposing, a universal ideal of justice on the parties, enforcing decisions on those parties and producing a division among the people between the good, the bad and the just arbiter. These divisions affect the people's perceptions of themselves and others, in turn affecting possibilities for united political action against dominant but minority groups like the bourgeoisie. There is then, too, a combination of the real effects generated by courts on other social spheres that are part of the real structure of French society.

Furthermore, Foucault argues that the bourgeois class position is an impediment to grasping social reality. As he states, "the bourgeoisie cannot have an accurate perception of real relations and processes" (Foucault 1980: 22). Crucial here is the word "cannot": it is not a matter of the bourgeoisie distorting the truth; rather, their position in a social hierarchy external to and independent of any particular bourgeois person or legal procedures for getting the facts of a case, constrains their capacity to have "an accurate perception of real relations and processes." The French class structure of relations between the bourgeoisie, workers, peasants and the common people is a mechanism generating an impediment to the capacity of the bourgeoisie to grasp the reality of French society itself.

In his discussion of the ideology of courts, Foucault stresses the spatial arrangement of people within it. As he describes it, the arrangement is composed of a table, and behind this table, which distances them from the two litigants, the "third party," that is, the judges. Their position indicates firstly that they are neutral with respect to each litigant, and secondly, this implies that their decision is not already arrived at in advance, that it will be made after an aural investigation of the two parties, on the basis of a certain conception and a certain number of ideas concerning what is just and unjust, and thirdly, that they have the authority to enforce their decision. (Foucault 1980: 8)

The very spatial staging of court practices produces, in ritual-like form (see Althusser 1971), ideological effects, like appearing to possess a god-like, universal capacity to pass just judgment. The bourgeois conception of justice treats justice as existing "in and for itself" (Foucault 1980: 29) and thus decontextualizes justice from society, history and the broad social divisions, struggles and conflicts that constitute social history.

While Foucault does not come out and define his conception of popular justice, we can distill one by following his reasoning. For him, popular justice refers to the immanent potential of the masses to mobilize the terms justice/injustice to indict and punish dominant classes who benefit from inequalities existing in a society. Popular justice needs to be elaborated through democratic political practices that respect differences and divisions in a society, lest it devolve into the ideological form of modern bourgeois court justice or other forms of bureaucratized tribunal overseen by an expert third party.

The merits of Foucault's realist approach can be summarized by noting the following:

- Foucault opposes any universalist conception of justice (popular or bourgeois-judicial);
- The meanings of justice and morality held by different groups in a society are external to legal discourse (they exist prior to and independently of it) and hence are real in relation to legal discourse;
- Laws depend on people accepting their administration as being just (minimally acceptable in the terms of widely held values);
- Justice concerns how the economy, state institutions, laws, morality, culture, religion, education and ideology are combined together;
- Bourgeois justice is ideological and this is an enduring consequence of the very material and practical structure of court justice; and
- Popular justice requires the punishment of dominant classes who benefit from an existing societal hierarchy that causes suffering and harm to many people.

Foucault's realist conception of popular justice is a kind of justice held in reserve by the people. It respects the bases of disputes in the political conflicts, struggles and inequalities in a society, especially as it concerns the harms and victimizations facilitated by power inequalities from which a dominant minority group benefits. We then have two quite different ways of theorizing justice — one nominalist and the other realist. But, they are at odds with each other on metatheoretical grounds. What can be done about this metatheoretical discrepancy?

DISCUSSION: RESOLVING THE METATHEORETICAL DISCREPANCY

The nominalist and realist approaches in Foucault's work are incompatible. It needs to be noted that this tension cannot be resolved by doing empirical research, but rather requires metatheoretical work. The main problem to be confronted is that nominalism makes it impossible to conceptualize the real possibilities of popular justice in the present. This is not least because popular justice, while having been actualized at times (such as the French Revolution), still remains a real potential, even if rarely actualized, that could again be used to judge police activities or those of Wall Street financiers, for instance. Foucault demonstrates that people have a sense of justice that frequently is unstated and, if it is unstated, no documentary evidence of it would exist. It is thus inaccessible to nominalist historical analysis on which to base a theory. Rather, popular justice is closer to a real but rarely manifested potential in the masses to refuse and resist social inequalities and impose their own sense of rightness and justice, doing so in a political and democratic way without relying on the state, laws and the courts (that is, bourgeois justice).

Foucault's realist approach to French society in the interview itself provides the theoretical means for resolving the impasses generated by nominalism. It requires that one treat the expert discourses about government as one among other institutions, like law, the economy or education. It involves stressing the need to appreciate the complex factors shaping political processes and transformations and appreciating that the capacity people have to act politically depends on "the different levels and functions which subjects can occupy in a domain which has its own rules of formation" (Foucault 1991: 70).

Crucially, we cannot see the big picture of the complexity of a society; humans do not have a god-like eye allowing us to empirically apprehend and follow all of the simultaneous happenings and connections that make social life possible. Here, nominalist approaches reach their limit. But, we can theorize this big picture combination of social forces by synthesizing and combining varieties of specific empirical investigations. Moreover, we need to do this kind of theoretical work or else we will miss all of the struggles over values and power inequalities brought to bear on state/bourgeois justice and broader beliefs about what counts as just that are circulating in a society. The struggle for theorizing justice in Foucault is very much about how to adequately conceptualize the internal workings of state laws and courts, which are situated in a broader array of social forces external to what counts as law.

Most compellingly, Foucault's realism about justice indicates that the place from which the people articulate their conception of justice in a moment of mass uprising remains real even if people aren't engaged in an uprising or protest. That place is, in many respects, a non-place in that when people engage in acts of popular justice they are not in the places where ruling classes ordain they should be (such as at work or at home). Should the people feel that the dominant classes have crossed the line about what is acceptable for them to do and not to do, the place of popular justice may become occupied and the people can pass their judgment. The non-place of popular justice is a place held in reserve by the people, and even if they do not take to the streets, it is really there.

CONCLUSION: FOUCAULT'S REALISM, FOUCAULT'S JUSTICE

Foucault's theoretical sensibilities about justice, politics, inequality and law as evinced in his interview "On Popular Justice" are an important but neglected resource for theorizing justice. Taking Foucault's realism seriously allows one to surpass the limits of his nominalism and the consequent argument about the displacement of justice by development that follows from his analysis of the dominance of governmentality. Foucault's case then, is an instructive one about why it might be desirable, via careful metatheoretical work, to overcome the divide between internalist (nominalist) and externalist (realist) approaches to thinking about justice. The logic of Foucault's sociologically realist approach to popular justice strikes me as a quite novel. It is one worth exploring further in light of Foucault's comments on the Iranian Revolution (Afray and Anderson 2005) and the current Occupy Wall Street movement.[5] Manifestations of popular justice serve as a reminder that the people reserve judgment and hold justice itself in reserve in a place external to the (bourgeois) justice system — the workings of state governance, security, law and the courts — as justice is not exhausted by the law. This reminds us that justice cannot be reduced to the workings of state law but concerns whether or not people will tolerate how their society is organized and governed. Foucault's realist approach suggests that we keep this in mind when we theorize justice.

Notes

1. My approach draws on the theoretical tradition in the sociology of law found in Pearce (2001); Hunt (1978, 1993); Pearce and Tombs (1998); Cotterrell (1992); Woodiwiss (1990); and Norrie (1996).
2. I wish to thank Frank Pearce, Alan Hunt, Jonathan Frauley, Kelly Gorkoff and Heidi Rimke for sharing many stimulating thoughts about justice with me, and for posing more than a few pointed questions. Mark Brownlee and Ariane

Hanemaayer were helpful research assistants at various stages of this project. A University of Windsor Travel Grant facilitated my attendance at the "Theorizing Justice" conference (University of Winnipeg, 2009) that served as a catalyst for this paper. I alone remain responsible for any errors or oversights in the position elaborated below.

3. Golder and Fitzpatrick (2009) have offered a substantial challenge to Hunt. My own view is that Golder and Fitzpatrick have unwittingly reinvented Hunt's conception of "law as a constitutive mode of regulation" and thus their criticism is misplaced.

4. The working class/proletariat is comprised of all those who must work for someone else in order to obtain money (an income in the form of either a wage or a salary) so they can purchase what they need in order to survive (for example, housing, clothing, food and child care). They are thus subordinated to the control of their bourgeois employers, and the contributions of the proletariat to wealth creation is exploited by the bourgeois pursuit of profit, not least by the threat of unemployment.

5. According to <occupywallst.org>: "Occupy Wall Street is a people powered movement that began on September 17, 2011 in Liberty Square in Manhattan's Financial District, and has spread to over 100 cities in the United States and actions in over 1,500 cities globally. #OWS is fighting back against the corrosive power of major banks and multinational corporations over the democratic process, and the role of Wall Street in creating an economic collapse that has caused the greatest recession in generations. The movement is inspired by popular uprisings in Egypt, Tunisia, Spain, Greece, Italy and the UK, and aims to expose how the richest 1% of people who are writing the rules of the global economy are imposing an agenda of neo-liberalism and economic inequality that is foreclosing our future."

References

Afray, J., and K.B. Anderson. 2005. *Foucault and the Iranian Revolution*. Chicago: University of Chicago Press.

Althusser, L. 1971 "Ideology and Ideological State Apparatuses." *Lenin and Philosophy and Other Essays*. London: New Left Books.

Bhaskar, R. 1975. *A Realist Theory of Science*. Brighton: Harvester Press.

___. 1979. *The Possibility of Naturalism*. Brighton: Harvester Press.

___. 1986. *Scientific Realism and Human Emancipation*. London: Verso.

___. 1989. *Reclaiming Reality*. New York: Verso.

Brodie, J. 2007. "Reforming Social Justice in Neoliberal Times." *Studies in Social Justice* 2.

Cotterrell, R. 1992. *The Sociology of Law: An Introduction*. London: Butterworths.

Datta, R P. 2007. "From Foucault's Genealogy to Aleatory Materialism: Realism, Nominalism and Politics." In J. Frauley and F. Pearce (eds.), *Critical Realism and the Social Sciences: Heterodox Elaborations*. Toronto: University of Toronto Press.

___. 2011. "Security and the Void: Aleatory Materialism contra Governmentality." In. M. Neocleous and G. Rigakos (eds.), *Anti-Security*. Ottawa: Red Quill Books.

Datta, R.P., J. Frauley and F. Pearce. 2010. "Situation Critical: For a Critical, Reflexive,

Realist, Emancipatory Social Science." *Journal of Critical Realism* 9, 2.

Deleuze, G. 1979. "Forward: The Rise of the Social." In J. Donzelot, *The Policing of Families*. New York: Pantheon Books.

Donzelot, J. 1979. *The Policing of Families*. New York: Pantheon.

Dupont, D., and F. Pearce. 2001. "Foucault Contra Foucault: Re-reading the Governmentality Papers." *Theoretical Criminology* 5, 2.

Ewald, F. 1990. "Norms, Discipline and the Law." *Representations* 30.

Fitzpatrick, P. 1992. "The Impossibility of Popular Justice." *Social and Legal Studies* 1 (2): 199–215.

Foucault, M. 1972. *The Archaeology of Knowledge*. New York: Pantheon.

____. 1973. *The Birth of the Clinic*. New York: Vintage Books.

____. 1979. *Discipline and Punish: The Birth of the Prison*. New York: Vintage Books.

____. 1980. "On Popular Justice: A Discussion with Maoists." In C. Gordon (ed.), *Power/Knowledge*. New York: Pantheon Books.

____. 1991. "Politics and the Study of Discourse." In G. Burchell et al. (eds.), *The Foucault Effect*. Chicago: University of Chicago Press.

____. 1994a. *The Order of Things: An Archaeology of the Human Sciences*. New York: Vintage Books.

____. 1994b. *The History of Sexuality: The Will to Know*. New York: Vintage Books.

____. 1996. "What Our Present Is." In S. Lotringer (ed.), *Foucault Live*. New York: Semiotex(e).

____. 2003a. "On the Genealogy of Ethics: An Overview of Work in Progress." In P. Rabinow and N. Rose (eds.), *The Essential Foucault*. New York: New Press.

____. 2003b. "Omnes et Singulatim." In P. Rabinow and N. Rose (eds.), *The Essential Foucault*. New York: New Press.

____. 2003c. "The Subject and Power." In P. Rabinow and N. Rose (eds.), *The Essential Foucault*. New York: New Press.

____. 2003d. "Preface to the History of Sexuality Volume Two." In P. Rabinow and N. Rose (eds.), *The Essential Foucault*. New York: New Press.

____. 2003e. "Questions of Method." In P. Rabinow and N. Rose (eds.), *The Essential Foucault*. New York: New Press.

____. 2006a. *Psychiatric Power*. New York: Palgrave-Macmillan.

____. 2006b. *Security, Territory, Population*. New York: Palgrave-Macmillan.

____. 2006c. *The History of Madness*. New York: Routledge.

____. 2008. *The Birth of Biopolitics*. New York: Palgrave-Macmillan.

Fraser, N. 2005. "Reframing Justice in a Globalising World." *New Left Review* 36, Nov.–Dec.

Frauley, J., and F. Pearce. 2007. "Critical Realism and the Social Sciences: Methodological and Epistemological Preliminaries." In J. Frauley and F. Pearce (eds.), *Critical Realism and the Social Sciences: Heterodox Elaborations*. Toronto: University of Toronto Press.

Frisby, D., and D. Sayer. 1986. *Society*. New York: Routledge.

Golder, B., and P. Fitzpatrick. 2009. *Foucault's Law*. New York: Routledge.

Gordon, C. 1991. "Governmental Rationality: An Introduction." In G. Burchell et al. (eds.), *The Foucault Effect: Studies in Governmentality*. Chicago: University of Chicago Press.

Hunt, A. 1978. *The Sociological Movement in Law*. London: Macmillan.

___. 1993. *Explorations in Law and Society*. New York: Routledge.

Hunt, A., and G. Wickam. 1994. *Foucault and Law*. London: Pluto.

Kelly, M.E. 2009. *The Political Philosophy of Michel Foucault*. New York: Routledge.

Lopez, J. 2003. *Society and Its Metaphors*. London: Continuum Books.

Macey, D. 1993. *The Lives of Michel Foucault*. New York: Pantheon Books.

Norrie, A. 1996. "From Law to Popular Justice: Beyond Antinomianism." *Social & Legal Studies* 5, 3.

Osborne, Thomas. 1996. "Security and Vitality: Drains, Liberalism and Power in the Nineteenth Century." In A Barry, T. Osborne and N. Rose (eds.), *Foucault and Political Reason*. London: UCL Press.

Pearce, F. 2001. *The Radical Durkheim*, second edition. Toronto: Canadian Scholars Press International.

Pearce, F., and S. Tombs. 1998. *Toxic Capitalism: Corporate Crime and the Chemical Industry.* London: Ashgate.

Pearce, F., and T. Woodiwiss. 2001. "Reading Foucault as a Realist." In J. Lopez and G. Potter (eds.), *After Postmodernism: An Introduction to Critical Realism*. London: Athlone.

Rajchman, J. 1985. *Michel Foucault: The Freedom of Philosophy*. New York: Columbia University Press.

Rose, N., and P. Miller. 1992. "Political Power Beyond the State: Problematics of Government." *British Journal of Sociology* 43, 2.

Steiner, P. 2010. *Durkheim and the Birth of Economic Sociology*. Princeton: Princeton University Press.

Turner, B.S. 2006. "Classical Sociology and Cosmopolitanism: A Critical Defence of the Social." *British Journal of Sociology* 57, 1.

Valverde, M. 2007. "Genealogies of European States: Foucauldian Reflections." *Economy & Society* 36, 1.

Veyne, P. 2010. *Foucault: His Thought, His Character*. Cambridge: Polity Press.

Woodiwiss, A. 1990. *Social Theory After Postmodernism*. London: Pluto Press.

___. 2005. *Scoping the Social*. New York: Open University Press.

Zedner, L. 2006. "Policing Before and After the Police: The Historical Antecedents of Contemporary Crime Control." *British Journal of Criminology* 46.

___. 2007. "Pre-Crime and Post-Criminology?" *Theoretical Criminology* 11, 2.

CHAPTER SIX

DISCIPLINING CAPITAL
Corporate Crime and the Neo-Liberal State
Steven Bittle

INTRODUCING CANADA'S CORPORATE CRIMINAL LIABILITY LEGISLATION

In March 2004 the Canadian government introduced, for the first time, Criminal Code legislation aimed at holding corporations accountable for serious injury and death in the workplace.[1] *Bill C-45, An Act to Amend the Criminal Code (criminal liability of organizations)*, imposes a legal duty for "all persons directing work to take reasonable steps to ensure the safety of workers and the public," attributes criminal liability to an "organization" if a senior officer knew or ought to have known about the offence and introduces sentencing provisions specifically crafted for the organizational setting.[2] Colloquially referred to as the "Westray Bill," the law was introduced in response to the deaths of twenty-six miners in 1992 in an underground explosion at the Westray mine in Pictou County, Nova Scotia — a disaster caused by unsafe and illegal working conditions.

The federal government believed that the Westray bill would significantly expand "the circumstances in which an organization can be held criminally responsible for the actions taken in its name by its representatives" (Liberal Member of Parliament, Paul Harold Macklin, 27 October 2003).[3] Pundits predicted that it would revolutionize corporate criminal liability (Archibald, Jull and Roach 2004: 368), ending the lenient treatment of corporations through the introduction of "stricter penalties" and improved "enforcement tools" (Mann 2004: 29). However, peeling back the veneer of the state's crackdown on corporate crime reveals a much different picture. To start, the law's introduction was anything but expeditious, subject to a long and drawn-out process in Canada's Parliament that raised questions about the need for reform. What is more, in the six or more years since the law took effect there have been only three charges and one conviction — not exactly a revolution in corporate accountability.

This chapter critically examines Canada's corporate criminal liability legislation, focusing on the role of the state in the constitution of corporate crime and its control. It attempts to extend beyond questions of how state power operates to explore why state power takes certain forms (Coleman et al. 2009: 18). It argues that an examination of the Westray bill's evolution reveals three ways in which the state was implicated and complicit in the production of corporate crime and corporate criminal liability (Tombs 2009). First, it helped create the conditions within which the Westray disaster occurred. Second, while contemplating the Westray bill's introduction it provided the ideological space for particular legal and economic discourses to downplay the seriousness of corporate crime and limit the reform options that were given serious consideration. Finally, it has failed to enforce the new law, despite expectations to the contrary and regardless that incidences of workplace injury and death continue unabated (Association of Workers' Compensation Boards of Canada 2006; Sharpe and Hardt 2006).[4]

Empirically, this chapter examines the hearings of the Standing Committee on Justice and Human Rights (hereafter referred to as the Committeee), a multi-party parliamentary committee directed to examine issues of corporate criminal liability (see also Bittle and Snider 2006). Throughout the spring of 2002, the Committee received briefs, heard testimony and asked questions of witnesses representing a wide range of opinions and positions, including lawyers from the Department of Justice and academia, union representatives, sociologists, criminologists, family members of victims of corporate disasters and representatives of non-governmental organizations. This evidence, as interpreted, incorporated or dismissed by members of the Committee and drafting experts from the Department of Justice, ultimately produced the law that became the Westray bill. This chapter also draws from the results of interviews with twenty-three individuals (such as lawyers, government officials and representatives from union, labour and non-governmental organizations) regarding the Westray bill's introduction and enforcement.[5]

Together, these arguments suggest that holding corporations to account for their harmful and illegal acts requires a better understanding of the state's constitutive role in corporate crime. More broadly, these arguments demonstrate that the apparatuses of justice that society turns to in order to resolve concerns in times of crises ironically contribute to and, in essence, create the necessary conditions for tragic consequences. The state's functions and its interactions with capital interests ought to be interrogated and examined critically in this regard. Regulatory and criminal regimes are espoused as sites of justice to be delivered and meted out through society. However, these regimes often disguise injustices at the hands of states and powerful capital interests camouflaging real harm as amelioration of dire consequences for Canadians.

CORPORATE CRIME, LAW AND THE STATE

A dominant and defining feature of Canadian society over the past thirty years has been the "tectonic shift" in public policy towards privatization (Fudge and Cossman 2002: 3). Previous actions of the state were rooted in Keynesian principles that embraced, at least theoretically, the benefits of "full employment" and "universal welfare" (Fudge and Cossman 2002: 10) — what has come to be called the welfare state. Confronted with declining profit levels and economic recessions throughout the 1980s and early 1990s, neo-liberal political and economic reasoning provided the basis for questioning the continued viability of the welfare state (Fudge and Cossman 2002: 13), raising caution against "government overreach and overload" and downplaying the state's responsibility for addressing social and economic ills (Rose and Miller 1992: 198). In response, successive federal governments (both Conservative and Liberal) proceeded to disassemble the welfare state, introducing crippling cutbacks to unemployment insurance and provincial transfers for "welfare, social services, and post secondary institutions" (Fudge and Cossman 2002: 15–16).

Meanwhile, deregulation of the economic realm became the dominant mantra within neo-liberal circles (Snider 2002). Fuelled by visions of bureaucratic "red tape" and "regulatory burden," governments in most Western nations jettisoned many forms of regulation deemed to stand in the way of so-called economic progress (Tombs and Whyte 2007: 158). Fudge and Cossman (2002: 19–20) characterize this as a period of re-regulation, not full deregulation, in which the state actually reconfigured, rather than dismantled, its regulatory responsibilities, but in pro-business ways. According to Snider (2000: 181), it was during this time that corporate crime disappeared as both a concept and in law, washed away by knowledge claims that were "compatible with hegemonic [business] interests." In particular, while the state was busy befriending corporate capitalism, it was at the same time sharpening its regulatory teeth in relation to traditional street crimes (Fudge and Cossman 2002: 20; Tombs and Whyte 2007: 158).

There has been much written in recent years about the impact of neo-liberalism on crime and its control (for example, Ericson and Haggerty 1997; Garland 1999, 2001; Shearing 2001; Valverde 2003). Of all this writing, what is important here is how it conceptualizes the role of the state. David Garland (2001: 124–26), for example, suggests that neo-liberal crime control strategies divest responsibility for crime from the state to the individual. Obscuring the broader structural factors of crime, these "responsibilization" strategies abstract the individual from his or her social circumstances and challenge them to act in a prudent manner (Hannah Moffat 2001: 522; Rose 2000: 327). For many criminologists and socio-legal scholars, this shift indicates how the state has become one of a plurality of sites of governance and control in contemporary society (Barry et al. 1996; Haggerty and Ericson 2006; Shearing and Stenning 2003). Referred to by Coleman et al. (2009: 7–8) as the "new pluralism," the state's monopoly over crime control has been uprooted by various mechanisms of social control (such as surveillance and risk assessments) — new forms of power that are beyond the state.

While not denying this contribution to our understanding of contemporary crime control measures, some critical scholars caution against its downplaying of the state (Coleman et al. 2009; Hall 2009; Pearce and Tombs 1999; Tombs and Whyte 2007), along with its failure to consider corporate crimes (Tombs and Whyte 2007; 2009; Braithwaite 2003). According to Coleman et al. (2009: 7–9), the state has been "airbrushed out of critical analysis" through a non-reflexive and uncritical acceptance of official definitions of crime that deem the most effective crime control strategies to include communities, private enterprise and government partnerships (2009: 7–9). Failure to unpack these claims has led to the conceptual mistake of reducing state power to "the organizational form that delivers policy." However, as Coleman et al. (2009: 9, emphasis in original) note, the state is not a thing, but "a *process* that, in its shifting boundaries and ensembles, provides the arena for the organization of social forces." We therefore need to examine the state beyond its "organizational forms" to consider how various manifestations of power flow through the state to produce material effects (2009: 18).

Critical scholars working within neo-Marxist frameworks have endeavoured to conceptualize the state as one of many different mechanisms within society that play an important, but not automatic, role in (re)producing capitalist market conditions (Jessop 2002, 2008). As Jessop (2002: 41) notes, the state is both "operationally autonomous" and "institutionally separate" from the capitalist market, meaning there is no *a priori* guarantee that the state will either advance or challenge the interests of capitalists. The operational autonomy of the state is underscored by the fact that, in addition to helping valorize the capitalist mode of production, the state also has the "overall political responsibility for maintaining social cohesion in a socially divided, pluralistic social formation" (Jessop 2002: 21; see also Resnick and Wolff 1987: 231–32; Tombs and Whyte 2007).[6] For example, laws that support the creation of corporations or the freedom to purchase and sell labour exemplify how the state provides ongoing support to capitalist endeavours (Resnick and Wolff 1987: 235). At the same time, however, the state must and does occasionally enact laws that do not necessarily favour capitalist class interests, as with the introduction of the Westray bill.

There are at least two ways to build on these critical accounts to examine the constitutive role of the state in the evolution of Canada's corporate criminal liability legislation. First, concerns must extend beyond criminology's myopic and distorted acceptance of crime as a "punishment of the poor project" (Braithwaite 2003: 7) to consider the state's attempts to regulate crimes of the powerful (Pearce 1976). Responses to corporate offences have differed significantly from the zero tolerance approaches towards street crimes in recent decades (Briathwaite 2003: 14; Snider 2008). It is therefore important to understand why corporate crime receives differential treatment in law and what this means for regulating corporate wrongdoing. Second, concerns must conceive of the state as a social relation that is "embedded" within the broader social context (Jessop 2008: 7); as a site where different powers coalesce around particular conjunctures, a process in which various forces flow "in and through" state institutions and actors (Coleman et al. 2009: 9; Jessop 1990: 269–70). As we shall see, although relatively autonomous, the state's "symbiotic relationship" with corporate capitalism (Tombs and Whyte 2009: 114) significantly shapes and produces corporate crime and corporate criminal liability, even if the results of this relationship are far from automatic, always contingent and never complete (Jessop 2008; Tombs and Whyte 2009).

THE WESTRAY DISASTER AND THE STATE

On May 9, 1992, twenty-six workers at the Westray mine in Plymouth, Nova Scotia, were killed in a methane gas explosion that was so intense that "it blew the top off the mine entrance, more than a mile above the blast centre" (McMullan 2001: 135), shaking houses and breaking windows in nearby communities (McMullan 2005: 24). Rescue workers frantically searched for survivors, but the explosion's devastating impact meant that death was probably immediate and certainly inevitable (McMullan 2005: 24; Comish 1993). Although the mine owners, Curragh Resources, were eventually charged criminally, no one was convicted. A combination of prosecutorial mishaps and difficulties determining legal responsibility conspired to ensure that no one was held to legal account (McMullen 2001: 136; McMullan, 2005: 30; also see Glasbeek 2002).

The report of the Nova Scotia government's public inquiry on the disaster, *The Westray Story: A Predictable Path to Disaster* (Richard 1997), characterized the tragedy as "foreseeable and preventable," unearthing evidence that management had been warned over fifty times prior to the explosion about workplace health and safety violations, all of which were ignored (Glasbeek 2002: 62). The inquiry chair, Justice Peter K. Richard, saved particular rebuke for the mine's management and labour officials for failing to ensure that the mine's operations complied with provincial safety regulations (Richard 1997: 605). Particularly concerning was that mine management, who were unqualified, ignored input from workers regarding the mine's working conditions and failed to ensure that workers received proper training in mine safety and operations (Richard 1997: 611). Even in situations that required obvious and immediate safety measures, such as neutralizing the excessive build-up of explosive coal dust through its removal or by the spreading of stone dust, management chose not to respond (Richard 1997: 617).

In many respects, the state's role in the Westray disaster encapsulates the political economy of liberal capitalist societies. The mine's opening in 1992 directly corresponded to the federal Conservative government's ideologically driven campaign to promote pro-business, anti-regulation ideals (Snider 1993). Elmer MacKay, the Conservative Member of Parliament in the riding where the mine was located, successfully convinced Brian Mulroney, Conservative leader and Prime Minister, of the mine's political and economic saleability (Jobb 1994: 13; also see Comish 1993: 52–53). While prohibitive production costs and the inability to secure adequate financing had discouraged other companies from opening Westray, Curragh Resources successfully secured the federal government as the guarantor on 85 percent of a $100 million loan to set up the mine's operations. The provincial Conservative government also contributed by providing a low interest loan and agreeing to purchase a set amount of coal from the mine at well above market value, regardless of how much coal was produced (Glasbeek 2002: 62; Richard 1997: 610). In addition to being an enticing deal for someone interested in a risky business venture, Westray was a good news story for a government keen on promoting its business-friendly image.

Framed by powerful economic and political forces, the state's support of the Westray mine ignored the long and deadly history of mining this particular coal seam (Comish 1993: 1–3; Glasbeek 2002: 61–66; Glasbeek and Tucker 1993: 16; Richard 1997). It meant glossing over questions about the ability to safely operate the mine, including concerns raised by the federal government's own geological experts (Glasbeek and Tucker 1993; Jobb 1994). After the mine began production, and as working conditions deteriorated, there were suggestions that those involved in lobbying for the mine's opening failed to see that something disastrous was about to happen (Glasbeek and Tucker 1993; Richards 1997). What is more, as the Westray Inquiry report revealed, the state's decision to negotiate a set production schedule was an important element in the disaster (Richard 1997: 610). At the time of the explosion, the mine's owners had been struggling to meet production quotas, pushing the production schedule at the expense of addressing the mounting and obvious safety concerns (Comish 1993; Jobb 1994).

The state was also implicated in the Westray disaster through its failure to properly regulate workplace safety. With both federal and provincial government priorities so closely tied to the success of the Westray mine, and fuelled by the perception that there are inherent risks to coal production (Glasbeek and Tucker 1993: 20; see also Slapper and Tombs 1999; Tombs and Whyte 2007), the provincial government made few attempts to seriously regulate workplace safety pursuant to their responsibilities for provincial workplace health and safety (Glasbeek 2002: 62). In the face of overwhelming evidence of serious and ongoing safety violations, Department of Labour regulators, who had helped create a "culture of indifference" between mine management and inspectors (McMullan 2005: 26), did nothing to ensure the mine's safe operation (Glasbeek 2002: 62; Richard 1997). Consistent with dominant neo-liberal reasoning that regulation was burdensome and therefore bad for business and the economy, concerns with workplace safety were largely ignored (Tillman and Indergaard 2005: 15–16). "After all," as Glasbeek (2002: 62) argues, "demands for compliance might require spending money or slow down operations, lessening the profitability of the enterprise and thereby the prestige of the supporting politicians."

Beyond Westray: The State and Law Reform

Following the disaster, the state was implicated further in the production of corporate crime through the ways that it characterized corporate wrongdoing and how it should be dealt with. Prior to the Westray bill, corporate criminal liability was established through the "identification doctrine," a common law standard that attributed liability to a company when a crime could be traced to senior employees, namely the "directing mind" of the corporation (*Canadian Dredge and Dock Co.* 1985). A person was deemed the directing mind when he or she was responsible for a particular department or unit, and the crime benefited the corporation in some way (Department of Justice Canada 2002). However, the challenges to tracing responsibility within large and complex companies (Department of Justice Canada March 2002; Cahill and Cahill 1999: 154) often effectively shields the corporation and corporate executives from criminal liability.

In recognition of the difficulties of holding corporate executives to legal account, something that was glaringly obvious in the Westray disaster, the Westray Inquiry report recommended:

> The Government of Canada, through the Department of Justice, should institute a study of the accountability of corporate executives and directors for the wrongful or negligent acts of the corporation and should introduce in the Parliament of Canada such amendments to legislation as are necessary to ensure that corporate executives and directors are held properly accountable for workplace safety. (Richard 1997: 600–01)

The seeds of reform were laid. It was now up to the federal government to decide whether to heed Justice Richard's advice. However, despite the Westray bill's eventual enactment, there was little sense of urgency on the federal government's part to introduce changes to the law.

In contrast to the unabashed support for opening the Westray mine, the government was less than enthusiastic in its embrace of corporate criminal liability legislation. It was more than six years after the Westray Inquiry report, and ten years after the disaster, before the law was introduced. What is more, if not for the efforts of union officials and opposition MPs, it is questionable whether the Westray bill would have seen the light of day. In addition to a motion in Parliament from the then Progressive Conservative Party requesting that the government accept the recommendation of the Westray Inquiry report, the New Democratic Party (NDP) tabled several private member's bills in an attempt to introduce corporate criminal liability legislation. The union representing the Westray workers (United Steelworkers of America) extensively lobbied federal politicians to introduce reforms.[7] In this respect it took considerable effort for the state not to act, to avoid changing the law.

Eventually, however, the contradictions became too great; it was increasingly difficult for the government to ignore the calls to better regulate workplace safety, particularly in that a (supposed) hallmark of the liberal democratic state is the protection of life and liberty. It also was becoming more and more politically viable to contemplate measures to punish corporations after the stock market/financial scandals of 1999/2000 revealed that the profits of many highly respected corporations (for example, Parmalat, Enron and WorldCom) were built on corruption, dishonesty and fraud (Laufer 2006). It was thus timely, and perhaps unavoidable, for the federal Liberal government to consider corporate criminal liability legislation by sending it to the Committee for its study and review.

Legal Discourses

The Committee's examination of corporate criminal liability provided a powerful frame for the state's legislative response. In particular, dominant conceptualizations of law fundamentally shaped the parameters of corporate criminal liability. In contemporary capitalist societies — particularly those steeped in common law traditions — law is a potent discourse, one that plays a prominent role in ordering relations of power (Fudge and Cossman, 2002: 30; Smart 1989). Although not a "homogenous force" that determines how various social relations (gender, race and class) will unfold, law "plays a significant role in the process of governing life" (Chunn and Lacombe, 2000: 14). Throughout the Westray bill reform process, law was treated as a specialized form of knowledge with unique rules and parameters — it was assigned "capital 'T' Truth" and given scientific-like status (Smart 1989).

Corporate Mens Rea

To be considered feasible, any reform option that was given serious consideration could not be seen as straying too far from traditional notions of *mens rea*, or the guilty mind. Legislators therefore had difficulty conceptualizing how to hold senior executives and the corporation responsible for something they did not do, for something they might not have known about even though they ought to have. Take, for example, comments from the following Committee MPs about the difficulty of establishing the criminal responsibility of corporate executives:

> How far up the chain do we attach accountability and liability? Some folks have said that the directors should be responsible for virtually everything done by their employees.... If you're talking about a large corporation that may have directors in Vancouver and something happens at a plant in Toronto, how liable is the director in Vancouver for what happens in Toronto? That's what I'm struggling with. (Chuck Cadman, Canadian Alliance, Standing Committee on Justice and Human Rights, May 23, 2002)

> But if I'm sitting in a corporate boardroom in Halifax or Vancouver or Toronto or Montreal, General Motors perhaps, realistically, how can I be held liable because a health and safety supervisor in the General Motors plant in Oshawa is incompetent or negligent? (John Maloney, Liberal, Justice Committee 22 May 2002)

Corporate Culture
The fate of the NDP's private member's bill is indicative of the common sense of individual responsibility that animated the Committee's work. The NDP's proposed legislation represented a significant departure from the common law identification doctrine, proposing criminal offences for directors and officers when staff of a corporation committed an offence and corporate management "knew or should have known of the act or omission or condoned or was wilfully blind to it." It also included the concept of "corporate culture," wherein senior management could be held criminally liable if a set of defining and driving values allowed or encouraged law violation or facilitated law avoidance (Department of Justice 2002).[8] In addition to implying a collective responsibility for corporate crime, for allowing criminogenic conditions to become dominant (Department of Justice Canada, March 2002), the concept of corporate culture signified that in any profit-making business there is always ample motivation to justify or ignore unsafe working conditions (Glasbeek 2002; Tombs and Whyte 2007).

From the outset it was clear that reference to corporate culture was a problematic concept for many MPs and witnesses, too vague and imprecise to be considered a viable reform option. The testimony of Professor Patrick Healy and Mr. William Trudell, from the Canadian Association of Criminal Defence Lawyers, was accorded special status by Committee MPs, in that their legal expertise provided the backdrop to their presentations and subsequent exchanges with members. Both were against the notion of corporate culture, employing the language of legal precision in their arguments. Healy argued that the concept of corporate culture was incongruent with notions of individual liability:

> As for the corporate culture point, I don't mean to be flippant about it, but the idea is, was it in the air that this kind of activity would be tolerated on behalf of the corporation? That obviously is a much more nebulous notion, a wider notion, and one that raises, in my respectful opinion, severe evidentiary problems, since, at the end of the day, criminal liability requires proof beyond a reasonable doubt. (Patrick Healy, Justice Committee 28 May 2002)

Trudell shared Healy's concern. "As far as I'm concerned, the... definition of corporate culture... creates problems. It is defined as 'an attitude, policy, rule, course of conduct or practice.' It's vague" (Justice Committee 28 May 2002).

Economic Discourses

Economic discourses also provided a dominant frame to evaluate and speak about corporate crime and corporate criminal liability. Throughout the Westray bill reform process there was frequent concern expressed that any attempts to hold corporations and corporate executives and board members to account for their harmful acts should not be too stringent; after all, we should avoid measures that have the potential to impede a corporation's ability to produce and accumulate profit. The dominant message was (and is) that corporations are an unequivocal good, a mechanism that will contribute to society's overall well being — profitable corporations are in everyone's best interests (Glasbeek 2002; Pearce and Snider 1995).

Many legislators said an overly harsh law would mean that corporations would no longer be able to attract the best and the brightest as board members, referred to as "director chill" throughout the Committee's hearing. Glasbeek (2002: 13) refers to arguments against holding corporate directors and officers to legal account as being groundless and "touched by arrogance":

> There is unconcealed anger that lawmakers are seeking to make directors and officers of corporations, that is, corporate actors, answerable as if they were ordinary mortals like you and me. There are vehement (unsupported) claims that the best and brightest will no longer make themselves available to serve corporations. Then we — the rest of us — would truly be sorry. (Glasbeek 2002: 13)

In the context of the Westray bill, this anger and arrogance was channelled through those with the responsibility for legislating against corporate illegality. Consider, for example, the comments of two MPs:

> People become directors for a lot of reasons. Some of the reasons are very good reasons and some of the reasons are not particularly good reasons. You've [a witness at the Committee] frequently used the phrase "sending a message." I would suggest to you that by engaging in legislation, we are sending a message. The message may not be heard in the same way by all people at all times, particularly by directors who may well have to reconsider their positions as directors. (John MacKay, Liberal, Justice Committee 23 May 2002)

> We do not want to create the situation where we dissuade competent people from being the directing minds of corporations. We want to encourage competent people who exercise sound skill and judgment to continue working through the vehicle of corporations to ensure that jobs are preserved and created in Canada. (Vic Toews, Canadian Alliance, 20 September 2001)

A related concern was that corporations would leave the country in the face of overly stringent laws, a decision with potentially devastating effects for the economy, or so we were told. As one MP suggested:

> You have to be very careful, if you believe all these Canadian corporations and companies are just going to stay around if we put in something that's a little too tough on them. I'm not suggesting that's what you've been proposing here. But I can tell you, there are many companies right now who look at our tax laws and other laws and are on the verge of heading somewhere else. (Kevin Sorenson, Canadian Alliance, Justice Committee 2 May 2002)

Corporations will threaten to relocate when confronted with laws that they perceive to be overly stringent or reduce profitability, or to strong-arm the government to reduce taxes or provide low interest loans. However, these threats are more apparent than real, with few corporations having the ability to pack up and leave a particular country on a moment's notice. In addition to requiring access to a skilled workforce in regions with "social, economic and political stability," something that is not always available in countries with cheap labour, many corporations are constrained geographically by the markets that they need access to for purchasing materials and selling their products (Hirst and Thompson 1996: 198; Pearce and Snider 1995; Pearce and Tombs 1998: 54).

Overall, the legal and economic discourses that flowed through the Committee's work contained a "mutually reinforcing" character that downplayed the seriousness of workplace injury and death and limited the reform options that were given serious consideration (Tombs and Whyte 2007: 69). The dominant frame ruled out any consideration of the structural causes of workplace death, any examination of the roots of corporate power or the privileged legal status and extensive rights conferred by limited liability (Glasbeek 2002; Tombs and Whyte 2007). The overwhelming moral, political, economic and social capital of the corporation was thus judged irrelevant from the get-go. It also meant that those in positions of power, the individual executives and directors who make the decisions and reap the financial rewards, remain largely hidden behind the corporate veil. While the Westray bill means that some corporations will be, and have been, held to account for their harmful acts, individual responsibility within the Criminal Code remains unchanged. In this respect, the new law was deemed necessary only for the Westrays of the world, the so-called rogue corporations that represent the exception to the rule. It was definitely not needed for crime, and certainly not for the result of a problematic corporate culture or the structural realities of corporate capitalism.

THE WESTRAY BILL IN ACTION

The state's role in the production of corporate crime and corporate criminal liability does not end with the Westray bill's introduction. Examining the differences between "law-as-legislation" and "law-in-practice" illustrates that what the law promises on paper is oftentimes substantially different than what is achieved through its enforcement.

Following its enactment, the Westray bill quickly faded into the background, overshadowed by the priorities of a criminal justice system more accustomed to dealing with guns and gangs than corporate miscreants. In the more than six years since the law was first introduced, there have been only three charges and one conviction.[9] In addition, all of the charges laid thus far have involved small companies where there was (or probably will be) little difficulty tracing the chain of responsibility throughout the organization — hardly the sort of corporate complexity that proponents had in mind when arguing for changes to the identification doctrine.

One factor animating the Westray bill's lack of enforcement, and further implicating the state in the production of corporate crime, is the occupational health and safety regulatory environment. Canada's corporate criminal liability legislation is set against a backdrop of a well-established set of provincial workplace safety regulations. That is, it operates within the context of a "bifurcated model of criminal process" (Tombs and Whyte 2007: 110) in which attempts to "assimilate" corporate wrongdoing into the criminal law have had to develop alongside a robust regulatory frame that involves a separate, non-criminal means of dealing with health and safety offences. As a private sector representative[10] suggested in an interview regarding the Westray bills' impact,

> You know, the thing that struck me at the time and I think is probably still the case is that clearly there is health and safety legislation in every province and that would be the natural thing that people would look to... to go the *Criminal Code* route you'd have a much higher burden of proof.

A related factor is the poor knowledge of, and disinterest in, this legislation among police and Crown prosecutors. In an interview, a corporate lawyer cited the lack of education and training for police and prosecutors as the "biggest single impediment to the enforcement of this law."[11] Unfortunately, he continued, Crown prosecutors do not have the time, expertise or requisite training to learn about the new legislation, particularly in comparison to the legion of well-paid corporate lawyers that stand waiting to defend against criminal charges.

The state also is implicated in the production of corporate crime through the priorities accorded (or not accorded) the policing of corporate offending. Glasbeek (2002: 149) argues that there is an ideological bias against criminalizing corporations and corporate actors that "saturates the efforts of the police forces, prosecutorial offices, and policymaking institutions." A union representative[12] noted that police tend to conceptualize violence from a narrow, stereotypical perspective:

> Another part of the problem is that the police, when they end up where there's been a death, work-related, their only concern... is to make sure that it is not a murder that has been camouflaged by a work accident, that it is really an accident. That is their concern. It seems that their approach, the way they are looking at work accidents, hasn't changed.

Similar concerns were expressed in reference to Crown prosecutors, who generally do not consider occupational health and safety offences as an important part of their work. According to a legal academic, "I just don't know that most criminal prosecutors think about this realm of criminal law when they are thinking about being a prosecutor in law school, or even before law school."[13]

Informed by dominant, culturally ingrained beliefs that corporations are not really criminals, the state's corporate criminal liability law has thus far been largely ineffectual. Although there is symbolic import to new corporate criminal liability legislation which signals an official approbation of corporate harm and wrongdoing, its lack of enforcement raises questions about the ability to hold corporations and their senior executives to account for serious injury and death in the workplace. As Snider (2004: 180) argues, "if neither the law nor the public can 'see' crime except through the body of the individual bad acts, the possibilities of disciplining the most powerful entities in the modern social order — the organizations dominating our economic and political system — appear slim." While the Westray bill will hold some corporations and corporate actors accountable — and thus far it has been the smallest and weakest that have been subject to the law's gaze — the primary causes of workplace injury and death (that is, the tension between profit maximization and the costs of safety and the relative worth of workers/employees versus owners and investors) will continue.

UNDERSTANDING THE PRODUCTION OF CORPORATE CRIME AND THE CORPORATE CRIMINAL

The state plays a constitutive role in the production of corporate crime and corporate criminal liability. Using the Westray bill as an empirical focus, we see that, while the state was not present in the explosion that killed twenty-six people, it helped create the conditions within which the Westray disaster occurred, putting the interests of corporate capitalism and the pursuit of profit before workplace safety, thus allowing the mining corporation to ignore its health and safety responsibilities (Glasbeek and Tucker 1993; Glasbeek 2002). The state also provides the space within which dominant legal and economic discourses helped to ensure that Canada's corporate criminal liability legislation was not overly ambitious or punitive in its nature and scope. As Comack (1999: 67, emphasis original) reminds us, "the state could be said to *condense* the relations of power in society, and one of the ways it does so is through discourse." Finally, the state's complicity in, or perhaps, condonation of corporate crime continues through the Westray bill's virtual non-enforcement by failing to address the structural and ideological biases against the policing of corporate crime.

These arguments do not suggest that the Canadian state or any other state automatically or necessarily (re)produces capitalist power relations, or makes it impossible to hold corporations to legal account. The mere fact that the Westray bill was introduced shows the problems of such deterministic, conspiratorial formulae. However, they do suggest that it is empirically incorrect and theoretically blind to ignore the state's role as a site where powerful forces coalesce to animate particular legal and policy matters (Comack 1999; Tombs and Whyte 2009), a process that, in the case of the Westray bill, also helps reproduce capitalism's hegemonic status (Jessop 2002). In this respect, as Tombs and Whyte (2009: 114) argue, "corporate crime is not simply a result of the success or lack of success of the state acting as 'policeman,' but is produced as a result of the symbiotic relationship between states and markets."

In the end, while we cannot ignore the symbolic importance of the Westray bill, the story thus far does not bode well for those interested in holding corporations and corporate actors to legal account. It suggests that there are "*limits upon*, and *no-go areas for*, regulation on the part of the *capitalist* state" (Tombs and Whyte 2009: 108, emphasis original), including that state processes and state actors are organized in ways that restrict the manner in which corporations are disciplined (Snider 2009). We therefore need to understand and challenge the state's role in the production of these limits if we are to imagine and realize the effective control of corporate crime, "even for brief moments" (Tombs and Whyte 2009: 114). Ultimately, it is apparent that the state plays a material role in allowing incidents of corporate wrongdoing to persist, and even thrive. This analysis demonstrates how the socio-legal structures of regulatory- and criminal–law-based regimes can contribute to, even produce, tragic and counterintuitive results from formal systems of justice. Understanding justice requires that we examine the broader effects of these systems to reveal the hidden ironies, such as state-sanctioned criminality. The responses to the Westray affair suggest that the state's sanctioning of this result may well continue so long as capital interests persist and remain paramount. We must continue to unpack these inadequacies to reveal the nature and quality of justice that such regimes sustain.

Notes

1. Thank you to Laureen Snider and Ruth Code for their helpful comments. Address correspondence to: Steven Bittle, Assistant Professor, Department of Criminology, University of Ottawa, 25 University (120) Ottawa, ON, Canada, K1N 6N5. Telephone: (613) 562-5800, ext.1561; email: steven.bittle@uOttawa. ca.

2. An organization can be found guilty of an offence involving negligence if the Crown can prove that "employees of the organization committed the act and that a senior officer should have taken reasonable steps to prevent them from doing so" (Department of Justice Canada 2003: 6). The senior officer must have "departed markedly" from standards that could be reasonably expected to be followed to prevent the employee from committing the offence (*Criminal Code,* s.22.1; Archibald et al. 2004: 385). For offences requiring subjective intent, there must be evidence that the harmful actions of senior officers somehow benefited the organization (*Criminal Code,* s.22.2; Department of Justice Canada 2003: 70). Sentencing provisions include probation orders for organizations, such as orders to improve safety policies (individuals are subject to penalties already in the Criminal Code) (*Criminal Code* s.732.1; also see Archibald et al. 2004: 389–92; Department of Justice Canada 2003: 9).

3. Hansard is the official recording of all proceedings in Parliament (Hansard Association of Canada, online: <hansard.ca> accessed 15 August 2009). All

proceedings referenced throughout this chapter are from the Parliament of Canada's website: <parl.gc.ca>. References include date of parliamentary proceeding or Committee meeting and, where appropriate, the individual speaker and his or her political party.

4. In Canada, there were 928 fatalities in the workplace in 2004 (Association of Workers' Compensation Boards of Canada 2006) and 1,097 in 2005 (Sharpe and Hardt 2006).

5. The interviews were conducted by the author for a larger study regarding the evolution of the Westray bill.

6. For Jessop (2009: 9; 1990: 341), the state is a "distinct ensemble of institutions and organizations whose socially accepted function is to define and enforce collectively binding decisions on a given population in the name of their 'common interest' or 'general will.'"

7. The main political parties in Canada's Parliament at the time were the Liberal Party (the government, centrist in orientation), the Canadian Alliance (right-wing/conservative), the Progressive Conservatives (centre-right), the Bloc-Québécois (independence movement/centre-right) and the New Democratic Party (left-wing).

8. The concept of corporate culture was pioneered by the federal government of Australia in 1995, defining corporate culture as an "attitude, policy, rule, course of conduct or practice existing within the body corporate generally or in the part of the body corporate in which the relevant activities take place" (Department of Justice Canada, March 2002).

9. The first charge was laid on April 19, 2004. Domenico Fantini, a sixty-eight-year-old owner/supervisor of a small construction company was charged with one count of criminal negligence causing death after a trench collapsed at the site of a private house renovation, killing an employee (Brown 2004; York Regional Police 26 August 2004). The criminal charges were dropped when Mr. Fantini pled guilty to provincial health and safety offences. The second charge, and only conviction, was against Transpavé, a manufacturer of concrete patio blocks, after a worker was crushed to death by a machine that stacks concrete stones onto wooden pallets (Edwards and Conlin 2006; Keith and Walsh 2008; Milan 2008). As part of a plea agreement, Transpavé pled guilty to criminal negligence causing death and paid a $100,000 fine, plus a $10,000 victim surcharge (Canadian HR Reporter 2008; Keith and Walsh 2008). The most recent charge was laid in February 2010 against a crane rental company and its owner and operator, after a crane fell into an excavation, crushing a worker to death (De Guzman 2010; Edwards, Todd and Warning 2010). The case is currently before the court.

10. Interview conducted by author with private sector representative, November 18, 2008.

11. Interview conducted by author with corporate lawyer, October 9, 2008.

12. Interview conducted by author with union representative, November 20, 2008.

13. Interview conducted by author with legal academic, October 8, 2008.

References

Archibald, T., K. Jull and K. Roach. 2004. "The Changed Face of Corporate Criminal Liability." *The Criminal Law Quarterly* 48.

Association of Workers' Compensation Boards of Canada. 2006. *National Work Injuries Statistics Program — February 2006*. <awcbc.org/english/Statistics.asp> accessed 20 September 2007.

Barry, A., T. Osborne and N. Rose. 1996. *Foucault and Political Reason: Liberalism, Neo-Liberalism and Rationalities of Government*. Chicago, IL: University of Chicago Press.

Bill C-45, *An Act to Amend the Criminal Code (criminal liability of organizations)*. Statutes of Canada: 2003, c. 21.

Bittle, S., and L. Snider. 2006. "From Manslaughter to Preventable Accident: Shaping Corporate Criminal Liability." *Law and Policy* 28, 4 (October).

Braithwaite, J. 2003. "What's Wrong with the Sociology of Punishment." *Theoretical Criminology* 7, 1.

Brown, D. 2004. "Criminal Charges Laid Under New Corporate Killing Law." *Canadian HR Reporter* 17, 16 (September 27).

Cahill, S., and P. Cahill. 1999. "Scarlet Letters: Punishing the Corporate Citizen." *International Journal of the Sociology of Law* 27.

Canadian Dredge and Dock Co. v. The Queen [1985] 1 S.C.R. 662.

Canadian HR Reporter. 2008. "Quebec Company Fined $110,000 in Worker's Death." Carswell Business Publication.

Chunn, D., and D. Lacombe (eds.). 2000. *Law as a Gendering Practice*. Oxford University Press.

Coleman, R., J. Sim, S. Tombs and D. Whyte. 2009. "Introduction: State, Power, Crime." In *State, Power, Crime*. Los Angeles, London, New Delhi, Singapore, Washington DC: Sage Publications.

Comack, E. (ed.). 1999. *Locating Law: Race/Class/Gender Connections*. Halifax, NS: Fernwood Publishing.

Comish, S. 1993. *The Westray Tragedy: A Miner's Story*. Halifax, NS: Fernwood Publishing.

Crime Post Bill C-45." *OH&S Due Diligence Update*. Toronto, ON: Stringer Brisbin Humphrey, Management Lawyers.

Criminal Code of Canada, R.S.C., c. C-46.

De Guzman, M.L. 2010. "Use It or Lose It." Canadian Occupational Safety <cos-mag.com/201004071847/legal/legal-columns/use-it-or-lose-it.html>.

Department of Justice Canada. 2002. *Corporate Criminal Liability: Discussion Paper*. March. Ottawa: Department of Justice Canada.

____. 2003. *Criminal Liability of Organizations: A Plain Language Guide to Bill C-45*. Ottawa: Department of Justice Canada.

Edwards, C.A., and R.J. Conlin. 2006. "First Corporate Charged with Workplace Safety Crime Post Bill C-45." OH&S Due Diligence Update. Toronto, ON: Stringer Brisbin Humphrey, Management Lawyers.

Edwards, C.A., S.D. Todd and J. Warning. 2010. "Bill C-45 Lives: Worker Death Sparks Criminal Negligence Charges." Canadian Occupational Health and Safety <cos-mag.com/201003051820/legal/legal-stories/bill-c-45-lives-worker-

death-sparks-criminal-negligence-charges.html>.

Ericson, R., and K.D. Haggerty. 1997. *Policing the Risk Society*. Oxford: Claredon Press.

Fudge, J., and B. Cossman. 2002. "Introduction." *Privatization, Law and the Challenge to Feminism*. University of Toronto Press.

Garland, D. 1999. "'Governmentality' and the Problem of Crime." In Russell Smandych (ed.), *Governable Places: Readings on Governmentality and Crime Contro*. Aldershot, Brookfield USA, Singapore, Sydney: Ashgate Dartmouth.

____. 2001. *The Culture of Control: Crime and Social Order in Contemporary Society*. Chicago: University of Chicago Press.

Glasbeek, H. 2002. *Wealth by Stealth: Corporate Crime, Corporate Law, and the Perversion of Democracy*. Toronto: Between the Lines.

Glasbeek, H., and E. Tucker. 1993. "Death by Consensus: The Westray Mine Story." *New Solutions* 14.

Haggerty, K.D., and R. Ericson (eds.). 2006. *The New Politics of Surveillance and Visibility*. Toronto: University of Toronto Press.

Hall, S. 2009. "Preface." In R. Coleman, J. Sim, S. Tombs and D. Whyte (eds.), *State, Power, Crime*. Washington, DC: Sage Publications.

Hannah-Moffat, K. 2001. *Punishment in Disguise: Penal Governance and Federal Imprisonment of Women in Canada*. Toronto: University of Toronto Press.

Hirst, P.Q., and G. Thompson. 1996. *Globalization in Question: The International Economy and the Possibilities of Governance*. Cambridge, MA: Blackwell.

Jessop, B. 1990. *State Theory: Putting Capitalist States in their Place*. Cambridge, MA: Polity Press.

____. 2002. *The Future of the Capitalist State*. Cambridge, UK: Polity Press.

____. 2008. *State Power*. Cambridge, MA: Polity Press.

Jobb, D. 1994. *Calculated Risk: Greed, Politics and the Westray Tragedy*. Halifax, NS: Nimbus Publishing.

Keith, N., and C. Walsh. 2008. "Bill C-45 Alert: Sentence Handed Down in First OHS Criminal Negligence Conviction." *OHS Law NewsFlash*, March <gowlings.com>.

Laufer, W. 2006. *Corporate Bodies and Guilty Minds*. University of Chicago Press.

Mann, M. 2004. "Corporate Criminals." *Canada Business* 77, 2.

McMullen, J. 2001. "Westray and After: Power, Truth and News Reporting of the Westray Mine Disaster." In Susan Boyd, Dorothy E. Chunn and Robert Menzies (eds.), *[Ab]Using Power: The Canadian Experience*. Halifax, NS: Fernwood Publishing.

____. 2005. *News, Truth and Crime: The Westray Disaster and Its Aftermath*. Halifax, NS: Fernwood Publishing.

Millan, L. 2008. "Company Fined $110,000 for Death of Employee." *The Lawyers Weekly* 27, 44 (March 28).

Pearce, F. 1976. *Crimes of the Powerful: Marxism, Crime and Deviance*. London: Pluto Press.

Pearce, F., and S. Snider (eds.). 1995. *Corporate Crime: Contemporary Debates*. Toronto: University of Toronto Press.

Pearce, F., and S. Tombs. 1999. *Toxic Capitalism: Corporate Crime and the Chemical Industry*. Toronto: Canadian Scholars' Press.

Resnick, S.A., and R.D. Wolff. 1987. *Knowledge and Class: A Marxian Critique of Political*

Economy. University of Chicago Press.

Richard, Justice P.K. 1997. *The Westray Story: A Predictable Path to Disaster*. Report of the Westray Mine Public Inquiry. Justice K. Peter Richard, Commissioner. Province of Nova Scotia.

Rose, N. 2000. "Government and Control." *The British Journal of Criminology* 40, 2.

Rose, N., and P. Miller. 1992. "Political Power beyond the State: Problematics of Government." *British Journal of Sociology* 43, 2.

Sharpe, A., and J. Hardt. 2006. *Five Deaths a Day: Workplace Fatalities in Canada: 1993–2005*. Centre for the Study of Living Standards. Research Paper 2006-04.

Shearing, C. 2001. "Punishment and the Changing Face of Governance." *Punishment and Society* 3, 2.

Shearing, C., and P.C. Stenning. 2003. "From the Panopticon to Disney World: The Development of Discipline." In E. McLaughlin, J. Muncie and G. Hughes (eds), *Criminological Perspectives: Essential Readings*. Milton Keynes: Open University Press.

Slapper, G., and S. Tombs. 1999. *Corporate Crime*. Essex, UK: Pearson Education Limited.

Smart, C. 1989. *Feminism and the Power of Law*. London and New York: Routledge.

Snider, L. 1993. *Bad Business: Corporate Crime in Canada*. Nelson Canada.

___. 2000. "The Sociology of Corporate Crime: An Obituary (or: Whose Knowledge Claims Have Legs?)" *Theoretical Criminology* 4, 2.

___. 2002. "Theft of Time: Disciplining Through Science and Law." *Osgoode Hall Law Journal* 40, 1.

___. 2004. "Poisoned Water, Environmental Regulation, and Crime: Constituting the Nonculpable Subject in Walkerton, Ontario." In Law Commission of Canada (ed.), *What Is a Crime? Defining Criminal Conduct in Contemporary Society*. Toronto, Vancouver: UBC Press.

___. 2008. "'But They're Not Real Criminals': Downsizing Corporate Crime." In B. Schissel and C. Brooks (eds.), *Marginality & Condemnation*. Halifax, NS: Fernwood Publishing.

Tillman, R.H., and M.L. Indergaard. 2005. *Pump and Dump: The Rancid Rules of the New Economy*. New Brunswick: Rutgers University Press.

Tombs, S. 2009. "Conference Presentation." European Developments in Corporate Criminal Liability. Hosted by Clifford Chance, London, U.K., 18 and 19 September.

Tombs, S., and D. Whyte. 2007. *Safety Crimes*. Cullompton, Devon, UK: Willan Publishing.

___. 2009. "The State and Corporate Crime." In R. Coleman, J. Sim, S. Tombs and D. Whyte (eds.), *State Power Crime*. Los Angeles, London, New Delhi, Singapore, Washington, DC: Sage Publications.

Valverde, M. 2003. *Law's Dream of a Common Knowledge*. Princeton University Press.

York Regional Police. 2004. "Charges in King Trench Collapse." Media Release. 25 August.

CHAPTER SEVEN

INFANTICIDE
The Will to Punish Through Equality and Reproductive Responsibility
Kirsten Kramar

GOVERNMENTALITY AND INFANTICIDE: AN OVERVIEW

This chapter examines the developing rationalities for reforming the law of infanticide, which governs the killing of newly born babies by their biological mothers, through the lens of "governmentality" (Foucault 1979, 1991a, 1991b, 2003). As an analytical framework, the governmentality lens enables scholars to draw attention to the ways of thinking and styles of reasoning that are embodied in various sorts of authoritative prescriptions for conduct, both within and beyond the state, and thus how we conduct ourselves. Governmentality is also a methodological approach that brings into focus the rationalities adopted by these authoritative claims-makers to "ask questions about how we govern and the conduct of both the governed and the governors" (Dean 1999: 28). According to Rose, O'Malley and Valverde (2006: 2) "governmentality" is in a "broad sense about the techniques and procedures for directing human behaviour. Government of children, government of souls and consciences, government of a household, of a state, or of oneself" (citing Foucault 1997: 82). In this sense, then, governing is not simply about the laws and regulations used by states to govern their societies, but includes a broad range of activities that offer prescriptions for how to be right in the world.

Governmentality studies can therefore help us to understand how social and political claims for social justice work in any given field of struggle. In general, this involves analyzing the claims-making activities of social justice advocates who advance arguments about how things ought to be. These power struggles over the way things ought to be in order to be socially just are generally advanced using claims that are rooted in what we call "discourses." For simplicity's sake, we can define discourses as expert forms of knowledge that are used to justify our claims about social justice — this can be sociological knowledge, psychological knowledge, environmental knowledge or scientific knowledge produced by experts in those fields to whom we sometimes turn when advancing particular political objectives of governance. But a governmentality analysis can also show us how discourses that contain resistance claims (by women's rights, disability rights, victims' rights and indigenous rights movements) and other identity-based emancipatory claims rest upon certain implicit assumptions. For example, one of these is the assumption that victims of oppression have a unique access to "capital 'T' Truth" on the basis of their victimization experience or identity and therefore have special access to knowledge for the purposes of resistance. According to a governmentality criticism, "the invocation of the expertise of the claimants themselves, and more generally of their agency and their capacity for active engagement with authorities of various kinds, no more steps outside relations of power, domination and subordination" (Dean 1999: 66) than any other sorts of claims about social justice. In this view, any sort of claim (whether in the pursuit of social justice or not) that is wedded to the idea of being free from some kind of effect of structural oppression (such as patriarchy, capitalism or colonialism) is also part and parcel of a matrix of power in which we are governed, or asked to govern ourselves in this or that way. Take another example — that of green consumerism. If you are concerned about the environment, you likely have a strong sense that recycling your tin cans and plastics and buying "environmentally friendly" products makes you a good citizen of planet Earth. Your sense of yourself as a good person is connected to your habits in relation to your garbage and shopping. From a governmentality perspective, the environmental movement and its claims about good citizenship have been successful in governing your actions in a particular way, partly because you feel good about yourself in relation to the habits you have developed or been asked to develop on the basis of particular knowledge claims about how best to proceed according to the governance objectives of green consumerism. That rationality seeks to target our shopping habits as opposed to, say, the habits of polluting corporations such as Alcoa Inc., the world's largest producer of aluminum products, or the deep sea drilling practices of British Petroleum to achieve their objectives. This example illustrates another central idea of governmentality studies, which is the insight that we are governed most effectively when we conduct ourselves according to these objectives using our own free will. This is what is known as governing through freedom. One of the central and critical claims of the governmentality literature "is the idea that we are 'governed' through and by means of our 'freedom'" (Garland 1997: 196).

Governing populations of citizens is more easily achieved when we govern ourselves freely according to the stated objectives of government broadly defined. A governmental objective can include the objectives of the environmental movement and the women's movement as well as the government or state. Generally, states are able to govern populations through free will more effectively than when they are required to apply direct regulatory force on the individual (such as through the use of criminal law that targets individual wrongdoers). Populations are more effectively governed through knowledge of the self that causes them to adopt particular habits that are in line with governing objectives. To take another example, some expert medical knowledge about the negative effects of too much alcohol causes many of us to freely choose not to drink too many martinis or glasses of red wine despite how good it may feel or the positive stress reduction benefit drinking may have in our daily lives. The objective of reducing alcohol consumption in any given population is achieved because citizens will freely choose to limit their intake of alcohol on the basis of a desire to be healthy, responsible citizens. That desire is tapped into by "governmental rationalities" that presume we are freely choosing citizens and asks us to reduce our own alcohol consumption "for our own good." It may be that the governmental rationality underpinning the notion that alcohol is bad for us is also linked to presumed costs to the healthcare system in a country that has socialized medicine. We are taught to avoid risks such as the overconsumption of martinis in an effort to avoid negative consequences to our health, but it may also have distinctly positive effects for the state in the form of reduced healthcare costs. Similarly, green consumerism targets the individual consumer leaving the mega-multinational corporations to pollute with little scrutiny from us because we are focused on recycling our cat food tins as part of an overall program of good citizenship. These are some of the unexamined effects of these different governmentalities.

What scholars working from within a governmentality perspective seek to draw attention to are the relations of power within which we are all immersed. Being committed to the justice of a movement like feminism or environmentalism does not take you outside relations of power and authority. From a governmentality perspective we can see that capital 'T' Truth claims of social justice claims-makers will result in differently configured matrices of power in which we all remain governed and governable in various different contexts by various different experts (scientific, legal, sociological, medical, psychological and so on) and in various different ways. The ideas may be different, but the governance structures may also remain just as oppressive as the ones they replace despite their claim of being linked to social justice, or achieve little in the way of the stated objectives of social justice advocates. In other words, there are no political programs (or prescriptions for social justice) that stand outside power/knowledge relations. Such an examination may also reveal that the most successful strategies (such as green consumerism) achieve very little in the way of social justice objectives. Understanding how certain governmental rationalities become dominant over others may be a social justice strategy in and of itself.

Because the governmentality approach enables us to consider how the effects of particular sets of prescriptive arguments (such as those offered by various feminist arguments for social change) may produce contradictory, often unintended, consequences with particular kinds of power effects, it can be very useful for understanding how social justice strategies work in practice. This approach is particularly useful for analyzing the ramifications of adopting particular ideals (such as emancipation, equality, liberty, freedom) to advance particular regimes of governing. According to Mitchell Dean (1999: 36–37):

> By making clear what is at stake when we try to govern in a particular way and employ certain ways of thinking and acting, an analytics of government allows us to accept a sense of responsibility for the consequences and effects of thinking and acting in certain ways… by noting that notions of "empowerment" are capable of being used by very different political stances and are themselves imbricated in definite sets of power relations, we produce a certain discomfort for the advocates of such notions of all political persuasions, particularly those who imagine themselves to be standing outside relations of power.

In this respect, the governmentality approach may appear to be at odds with social justice projects (such as those advanced by the various kinds of feminist arguments for empowerment or other kinds of revolutionary or emancipatory programs for social change) insofar as they advance proscriptive programs while perhaps ignoring the power effects of their own political objectives. Nevertheless, we can ask questions about the effects of emancipatory strategies and their relationship to existing power structures.

GOVERNMENTALITIES OF INFANT KILLING

Using the conceptual tools offered by the governmentality framework, this chapter examines the governmentalities of infant killing. These are made up of competing discourses about the nature of infant killing and its proper response in law. The Canadian infanticide law offers a mitigation framework that reduces the punishment for murder for those cases in which a biological mother kills a newly born baby. This reduced punishment framework is justified on the grounds that the strains of new motherhood in the context of social and economic hardship sometimes compels women to kill their unwanted babies. However, the authorities in a number of Canadian provinces have begun to problematize the infanticide law and its mitigation framework as a threat to men's equality against a backdrop of sweeping social and economic changes that have reconfigured the responsibility of the state towards those very populations of women now targeted through enhanced law-and-order approaches to infanticide. These broad positions are each lent support through a range of competing criminological, feminist and legal discourses to be examined here.

INFANTICIDE AND THE LAW

Prior to the passage of the 1948 Canadian infanticide law, women who killed children at birth or shortly afterwards were charged with the crime of murder. At that time, a murder conviction carried with it a mandatory penalty of death. The young women who committed infanticide were usually only convicted of murder when they confessed to killing the baby (Kramar 2005). Sometimes the women were victims of sexual assault or domestic violence and they were very often quite young. These young women found themselves compelled by social norms to hide their unwanted pregnancy and dispose of the infant at birth to conceal their extra-marital sexual activity or desperate circumstances. They were not motivated by any malice towards the infants, who were rarely seen as victims of callous women-murderers. The practice of concealing an unwanted pregnancy and giving birth in secret and disposing of the baby's body could lead to criminal charges for "murder," "concealment of birth" or "neglecting to obtain assistance in childbirth." However, jurors were so sympathetic to these women that they were disinclined to convict them, whatever the evidence, because infanticide was thought of as quasi-criminal.

During the nineteenth century there were a range of social factors that very strongly mitigated women's responsibilities, and women's "irrational" behaviour or impulses were seen as motivated not by evil but by morally pure intentions. Women who killed their illegitimate babies were seen as conforming to society's moral standards and were viewed in contradictory terms as acting both irrationally and properly because they were acting to protect their sexual reputations as well as the illegitimate baby, who would experience a life of stigmatization. Men who failed to live up to society's moral standards by seducing, abandoning or abusing the women were, therefore, the real criminals. Although women sometimes killed their babies in states of what we now refer to as post-partum psychosis brought about by hormonal changes associated with pregnancy, childbirth and lactation, the infanticide provision was originally enacted to address the killing of newly born babies by desperate women in desperate social circumstances for which the penalty for murder was entirely without basis in penological theory.

For example, in 1919 Viola Thompson suffocated her two-week-old daughter by stuffing her mouth with a cotton handkerchief and wrapping her nose and mouth with a bandage. The baby girl was later found beside a railway track, not far from where Thompson boarded a train to take her home. The baby, dressed in a flannelette nightdress, was frozen and dead. Thompson had attempted to put the baby in a home because her husband did not want it but the infants home required her to pay $125 and to stay with the baby for six months. She claimed to have been driven to commit the crime only as a last resort. The jury found the defendant guilty of murder, but with a strong recommendation of mercy. The defence tried to show that the defendant was not mentally responsible for her acts, but the evidence of insanity was rejected by the trial judge, who sentenced Thompson to death on September 27, 1919. Dozens of letters sent to the Department of Justice to request clemency sought to explain Thompson's actions.

Viola Thompson was repeatedly brutally assaulted by her husband Jim Thompson, whom she had married when she was seventeen and he was forty-eight. Mr. Thompson had seven children at the time of their marriage, and they had four more together. He was described as a madman. The letters written on her behalf described a man who was drunk most of the time and who beat her so badly she would often turn up at neighbours' homes bleeding and severely bruised. Given these circumstances, it was argued that Jim Thompson provoked her to kill her baby and that the baby's death was his responsibility. Viola Thompson begged the Minister of Justice for her release so that she could return to her four children, who had been left in the care of her husband. On February 15, 1926 Viola Thompson was granted a ticket of leave from Kingston Penitentiary, where she had been imprisoned for six and a half years.[1]

This case is one example of the social problem the infanticide law was intended to address. At the time the law was passed in both England and Canada, experts in mental medicine did not consider most of these women to have "diseased minds" associated with pregnancy, childbirth and lactation. They were rather more concerned with a mitigation framework that recognized the social pressures on the women in the context of a death penalty for murder in Canada (Kramar and Watson 2006). Moreover, by the 1940s, developments in psychiatric theories about "puerperal" or "exhaustion psychosis" had not the slightest relevance for Canadian legislators in 1948 whose only task was to provide a proven legal solution to a persistent legal problem (Kramar and Watson 2008: 247). It was only later that the infanticide laws were extended to include cases of maternal neonaticide when the mothers were suffering from post-partum illness.[2]

Contemporary Canadian infanticide law, which only applies to the biological mother of a victim in the first year of life, and which offers a kind of mitigation from a possible murder conviction, seems to link women's deviance to reproductive difference and pathology in the most obvious and unequivocal way. Passed into law in 1948, the relevant section of the *Criminal Code of Canada*, section 233, reads as follows:

> Infanticide — a female person commits infanticide when by a willful act or omission she causes the death of her newly-born child, if at the time of the act or omission she is not fully recovered from the effects of giving birth to the child and by reason thereof or of the effect of lactation consequent on the birth of the child the balance of her mind is then disturbed.

The maximum penalty for infanticide is five years' imprisonment. In practice, women found guilty are sentenced to shorter probationary periods in the community and sometimes in hospital if they are found to be mentally ill. The law is situated in the range of charges available for maternal neonaticide, which also include "concealment of birth" and "neglecting to obtain assistance in childbirth." The law was passed at a time when Canadian law carried the death penalty for murder, birth control and abortion were criminalized and the stigma attached to illegitimacy enforced through bastardy laws prevented children born out of wedlock from inheriting property and prior to the liberalization of divorce procedures. The victim's rights movement had yet to alter the prosecution process in the manner we see it today such that Crown prosecutors and experts, such as forensic pathologists, see themselves as legal advocates for infant-victims (see Roach 1999 on victims' rights and Kramar 2005, 2006 on the advocacy role played by forensic experts working for Coroner's Offices).

The passage of the law coincided with the rationalization of all punishment frameworks in Canadian law beginning in the mid-twentieth century. It can be viewed as an effort to prosecute these cases fairly and in a uniform manner across the provinces and territories. At this time, the Crown often failed to secure convictions for murder in cases of maternal neonaticide and the mandatory death penalties that accompanied the rare murder convictions in these circumstances were always commuted. That these problems provided the impetus for infanticide law, which was an attempt to fashion an appropriate homicide offence that could result in principled conviction and disposition, is accepted by all the commentators (Kramar & Watson 2006). In other words, the infanticide law was viewed as a just response to the crime of killing one's newly born child. In 1955, following *R. v. Marchello*, a case heard before the Ontario Court of Queen's Bench, the infanticide legal framework was amended in four significant ways: 1) infanticide became a lesser included finding on a charge of murder allowing judges and juries to convict women charged with murder for infanticide where the facts conformed to the infanticide scenario; 2) the phrase "effects of lactation" was added so as to expand the law to cover those cases in which the mother may be suffering from post-partum depression, understood then to be the result of the exhaustion associated with lack of sleep as a result of round-the-clock breast feeding; 3) the phrase "newly born" was defined as being a child up to twelve months of age, thereby expanding the infanticide provision to include children more than a few hours or days old; and 4) a clause was added that removed the Crown's evidentiary burden to prove the mental element beyond a reasonable doubt. That provision, section 663 of the *Criminal Code of Canada*, was aimed at reducing the burden on the Crown to prove the strong psychological element written into the law and reads as follows:

> No acquittal unless act or omission not wilful — Where a female person is charged with infanticide and the evidence establishes that she caused the death of her child but does not establish that, at the time of the act or omission by which she caused the death of the child, she was not fully recovered from the effects of giving birth to the:
>
> (a) child or from the effect of lactation consequent on the birth of the child, and that the balance of her mind was, at that time, disturbed by reason;
>
> (b) of the effect of giving birth to the child or of the effect of lactation consequent on the birth of the child she may be convicted unless the evidence establishes that the act or omission was not wilful.

Taken as a whole, these amendments brought the Canadian legal framework in line with the expanded English law of 1938 and can be seen as producing a kind of lay-psychiatric hybrid category to address a range of cases in which babies are killed by their mothers (Kramar and Watson 2008). These amendments would be clawed back in the late twentieth and early twenty-first centuries by judges and juries who did not want to allow for a lesser punishment framework when a single mother kills an unwanted baby in the context of post-partum depression, or when attempting to hide their sexual activity for religious or other kinds of socially proscribed moral reasons. This more recent development can be linked to women's formal legal equality, the achievement of reproductive freedom and advocacy for the infant-victim on the part of the authorities.

THE DISAPPEARANCE OF INFANTICIDE

Despite the efforts of legislators to implement a special infanticide law to address the socio-legal aspects of maternal neonaticide, research on reported Canadian cases reveals a trend from the 1990s onwards of charging filicidal women with murder (Cunliffe 2009). Cunliffe examined twenty-seven cases in which infanticide was a potential verdict in the period between June 1954 and August 2008, showing that, since the late 1990s, the authorities have seen it as their role to prosecute women who kill infants under twelve months of age with the full force of the punishment framework available for murder. The extension of harsh punishment in these cases is justified through classical notions of deterrence, which views women as rational actors who calculate the cost-benefit of committing such a crime. The punishment response is also justified on the grounds that the infanticide law is "outdated" because decades of social change have improved the lot of single mothers (Staples 2006: E6). Decades of law reform in the area of reproductive freedom now give women access to abortion and birth control such that, in the words of Supreme Court Justice Beverley McLachlin, "women faced with an unwanted pregnancy now have a number of less desperate alternatives available to them" (Staples 2006: A1). In addition, feminist academics have objected in principle to the "medicalization of women's deviance" in favour of under-standing women's criminal offending as a product of structural oppression (or the effects of patriarchy and capitalism). Few feminist commentators, other than O'Donovan (1984: 261), recognized that the "medicalization of infanticide" was a strategic move on the part of legislators because it had the advantage of providing a scientific mitigation framework that worked well with the legal requirement that individuals be held legally accountable even if society's social arrangements were to blame. According to O'Donovan (1984: 261):

> The Act was the product, not of nineteenth century medical theory about the effects of child-birth, but of judicial effort to avoid passing death sentences which were not going to be executed. But medical theory provided a convenient reason for changing the law.

The perceived absence of sociological mitigation factors, along with the reduction of infant mortality rates and the associated rise in status of the infant-victim and the rejection of the psychological mitigation framework by feminist sociologists, has resulted in a rational actor model of infanticide to justify sentences of life imprisonment with no possibility of parole for ten years. This retributive response framework is advanced as a solution for the problem of infanticide with little or no discussion of the failure of harsh sentences to deter crime. Instead, the women are presumed to be rational actors with viable alternative options. The governance strategy presumes a kind of formal equality among all women wherein it is presumed that there exists no religious or moral impediment to accessing birth control, abortion or adoption as alternatives, and where the stressors of round-the-clock breast feeding, multiple children and post-partum changes have no effect on the women. This rational actor model is also accepted by criminologists, such as Rosemary Gartner, who conclude that the victim image of the infanticidal woman has long been mistaken. "We believe that a greater proportion of these women more closely resemble the image of the killer as rational actor" (Staples 2006: A1). This conclusion is drawn on the grounds that some infanticidal mothers are never caught following the discovery of the corpse of a baby. Because the mothers successfully hid their crimes, Gartner argues that the killers acted with intent and with an eye towards hiding the evidence. This conclusion sees infanticidal mothers as being motivated by evil intent or malice, a forethought to justify harsh punishment of the women, rather than as sobering evidence about the challenges faced by women who feel compelled to preserve their sexual reputations or are unwilling to mother under harsh economic and social circumstances.

THE DISAPPEARANCE OF SOCIAL JUSTICE FRAMEWORKS: R. V. EFFERT AND R. V. L.B.

In September of 2006 a Wetaskiwin, Alberta, jury found twenty-year-old Katrina Effert guilty of second-degree murder for killing her baby following a concealed pregnancy and secret birth in the basement of her parent's home. Evidence suggested that she strangled the baby with her panties to stop its cries and then fell asleep from exhaustion. She later threw the dead baby over a neighbour's fence into their yard in an effort to conceal the body. Effert was given the mandatory sentence of life imprisonment without possibility of parole for ten years. It was the first time that a woman had been found guilty of murder for maternal neonaticide since the passage of the infanticide provision in 1948. In September 2007, the Alberta Court of Appeal overturned the conviction on the grounds that the judge's instructions to the jury with respect to the infanticide provision were flawed and ordered a new trial. Effert was re-prosecuted and found guilty of second-degree murder by a second jury who rejected the infanticide defence as well as the evidence that Effert suffered from an emotional disturbance at the time of the killing. In part, the aggressive prosecution may reflect a prosecution strategy to secure guilty pleas for infanticide. Nevertheless, the Effert case illustrates that life imprisonment is a viable option for jurors who see it as their job to protect the lives of infants through the application of a deterrence-based model of justice to simultaneously deter populations of women and manage risk of harm to infants.

Recently in Ontario, an infanticide finding provided the impetus for the Ontario government to challenge the validity of the infanticide law itself. In 2008 L.B. was convicted in Guelph, Ontario, on two counts of infanticide.[3] The woman admitted to smothering her ten-month-old infant son when she was seventeen and another infant son again four years later. The case provided the opportunity for the Crown to discredit the psychological mitigation framework by appealing the lower court's decision. That two children were killed marshalled a Crown strategy to seek an order from the

Court of Appeal that L.B. stand trial for first-degree murder, which carries a maximum penalty of life imprisonment with no possibility of parole. The case heard before the Ontario Court of Appeal centred on the legitimacy of the infanticide law as a lesser included defence to murder. The Women's Legal and Education Action Fund (LEAF) was granted leave to intervene in the case in order to present arguments on the proper interpretation of the infanticide provisions of the Criminal Code. According to LEAF, the Crown seeks to deny women the opportunity to access a regime of reduced culpability and sentence provided by the infanticide provision (LEAF 2010: para 2).

The sociological and psychological mitigation rationalities have given way to a rather more retributive style of governance that attempts to manage the future through deterrence and harsh punishment. Challenges to these efforts to repeal the infanticide law on the part of equality-seeking groups such as LEAF continue to advance the rights of women to have the social context of pregnancy and mothering recognized in homicide law (LEAF 2010). Retributive calls for infanticide law reform often seek to erase the gendered nature of infanticide, relying on discourses of formal equality and reproductive rights and responsibility that have historically been advanced by feminist sociologists. These produce a rational legal subject where society, characterized as having solved the problems of the past that mitigated responsibility for infanticide, has little or no role in the mitigation of responsibility. In addition, legal strategies adopted by Crowns suggest that the infanticide law ought to be repealed because, it is argued, post-partum mental disturbance has no connection to violence in these cases (CBC 2010).

The will to provide a mitigation framework in cases of mothers who conceal their pregnancies and subsequently kill their babies at birth and those in which the mother is suffering from a post-partum mental disturbance and who commit infanticide has fallen out of favour in some provinces among Crown prosecutors, jurors and the public. The argument is that the social conditions that compel women to commit infanticide no longer exist because either the feminist movement has achieved both formal legal equality and reproductive freedom for women, or they simply do not want to extend the reduced culpability framework that recognizes the relative "powerlessness of women charged with infanticide and the social and economic imposition on them alone of the stigma and responsibility for pregnancy and child-rearing" (LEAF 2010: para 13). In another ironic twist, the law is viewed by retributive reformers as a violation of the equality provision of the *Charter of Rights and Freedoms* because no such law exists for men. For example, University of Saskatchewan Dean of Law, Professor Sanjeev Anand, argues that women ought to be treated equally to men and charged with murder or that a kind of diminished capacity offence ought to be added to the legal framework to address the needs of men who kill newly born babies (CBC 2010). In other words, the category of equality (in the context of reproductive freedom) is deployed to allow for the potential application of harsher punishment for infanticide rather than develop a legal category to understand women's unique experiences of motherhood. The rationality underpinning the move towards retribution on behalf of the infant-victim also sometimes includes a critique of the infanticide law that appropriates the feminist critique of the medicalization of women's deviance in an overall attempt to discredit the infanticide law itself.

Infanticide, Gender Inequality and Justice

These emerging retributive rationalities privilege formal legal equality over the feminist recognition of ongoing gender inequality in their proposals for the abolishment of infanticide. Legal academic commentators such as Professor Anand, interviewed extensively about the Effert and L.B. infanticide cases, have suggested that the infanticide law be abolished because it medicalizes deviance and fails to provide a mitigation framework for men (CBC 2010). Anand's equality argument dovetails directly into a governmentality of reproductive responsibility and therefore criminal responsibility. But this rationality is at odds with the intended purpose of the sociological feminist critique of the individualization and medicalization of women's crime, legislators efforts to recognize the direct economic and emotional effects of women's inequality and the court's recognition of the mitigation regime offered by the infanticide law that, despite the wording of the law, includes social, economic, cultural, religious, psychological and other factors that can lead some women to experience a disturbance of the mind following pregnancy and childbirth.

Notes

1. See Kirsten J. Kramar 2005.
2. Maternal neonaticide refers to killing newly born babies. Infanticide is a legal term used to describe the offence and diminished capacity framework for the crime of maternal neonaticide. Maternal filicide refers to the killing of children (as opposed to neonates) by their mothers. Infanticide may or may not apply in cases of maternal filicide. Infanticide law applies only to biological mothers who kill their newly born babies. A newly born baby is considered to be under the age of twelve months.
3. Because L.B. was a young offender at the time of the offences she cannot be named.

References

Burchell, G., C. Gordon and P. Miller (eds.). 1991. *The Foucault Effect*. Hemmel Hempstead: Harvester Wheatsheaf.

CBC. 2010. "Infanticide." *The Current*. September 23. <cbc.ca/thecurrent/2010/09/

sept-2310---pt-2-infanticide.html>.

Cunliffe, E. 2009. "Infanticide: Legislative History and Current Questions." *Criminal Law Quarterly* 55.

Dean, M. 1999. *Governmentality: Power and Rule in Modern Society*. London: Sage Publications.

Foucault, M. 1991a. "Governmentality." In Graham Burchell, Colin Gordon and Peter Miller (eds.), *The Foucault Effect: Studies in Governmentality*. Chicago: University of Chicago Press.

___. 1991b. "On Questions of Method." In Graham Burchell, Colin Gordon and Peter Miller (eds.), *The Foucault Effect: Studies in Governmentality*. Chicago: University of Chicago Press.

___. 2003. *"Society Must Be Defended" Lectures at the Collège de France 1975–1976*. Trans. David Macy. New York: Picador.

Garland, David. 1997. "'Governmentality' and the Problem of Crime: Foucault, Criminology, Sociology." *Theoretical Criminology* 1, 2.

Kramar, K. 2005. *Unwilling Mothers, Unwanted Babies: Infanticide in Canada*. Vancouver: UBC Press.

___. 2006. "Coroners' Interested Advocacy: Understanding Wrongful Accusations and Convictions." *Canadian Journal of Criminology and Criminal Justice* 48, 5.

Kramar, K., and W. Watson. 2006. "The Insanities of Reproduction: Medico-Legal Knowledge and the Development of Infanticide Law." *Social & Legal Studies* 15, 2.

___. 2008. "Canadian Infanticide Legislation, 1948 and 1955: Reflections on the Medicalization/Autopoiesis Debate." *Canadian Journal of Sociology* 33, 2.

LEAF 2010. Facutum of the Intervener, *R. v. L.B.* C49467/C49468. Ontario Court of Appeal.

Makin, K. 2010. "'Infanticide' Not a Defence to Murder, Appeal Court Told." *Globe and Mail* 23 September<theglobeandmail.com/news/national/ontario/infanticide-not-a-defence-for-murder-appeal-court-told/article1721071/>.

McLachlin, B. 1991. "Crime and Women — Feminine Equality and the Criminal Law." *U.B.C. Law Review* 25.

O'Donovan, K. 1984. "The Medicalisation of Infanticide." *Criminal Law Review* 259.

R. v. Marchello (1951), 100 C.C.C. 137, [1957] 4 D.R.L. 751, 12 C.R. 7.

Roach, K. 1999. *Due Process and Victims' Rights: The New Law and Politics of Criminal Justice*. Toronto: University of Toronto Press.

Rose, N., P. O'Malley, and M. Valverde. 2006. "Governmentality." *Annual Review of Law and Social Science* 2.

Staples, David. 2006. "Baby Killers Surprisingly Rational, Study Finds: Evidence of Coverup in Many Cases Belies Image of the Mentally Unbalanced Mother." *Edmonton Journal* 12 November.

PART III

BRIDGING THE DIVIDE

In this section we explore areas of research that represent moments of inter-digitations between the internal and external approaches. The internal approaches we studied had called for changes in the system but, rooted in positivism, these were calls to return to baseline concepts of justice — for instance, rehabilitation, rule of law and responsible journalism. Our external approaches rejected such baselines and instead focused on the importance of method in understanding the power relations that operate in the justice system. These approaches sought to unpack, describe and even challenge accepted approaches about the nature of justice in the fields they studied.

The approaches in this section mark the spaces between the two approaches. Between the poles of the purely external and the purely internal lie a series of approaches that reject the notion of baseline, but that also accept that changes in justice policy would form part of an appropriate response to tangible problems of justice systems. The division points between the external approaches and the bridging perspectives is laid out nicely by comparing and contrasting Kramar's work in the last section with Malhotra's work in Chapter Eight. Both adopt Foucault's governmentality lens of analysis in their work to reveal inadequacies in the systems they are studying, yet Kramar stops short of suggesting policy changes that might ameliorate the problems revealed. Malhotra, while agreeing with many of the analytical tools that Kramar uses, is able to suggest that a nuanced understanding of disability, informed by Foucault and Goffman, could and should result in legal changes that would improve the lives of people with disabilities. While Malhotra uses an external lens of analysis, he uses that lens to prescribe a policy change and to redistribute justice. This is not a change to return us to baseline, unlike the internal approaches, and is not merely an external broad analytic of justice. Rather, the change here would lead to a new understanding of disability in the law and would affect the way the law reacts to people with disabilities.

Similarly, Hogeveen and Friedstadt, in Chapter Eleven, use external Derridean analysis to suggest that affording public spaces with hospitality, although challenging and fraught with difficulties, would be a better way of achieving justice in the context of marginalized youths in the city of Edmonton (and beyond). This is bridging the problematic of justice because it is an external analytic calling for prospective changes. Again, the changes do not call for a return to baseline but for something of a revolution in the way marginalized youths are treated.

The two other chapters in this section approach their studies from more commonly understood internal methodologies. Kohm, in Chapter Nine, uses survey data and Shaver, in Chapter Ten, uses comparative legal analysis to understand the social conditions they study. Neither adopts an external lens explicitly. Indeed, they both use methods with which an internalist would be comfortable. Yet, in reviewing their results, both authors become aware of the limitations faced by their respective fields of study. Kohm comes to understand the lack of voice given to marginalized populations as a fundamental deficit in the way we conceive of criminality and fear of crime in the inner city. Providing more voice to these residents represents an overhaul (or redistribution) of the way in which crime and fear of crime is conceived of by the state. Similarly, Shaver's observations, in respect of people who work in the sex trade and the regulation and criminalization of sex work, call for wholesale change of the operating legal regime in Canada. Neither sees justice in returning to baseline and neither would be satisfied by incremental change in the name of justice.

Thus, the spaces occupied by those who bridge the divide are united by their calls for change and their rejections of normative baselines of justice. They seek real change on the ground when it comes to justice policy. They may seek to approach their study using critical methodologies or theories or they may choose to gather data in more positivistic ways but the lenses through which they study in their respective fields call them to seek for a new order of things. They seek for a new justice in their conclusions, and this is justice that, to them, has been missing in previous iterations.

CHAPTER EIGHT

R. V. LATIMER AND EMPOWERING PEOPLE WITH DISABILITIES

Ravi Malhotra

Criminologists, legal scholars and other theorists of justice have understandably devoted considerable time and energy to demonstrating how the criminal justice system marginalizes various segments of the population, including people of colour and women (Aylward 1999; Valverde, MacLeod and Johnson 1995). However, people with disabilities have largely been ignored as a constituency that warrants scholarly attention. Critical disability theory (Devlin and Pothier 2006) seeks to remedy this deficiency, and I adopt this methodological approach to understanding certain problems in the Canadian justice system. The analytical lens I adopt demands that substantive justice through the achievement of equality be accomplished for all members of society, and that to reveal inequalities that inculcate the terrain of the socio-legal world, we must unpack these inequalities. Thinking about justice means that we must be unafraid to interrogate these spaces of inequality and demand more tolerance and recognition of difference from these spaces. On some occasions, this analysis may require a wholesale rethinking of the way society or popular conceptions seem to approach a socio-legal problem. This chapter discusses one such story.

Critical disability theory can shed important light on one pressing public policy problem, the murder of children with disabilities by their parents. I use this tool in part by combining the contributions of Erving Goffman's theory of stigma and Michel Foucault's concepts of bio-power and governmentality. In *R. v. Latimer*, Saskatchewan farmer Robert Latimer was ultimately prosecuted for the murder of his twelve-year-old daughter, Tracy, who had cerebral palsy. A critical disability theory analysis of the *Latimer* case and the accompanying media coverage illustrates how people with disabilities are a group entitled to justice in cases of violence, implying some suggestions for reform. In short, the media marginalized the voices of people with disabilities as well as the neo-liberal political economy context that structures the lives of parents of children with disabilities. To avoid confusion, I will refer to Robert Latimer throughout this chapter as Latimer and to his murdered daughter simply as Tracy.

CRITICAL DISABILITY THEORY

People with disabilities have typically been regarded as objects of pity and charity. Since the Enlightenment's establishment of scientific rationality as a key method of scholarly inquiry, their problems have been regarded as stemming from their physiological impairments. For instance, Lisa cannot climb stairs because she has a medical problem: her legs are paralyzed and must be cured through surgery or other medical treatment, where possible. If her impairments cannot be cured, however, her life is regarded as a personal tragedy. While the hegemonic rise of medical science was in fact a revolutionary advance over the obscurantist religious superstition that was predominant in medieval times, this paradigm has also been accompanied by much oppression and marginalization (Barnes 1991: 12–13).

Historically, those people with disabilities who were unable to independently engage in activities of daily living, such as bathing, dressing and toileting, were segregated in bleak institutional settings where physical and sexual abuse were commonplace (Braddock and Parish 2001). People who were labelled as having psychiatric disabilities, often with very little evidence, were similarly condemned in many cases to life in institutional settings where they were often expected to work to pay for the costs of their incarceration (Reaume 2000). In Alberta and British Columbia, sterilization boards influenced by eugenics theories, which sought to "improve" the quality of the human race, ordered the sterilization of thousands of young people with intellectual disabilities, disproportionately working class girls and members of ethnic minorities, without their consent. In Alberta alone, nearly three thousand people were sterilized, and the authorizing legislation, the 1928 Alberta *Sexual Sterilization Act* was not repealed until 1972 (Caulfield and Robertson 1996: 60–62; Pothier 2006: 307).

Until the 1980s, or in many cases even later, children and teenagers with physical disabilities were largely educated in segregated institutions where they were often subjected to demeaning practices such as regularly scheduled compulsory group medical examinations of the entire student body conducted in school gymnasia and observed by medical students in training, a practice the disability rights community has labelled "public stripping." Even students with disabilities who were fortunate enough to attend integrated educational settings with their able-bodied peers would frequently experience humiliating medical examinations during periodic medical consultations, sometimes photographed or videotaped for future training, in front of large numbers of physicians and medical students (Hansen 1992; Steinstra and Gucciardi 2002; Frazee, Gilmour and Mykitiuk 2006: 236–37; Saxton 1987; Sobsey 1994). A large percentage of people with disabilities continue to be excluded from the labour market and live marginal lives in deep poverty (Malhotra 2009a). Collectively, this focus on addressing the disabled person's physiological impairment through medical intervention and segregation has come to be known as the "medical model." Consequently, the dominant image of people with disabilities in the Canadian media has been as recipients of charities, exemplified by telethon broadcasts where children with disabilities are featured as pathetic and helpless in order to raise funds to find a cure (Dahl 1993).

Critical disability theory, in contrast, is based on the social model of disablement (Oliver 1990). Originating in the independent living movement in California in the 1960s and galvanized by returning disabled Vietnam veterans, it seeks to shift the focus to how societal barriers create handicaps that undermine the struggle of people with disabilities for equality, full citizenship and human rights. In other words, disability is regarded as a social construct that can be remedied: disability is the social barriers faced by people with bodies deemed outside the norm (Devlin and Pothier 2006: 13; Shapiro 1993: 57–58). Similarly, British activists such as Vic Finkelstein, a South African immigrant and wheelchair user who had been active in opposition to the racist apartheid regime, co-founded the Union of the Physically Impaired Against Segregation (UPIAS), which maintained that disability reflected a form of social oppression (Thomas 2007: 51–52). The World Health Organization embraced the social model to at least some extent in its landmark, if inadequate, 1980 document, the *International Classification of Impairments, Diseases and Handicaps*, which distinguished between physiological impairment and socially constructed handicaps (Bickenbach 1993: 23–25).

Some illustrations may clarify the conceptual framework. A social model approach would regard the lack of wheelchair access as handicapping Lisa's ability to get around, rather than focusing on her physiological capacity to ambulate. Similarly, it would regard the lack of community-based, client-directed attendant services, which offer assistance with activities of daily living, as the fundamental problem depriving people with disabilities of effective control over their lives (Krogh and Johnson 2006: 153). The social model has been applied to identify barriers in all spheres of life including employment, housing, transportation and education. It often, but not always, takes the form of advocacy for human rights legislation such as the *Americans with Disabilities Act* in the United States (Zames and Fleischer 2011, 2001) and the *Accessibility for Ontarians with Disabilities Act* in Ontario (Lepofsky and Graham 2009: 101). Disability rights advocates successfully lobbied Parliament for the inclusion of disability as a ground of discrimination in section 15 of the *Charter of Rights and Freedoms* (Lepofsky 1998: 161–64). It has also been used to deconstruct and interrogate arguments relating to quality of life that were so salient in the Latimer controversy.

Social Theory and Disability

One of the earliest scholars to anticipate some of the foundational concepts that lie at the heart of the social model is Erving Goffman. In his landmark text, written prior to the emergence of the modern disability rights movement, *Stigma: Notes on the Management of Spoiled Identity* (1963), Goffman documented how various characteristics, including but not limited to physical disabilities, are discreditable. They bring shame to the bearer of the characteristic, such as a limp or impaired vision, leading her to engage, where possible, in information control to "pass" for normal when interacting with able-bodied individuals, thereby undertaking creative strategies that avoid disclosure of the stigmatizing characteristic (Goffman 1963). Where passing is impossible and the person is already discredited, individuals with disabilities may attempt to engage in "covering," strategies designed to minimize the stigmatizing impact of the impairment (Goffman 1963: 102–04). While the notion of passing in queer theory, for example, is well documented (Yoshino 2006), Goffman's work on stigma and the dehumanization of people with disabilities was foundational in giving a theoretical language for the daily lived experience of people with disabilities and has influenced much scholarship in disability studies (Gill 2001: 355).

In a perceptive analysis, Ann Branaman (1997) comments on how Goffman built on his earlier work on the mortification of the self in psychiatric institutions and in the rehabilitation of incarcerated criminals. In this earlier work, Goffman identifies a number of processes by which an individual's self is mortified, including: role dispossession; the dispossession of name, property and personal clothing; the imposition of degrading postures, such as regulations on the governance of daily life, including strip searches; contaminative exposure by erasing privacy and documenting the past conduct of the patient; the disruption of attempts to separate an act from the actor whereby the incarcerated person's responses to humiliating treatment are themselves judged and evaluated as potentially deviant; and restrictions on self-determination, freedom of action and autonomy (Branaman 1997: liv–lvi). Goffman comments:

> In addition to personal defacement that comes from being stripped of one's identity kit, there is personal disfigurement that comes from direct and permanent mutilations of the body such as brands or loss of limbs. Although this mortification of the self by way of the body is found in few total institutions, still, loss of a sense of personal safety is common and provides a basis for anxieties about disfigurement. Beatings, shock therapy, or, in mental hospitals, surgery — whatever the intent of staff in providing these services for some inmates — may lead many inmates to feel that they are

in an environment that does not guarantee their personal integrity. (Goffman 1961/1997: 59)

Branaman observes that *Stigma* deepens this analysis of psychiatric institutions by suggesting, "society could be considered a total institution insofar as it is the basis of a single, universal system of honor that determines the complement of attributes individuals must possess in order to be accorded full-fledged humanity" (Branaman 1997: lviii).

Michel Foucault's theory of bio-power and governmentality is also helpful in understanding the marginalization of people with disabilities. In *Discipline and Punish*, Foucault documents how the daily life of French prisoners was highly regulated, with virtually every hour of the day structured and routinized (Foucault 1977). This is an example of what Foucault referred to as "bio-power," more modern disciplinary mechanisms that replaced public torture and execution through "external surveillance and internal self-regulation" (Thomas 2007: 37). Governmentality refers to the "development of micro-systems of social regulation that exercise normative control over individuals and populations" (Turner 2001: 253). Remarkably, the connection with disability rights and the regulation of the lives of people with disabilities is far from tenuous. Two illustrations may suffice. In his account, Foucault uses the phrase "minor civil servants of moral orthopaedics" to describe magistrates and others who dispense justice (Foucault 1977: 10). This clearly links the regulation of criminal morality with the regulation of the disabled body by orthopedic surgeons, physicians in general and a whole host of rehabilitation specialists such as physiotherapists and occupational therapists who require people with disabilities to undertake particular regimens. Making the connection even more clear, Foucault includes in the text a diagram on the orthopedic correction of children with disabilities (Foucault 1977: Plate 10).

Foucauldian concepts have been used to explain the marginalization of people with disabilities in many contexts, including the workplace (O'Brien 2005). As Tremain (2005) has noted, one could easily extend a Foucauldian reading to many other aspects of disablement including income support programs, segregated paratransit systems for people with mobility impairments, attendant services and, most relevant for the Latimer context, quality of life assessments. She has gone so far as to suggest that a Foucauldian theory of disability allows one to go beyond the traditional conception of the social model of disablement to develop a theory explicating how even biological impairment may be largely explained by the political arrangements of society (Tremain 2005: 5, 10–11).

One of the advantages of the approach developed in different ways by Goffman and Foucault is that they allow full engagement with a sociology of the body, or what might be characterized as "bringing the body back in."

While a comprehensive treatment of this issue is beyond the scope of this chapter, an engaged sociology of the body responds to feminist critiques, for example, that the social model ignores the fact that many people with disabilities, even when empowered through systemic barrier removal and anti-discrimination legislation through the social model, still experience some degree of pain and fatigue, often a feature of conditions particularly predominant among women with disabilities. In other words, it is impossible to completely ignore the impact of physiological impairment (Thomas 2007: 124–25). The work of Goffman and Foucault enables scholars and disability rights activists to simultaneously embrace the social model of disablement while acknowledging that all humans experience pain and fatigue at some point — what Thomas has eloquently called the "stubbornness of the 'real' body" (Thomas 2007: 128). We are able to move away from the stereotype of a (masculine) "Supercrip" who is all-powerful and acknowledge the complexity of life for people with disabilities (Thomas 2007: 124–25).

Such an analysis also facilitates a richer understanding of otherwise seemingly anomalous practices such as the public stripping experienced by many children and teenagers with physical disabilities in Canadian segregated schools and hospital clinics. An understanding of such practices conveys the dehumanization of people with disabilities and therefore helps to situate the context for understanding the *Latimer* case. While this practice has generally been understood as merely harmless learning opportunities for medical students, it in fact resembles the disciplinary power of medical science imposed on those regarded as Other and has devastating psychological effects on those that have been repeatedly subjected to it (Blumberg 1994: 73–77). Since a child with a physical disability violates the standard norms of agility, dexterity and mobility of the able-bodied, regular and comprehensive medical inspection is required to assess the patient's gait, flexion, range of motion and level of sensation in order to recommend the appropriate regimen of physiotherapy, occupational therapy and surgery. The child's privacy is invaded as she or he is required to strip and the use of photography or videotape magnifies the surveillance of her or his body by creating a permanent record of the episode. The mortification is compounded in the case of medical examinations conducted in segregated schools in the past because not only are numerous physicians and medical students inspecting the student, but little privacy is accorded to the student, who was frequently ordered to strip while being observed and then examined en masse with other students and often parents and even teachers in attendance (Hansen 1992). The very inclusion of regular medical exams in the school setting serves to regulate the disabled child or teenager and remind her or him of her or his impairments and the obligation to cooperate with medical professionals.

Given the small number of female physicians in Canada until quite recently, such examinations were particularly humiliating for teenage girls, who may have been examined nude or in their undergarments by as many as fifty male physicians (Frazee, Gilmour and Mykitiuk 2006: 236–37). The most intimate physiological details of the patient, a theme that we will return to when discussing the *Latimer* case, are documented, analyzed and discussed. An unwillingness on the part of the patient to comply with the instructions of physicians or other health care therapists, including reluctance to fully answer invasive medical questions, would typically be regarded as uncooperative conduct with the patient admonished and made to feel ashamed for misbehaviour (Saxton 1987: 53–54). Virtually all aspects of the mortification described by Goffman in psychiatric institutions are therefore replicated in the public stripping experienced by many disabled people. The regulation of the disabled body through the mechanisms analyzed so well by Foucault and Goffman applies all the more to those children and teenagers who are labelled as having both physical and intellectual disabilities. This was the case with Tracy Latimer.

THE MURDER OF TRACY LATIMER

In October 1993, Saskatchewan farmer Robert Latimer murdered his twelve-year-old daughter, Tracy, who had cerebral palsy, a medical condition that varies dramatically from person to person. Latimer placed his daughter in his pickup truck and then inserted a hose from the truck's exhaust pipe into the cab, beginning what would become one of the most notorious and lengthy sagas in Canadian legal history. Although Latimer initially claimed that Tracy died naturally, he confessed to the crime after an autopsy demonstrated that she died of carbon monoxide poisoning (Jenkins 2001: para. 5). Tracy's significant physical and intellectual disabilities, a result of cerebral palsy, prevented her from walking and communicating without much difficulty. Although Latimer never took the stand to testify about his precise motivations, evidence was presented by the Latimers that Tracy experienced severe pain and was scheduled to have future surgery at the time of her murder that her parents felt would cause further pain. However, she also attended school and enjoyed leisure activities including music and the circus, underscoring how Tracy was, in effect, just like any other child, able to participate in a variety of activities and entitled to human dignity (Peters 2001: para. 34; Janz and Hayward 2003; *R. v. Latimer (No. 2)* 2001: para. 8–13). Latimer was charged and convicted by a jury of second-degree murder. His original conviction was, however, quashed by the Supreme Court of Canada due to interference by the Crown with the jury selection process. A new trial was therefore ordered (*R. v. Latimer (No. 1)* 1997: para. 44).

At his second trial, Latimer was again convicted by a jury of second-degree murder. The trial judge ruled during the course of the trial that the defence of necessity was not available (*R. v. Latimer (No. 2)* 2001: para. 18). The jury, however, raised objections to the Criminal Code's mandatory minimum sentence of ten years for this offence. Therefore, the trial judge told the jury: 1) it should not consider the issue of sentencing until it reached a conclusion on Latimer's innocence; and 2) if it found Latimer guilty, it should feel entitled to recommend a sentence of its own choosing (*R. v. Latimer (No. 2)* 2001: para. 19–20). The jury convicted Latimer and recommended a prison term of one year before parole eligibility. The trial judge accordingly granted Latimer a constitutional exemption from the minimum mandatory sentence and sentenced him to a year in prison, to be followed by a year of parole (*R. v. Latimer (No. 2)* 2001: para. 20). This allowed the trial judge to avoid having to impose the minimum mandatory sentence specifically stipulated for second-degree murder in the Criminal Code. On appeal, the Saskatchewan Court of Appeal upheld Latimer's conviction but imposed the mandatory minimum sentence of ten years required by the Criminal Code (*R. v. Latimer (No. 2)* 2001: para. 21). I will not analyze the debates around Latimer's sentencing, including his unsuccessful claim that the mandatory minimum sentence violated the prohibition on cruel and unusual punishment in section 12 of the Charter. I need only note that deterrence is an important aspect of criminal justice in Canada, which is germane to the widespread reaction among both the Canadian media and scholarly commentators that Latimer did not engage in any wrongdoing whatsoever.

On further appeal to the Supreme Court of Canada, the Court unanimously upheld both the conviction and the sentence, bringing the eight-year saga to a close in 2001. The Court found that there are three elements to the defence of necessity that the accused must demonstrate in order to be acquitted. First, there is the requirement of imminent peril. Second, the accused must have had no reasonable legal alternative to the action taken. Finally, there must be proportionality between the harm inflicted and the harm avoided (*R. v. Latimer (No. 2)* 2001: para. 29–31). The Court held that the first two prongs of the test are to be judged on a modified objective standard. An objective standard typically judges the conduct of an accused based on what a reasonable person would have done in the circumstances regardless of the accused's actual belief (*R. v. Latimer (No. 2)* 2001: para. 32). A modified objective standard means "the accused person must, at the time of the act, honestly believe, on reasonable grounds, that he [or she] faces a situation of imminent peril that leaves no reasonable legal alternative open" (*R. v. Latimer (No. 2)* 2001: para. 33). The final prong, however, is to be judged on an objective standard. The Court held that proportionality must be determined on an objective standard to ensure that it reflects society's fundamental values with respect to what constitutes a transgression of its rules. The Court also made reference to the fact that one must consider the equality rights of people with disabilities enshrined in section 15 of the Charter (*R. v. Latimer (No. 2)* 2001: para. 34).

As this was a case before a jury that was to determine Latimer's guilt or innocence, the legal question was simply whether the trial judge acted appropriately in not putting the defence of necessity to the jury. The Court held that there must be an air of reality to each of the three prongs of the defence of necessity test before a trial judge would be required to put the defence to a jury. This means that there must be sufficient evidence for each prong of the defence so that a jury could acquit the accused (*R. v. Latimer (No. 2)* 2001: para. 35). On the facts, the Court concluded that there was no air of reality to any of the three prongs. First, the Court held that there was no imminent peril to either the defendant or to Tracy. The fact that she was scheduled to undergo surgery could not be equated with imminent peril as there was simply no evidence that Tracy's life was in danger. While her pain level was expected to increase as a result of the surgery, this did not constitute an imminent peril. Moreover, there was no evidence that the accused had a psychological condition that made him incapable of logically determining that there was no imminent peril (*R. v. Latimer (No. 2)* 2001: para. 38).

On the second prong, the Court held that there were clearly reasonable legal alternatives to Latimer's choice of murdering his daughter. The Court reasoned that Latimer could have either continued with the existing situation, given Tracy's stable medical condition, or he could have put Tracy in a group home or attempted to use a feeding tube, which was suggested to him to allow for better administration of pain medication. It was not open to him, however, to simply end his daughter's life (*R. v. Latimer (No. 2)* 2001: para. 39).

On the question of proportionality, the Court noted that it was not even clear that the defence of necessity is available for homicide given that it is difficult to identify circumstances where committing homicide might be interpreted as a proportional response that would ground the defence. Nevertheless, the Court assumed that defence of necessity would be available in principle and turned to analyze the situation before it. On the facts, the Court concluded that the harm inflicted on Tracy, resulting in her death, was completely disproportional to the harm avoided. The Court declined to equate the pain resulting from the scheduled surgery with the murder that ended her life (*R. v. Latimer (No. 2)* 2001: para. 40–42). After rejecting other highly technical procedural issues, the Court upheld Latimer's conviction.

A CRITICAL DISABILITY ANALYSIS OF THE LATIMER CASE

The *Latimer* case requires a careful analysis, especially as mainstream commentary has largely framed the issue as one of euthanasia, even though Tracy clearly never consented to her murder. On the one hand, the Supreme Court of Canada's affirmation of the conviction was a victory for those concerned about the equality rights of people with disabilities. Given that the context in question here was the right of people with disabilities to simply be alive, the Court's unwillingness to contemplate broadening a necessity defence in the context of murdering people with disabilities is an encouraging sign about the strength of the disability rights movement and its influence on Charter values. In other rulings, the Supreme Court, even where ruling against the particular complainants with disabilities on the facts, has demonstrated at least a partial embrace of the social model. For instance, the Court's earlier decision in *Granovsky* (2000), holding that disability pension benefit rules that exclude people with sporadic disabilities from entitlement do not violate section 15 of the Charter, commented:

> It is therefore useful to keep distinct the component of disability that may be said to be located in an individual, namely the aspects of physical or mental impairment, and functional limitation, and on the other hand the other component, namely, the socially constructed handicap that is not located in the individual at all but in the society in which the individual is obliged to go about his or her everyday tasks. (*R v. Granovsky* 2000: para. 34)

This suggests at least some awareness of the social model of disablement even though this decision has been widely regarded as a major defeat for disability rights advocates (Malhotra 2009b).

Nevertheless, the media reaction to and coverage of the *Latimer* case was disturbing to many disability rights advocates. Similarly, much legal scholarship that has purported to analyze the case betrays an ignorance of the social model of disablement by framing the issue in terms of mercy killing or compassionate homicide.

Tracy and Latimer in the Media

As Yvonne Peters has aptly observed, Tracy Latimer clearly became Other in the eyes of most media (2001: para. 40). With the ironic exception of marginal social conservative Christian commentators, such as *Alberta Report*, most media portrayed Tracy Latimer in an extremely medicalized way that implicitly called into question her right to life (by questioning the quality of her life) rather than portraying her as a twelve-year-old girl who was brutally murdered (Janz 1998). Just as criminal trials and the criminal justice system more generally have been correctly criticized for blaming and judging the victim in the case of women who complain about spousal abuse (Valverde, MacLeod and Johnson 1995), most mainstream media effectively put Tracy on trial. Whereas most media are harshly critical of accused murderers of able-bodied children and correctly focus on the conduct of the accused, in the case of Tracy Latimer, every aspect of her medical condition became subject to detailed public scrutiny. Hence, the Canadian public read in graphic detail of her toileting abilities, her eating abilities and her restricted mobility as if this had any bearing on whether or not she should be murdered (Malhotra 2001; Janz 1998: 66–67). Moreover, this was completely detached, for the most part, from the underlying political economy context: the withdrawal of the neo-liberal state from the provision of services that might make it easier for parents of children with disabilities to take care of them at home (Cossman and Fudge 2002).

The disciplinary aspects of the media coverage are hard to miss. As she failed to conform to the standard norms of able-bodied twelve-year-olds, Tracy was harshly disciplined in the media for her impairments. Largely, she was portrayed as a-human and incapable of pleasure, and the most graphic details of her life were publicized in furtherance of her "public stripping" (Malhotra 2001).

Both Goffman and Foucault note how documentation of medical conditions may be used to discipline those regarded as deviant (Goffman 1961/1997: 60–61). In the psychiatric setting, detailed medical documentation records are concealed in dossiers, which may be grounds for changes to treatment such as increased doses of medication or electroconvulsive therapy. In the case of physical disabilities, documented findings may prompt a recommendation for surgery or therapy. In the *Latimer* case, both the nature of the documentation and the objective are different. While medical documentation is undoubtedly detailed for many adults and children with disabilities and may be requested by other parties to determine eligibility for income support programs, for example, it is typically confidential and only available to medical professionals, the patients and the patients' families. This has been repeatedly confirmed by the courts, is true as a matter of both common law and statutory provisions and is even required by the codes of conduct of various health professions (Frazee, Gilmour, and Mykitiuk 2006: 233–34). However, in the *Latimer* case, the journalism about Tracy's health status was disseminated entirely in the public domain. Moreover, the detailed and graphic disclosure was not designed to provide health recommendations to improve her health. It was written posthumously to question whether such a person should be allowed to live (Malhotra 2001). It is also worth noting that much of the media and academic commentary is as graphic and critical about Tracy's physical impairments as her mental impairments (Malhotra 2001).

Some might dismiss this approach to Tracy's condition as an exercise in governmentality. The impact of this disciplinary mechanism, however, is not trivial and has real implications for the equality rights of Canadians with disabilities. The trial judge noted in his decision, in which he granted Latimer the extraordinary remedy of the constitutional exemption, that he had received hundreds of letters urging him to be lenient towards Latimer.

He also commented on the telephone calls he received as well as the editorial coverage that was overwhelmingly sympathetic to Latimer. Significant funds for Latimer's legal bills were also raised and petitions for a pardon by the federal cabinet, which was never granted, were widely circulated (Janz 1998: 68). This suggests that the effects of the media coverage in the *Latimer* case were significant.

Furthermore, it is important to understand the quality of life assumptions in the "public stripping" of Tracy. Given the history of eugenics against people with disabilities, disability rights activists are often skeptical of the merits of quality of life assessments. Indeed, studies have suggested that medical professionals typically rank the quality of life of people with disabilities as lower than the disabled clients themselves and possibly lower than the general public (Gill 2000: 530). Yet, the media reports in the *Latimer* case continually framed the issue as one of mercy killing, one where the very controversial notion that Tracy had a low quality of life was simply assumed. I would submit, however, that it is simply impossible to objectively evaluate quality of life. As noted above, quality of life assessments are far from being scientifically neutral, and can be regarded as sites where Foucauldian biopower is exercised by medical authorities over people with disabilities. They are inherently political and reflect socio-economic factors as much as any inherent medical science.

One particularly shocking example of disciplinary power was the subsequent controversy over a museum exhibit at the Alberta Provincial Museum in Edmonton entitled, "Anno Domini: Jesus Through the Centuries." Intended to analyze how Jesus Christ's Sermon on the Mount was applied by subsequent historical figures, it featured Mother Theresa, Mahatma Gandhi and Nelson Mandela along with Robert Latimer. Disability activist organizations vigorously protested this portrayal of Latimer with the historical figures. While museum officials denied that Latimer's inclusion in the exhibit implied endorsement for his actions, the very fact that he was included indicates how he is perceived and has great potential to communicate hostile attitudes toward people with disabilities. The museum exhibit is a subtle but nevertheless revealing way in which attitudes about people with disabilities are conveyed in mainstream society (CCD Online 2000b).

There is also the controversial question of whether the *Latimer* case has encouraged other parents of children with disabilities to take their children's lives. Obviously, the vast majority of parents of children with disabilities are law-abiding and supportive parents. A critical disability perspective should not be misinterpreted as trivializing the complicated challenges that parents of children with disabilities, especially those with both physical and intellectual disabilities like Tracy, face on a daily basis (Janz 1998: 67). Nevertheless, the dominant media portrayal was of Tracy as an intolerable burden, rather than emphasizing the neo-liberal impact on support services for parents with disabilities. But, there is evidence of copycat crimes, vindicating the fear of those in the disability community who expressed concerns that public approval for Latimer, especially if sanctioned by the courts, would make it easier for such crimes to take place. While more evidence is needed with respect to this particular claim, there have been numerous murders of disabled children by parents in Canada since the murder of Tracy Latimer, including the murder of fourteen-year-old Chelsea Craig by her mother, who survived a subsequent suicide attempt (CCD Online 2001) and the murder of Ryan Wilkinson, a child with cerebral palsy and other disabilities, by his mother, who subsequently killed herself (Couglin 1995).

Finally, there is the large gap between disability rights activists committed to the social model and legal scholars, who typically regarded the *Latimer* case as a philosophical issue about mercy killing that has no straightforward solution. A coalition of activists representing various groups of people with disabilities was granted intervener status at the Supreme Court of Canada. The coalition was comprised of the Council of Canadians with Disabilities, the Saskatchewan Voice of People with Disabilities, People in Equal Participation, the Canadian Association of Community Living, DisAbled Women's Network and People First Canada (CCD Online 2000a). They argued that it was in fact impossible to distinguish Tracy's pain from her disability. Whereas Latimer attempted to argue that he acted selflessly to relieve Tracy of her pain, the coalition maintained that, for some people with disabilities, a certain degree of pain is an inextricable part of the disability. They cited remarks by Justice Tallis of the Saskatchewan Court of Appeal, hearing the appeal in the first Latimer trial, who observed that one had to consider whether the same decision would have been made with respect to a child in extreme pain who had no disabilities. Since the answer clearly appears to be "no," it follows that Latimer's actions have implications for devaluing the lives of children with disabilities (CCD Online 2000a). They further maintained that the impact of pain on a given individual is extremely subjective, noting studies of Second World War veterans who were unaffected by serious war injuries that would have been debilitating to civilians (CCD Online 2000a).

In contrast to the view of disabled people themselves, scholarly commentary has tended, like media reports, to focus on a very medicalized interpretation of Tracy's life. In an article representative of the dominant scholarly analysis, Jenkins declines to take an explicit stand on the matter of responsibility, suggesting that extreme positions on both sides have flawed ideas (Jenkins 2001: 3). Nevertheless, her work is marred by a failure to appreciate the basic issues. Jenkins correctly suggests that supporters of Tracy may be interpreted as articulating a deontological stand: the notion that some actions are wrong regardless of the consequences (Jenkins 2001: 12). However,

Jenkins goes on to suggest that the moral dilemma posed by Latimer's actions would lead to the conclusion that only rational beings are entitled to dignity. While Jenkins is herself vague on this matter, she notes that someone like Tracy can be usefully distinguished from newborn babies and able-bodied children who have the future potential of rationality (Jenkins 2001: 13). This misses the entire point of the proposition that all people, including those with disabilities, have inherent worth and are, as enshrined in the Charter, equal before the law. Indeed, as she seems aware, her discussion of the controversial philosopher Peter Singer, who sees animals as more sentient than many people with disabilities, encompasses ideas that are anathema to the very precepts of disability rights (Jenkins 2001: para.15). Other philosophers like Martha Nussbaum and Licia Carlson have thoughtfully rejected this Kantian requirement of rationality as a precondition for equality rights for people with disabilities (Nussbaum 2006; Carlson 2010).

Given this analysis, there is still a question about whether or not a reliance of people with disabilities on the Charter for their equality rights for will merely reinscribe an oppressive governmentality that marginalizes them by flattening their rich experiences into the narrow one-dimensional language of the law. While a huge topic, I will say that, against the governmentality of the media, Charter values and Charter arguments should be used selectively and skeptically. There is a real risk of further marginalization through the regulation of legal discourse, especially when making use of the criminal law. Legal categories established by courts, for instance, set legal precedent, and a precedent-based approach to disability risks being locked in time and may not be nimble enough to contain the multiple contexts of marginalized communities. But, so long as advocates of social justice do not rely exclusively on legal discourse and leave open the option of political forms of protest such as street demonstrations and direct lobbying, legal discourse is simply too important to dismiss entirely (see Armstrong 2003, Sheldrick 2004). Simply put, I submit that the perils of engaging in legal discourse are outweighed by the potential gains.

CONCLUSION

I have tried to provide an account of critical disability theory and demonstrate its value by thinking through one urgent public policy problem. At its root, critical disability theory seeks to show that it is social structural barriers that actually handicap people with disabilities. Tracy's tragic murder was governed by the powers of the media and academic representation rather than the social and lived realities of people with disabilities.

Yet, this same governmentality should not allow one to be complacent in accepting the status quo of those among us who face real injustices — those among us who are routinely "publicly stripped" and dehumanized in the regulatory and regulated world. Critical disability theory allows for the explosion of these uneasy explications of dehumanization and for the possibility of incremental changes to move further away from these sites of injustice. Critical disability theory also requires that we not be complacent in accepting the incremental changes as an ultimate solution, since we are always governing and being governed and must always be aware that each liberation (that is, each legal victory) contains a potential for enslavement (new forms of injustice and marginalization).

References

Armstrong, Sarah. 2003. "Disability Advocacy in the *Charter* Era." *Journal of Law and Equality* 2, 1.

Aylward, Carol A. 1999. *Canadian Critical Race Theory: Racism and the Law.* Halifax: Fernwood Publishing.

Barnes, Colin. 1991. *Disabled People in Britain and Discrimination: A Case for Anti-Discrimination Legislation.* London: Hurst & Co.

Bickenbach, Jerome E. 1993. *Physical Disability and Social Policy.* Toronto: University of Toronto Press.

Blumberg, Lisa. 1994. "Public Stripping." In Barrett Shaw (ed.), *The Ragged Edge: The Disability Experience from the Pages of the First Fifteen Years of the Disability Rag.* Louisville, KY: Advocado Press.

Braddock, David L., and Carol L. Parish. 2001. "An Institutional History of Disability." In Gary L. Albrecht, Katherine D. Seelman and Michael Bury (eds.), *Handbook of Disability Studies.* Thousand Oaks, CA: Sage Publications.

Branaman, Ann. 1997. "Goffman's Social Theory." In Charles Lemert and Ann Branaman (eds.), *The Goffman Reader.* Oxford: Blackwell.

Carlson, Licia. 2010. *The Faces of Intellectual Disability: Philosophical Reflections.* Bloomington: Indiana University Press.

Caulfield, Timothy, and Gerald Robertson. 1996. "Eugenic Policies in Alberta: From the Systematic to the Systemic?" *Alberta Law Review* 35.

CCD Online. 2000a. "Latimer Case Factum 2000." At <ccdonline.ca/en/human-rights/endoflife/latimer/factum2000#pain>.

___. 2000b. "Provincial Museum of Alberta Promotes Murder of Disabled Children Says ACL Web Site." At <ccdonline.ca/en/humanrights/endoflife/latimer/2000/11>.

___. 2001. "The Toll Mounts: Another Child Killed." At <ccdenligne.ca/en/humanrights/endoflife/latimer/2001/03>.

Charter of Rights and Freedoms. Part I of the *Constitution Act, 1982*, being Schedule B to the *Canada Act, 1982* (U.K.), 1982, c. 11.

Cossman, Brenda, and Judy Fudge. 2002. *Privatization, Law and the Challenge to Feminism.* Toronto: University of Toronto Press.

Coughlin, Joe. 1995. "Open Season." *Abilities Magazine* (Spring). At <abilities.ca/social_policy/1995/03/01/open_season/>.

Dahl, Marilyn. 1993. "The Role of the Media in Promoting Images of Disability — Disability as Metaphor: The Evil Crip." *Canadian Journal of Communication*

18, 1.

Devlin, Richard, and Dianne Pothier. 2006. "Introduction: Toward a Critical Theory of Dis-Citizenship." In Dianne Pothier and Richard Devlin (eds.), *Critical Disability Theory: Essays in Philosophy, Politics, Policy and Law*. Vancouver: University of British Columbia Press.

Fleischer, Doris Z., and Frieda Zames. 2011 and 2001. *The Disability Rights Movement: From Charity to Confrontation*. Philadelphia: Temple University Press.

Foucault, Michel. 1977. *Discipline and Punish: The Birth of the Prison*. Trans. Alan Sheridan. Toronto: Random House.

Frazee, Catherine, Joan Gilmour and Roxanne Mykitiuk. 2006. "Now You See Her, Now You Don't: How Law Shapes Disabled Women's Experience of Exposure, Surveillance, and Assessment in the Clinical Encounter." In Dianne Pothier and Richard Devlin (eds.), *Critical Disability Theory: Essays in Philosophy, Politics, Policy and Law*. Vancouver: University of British Columbia Press.

Gill, Carol J. 2000. "Health Professionals, Disability and Assisted Suicide: An Examination of Relevant Empirical Evidence and Reply to Batavia." *Psychology, Public Policy and Law* 6, 2.

____. 2001. "Divided Understandings: The Social Experience of Disability." In Gary L. Albrecht, Katherine D. Seelman and Michael Bury (eds.), *Handbook of Disability Studies*. Thousand Oaks, CA: Sage Publications.

Goffman, Erving. 1961/1997. "The Characteristics of Total Institutions." In Charles Lemert and Ann Branaman (eds.), *The Goffman Reader*. Oxford: Blackwell.

____. 1963. *Stigma: Notes on the Management of Spoiled Identity*. New York: Simon & Schuster.

Granovsky v. Canada (Minister of Employment and Immigration). 2000. 1 *Supreme Court Reports* at 703.

Hansen, Nancy. 1992. "Surmounting Perfect Body Syndrome: Women with Disabilities and the Medical Profession." In Houston Stewart, Beth Percival and Elizabeth R. Epperly (eds.), *The More We Get Together*. Charlottetown, PE: Gynergy Books.

Janz, Heidi L. 1998. "Disabling Images and the Dangers of Public Perception: A Commentary on the Media's 'Coverage' of the *Latimer* Case." *Constitutional Forum* 9, 3.

Janz, Heidi L., and Sally Hayward. 2003. "The Latimer Case and the Media: If the Right Has It Right, What's Wrong with the Left?" In James Gifford and Gabrielle Zezulka-Mailloux (eds.), *Culture and the State: Disability Studies and Indigenous Studies*. Edmonton: University of Alberta.

Jenkins, Maricarmen. 2001. "Moral Judgment and the Case of Robert Latimer." *Saskatchewan Law Review* 64.

Krogh, Kari, and Jon Johnson. 2006. "A Life Without Living: Challenging Medical and Economic Reductionism in Home Support Policy for People with Disabilities." In Dianne Pothier and Richard Devlin (eds.), *Critical Disability Theory: Essays in Philosophy, Politics, Policy and Law*. Vancouver: University of British Columbia Press.

Lepofsky, M. David. 1998. "The *Charter*'s Guarantee of Equality to People with Disabilities — How Well Is It Working?" *Windsor Yearbook of Access to Justice* 16.

Lepofsky, M. David, and Randall N.M. Graham. 2009. "Universal Design in

Legislation: Eliminating Barriers for People with Disabilities." *Statute Law Review* 30, 2.

Malhotra, Ravi. 2001. "Tracy Latimer, Disability Rights and the Left." *Canadian Dimension* 35, 3.

___. 2009a. "A Tale of Marginalization: Comparing Workers with Disabilities in Canada and the United States." *Journal of Law and Society* 22.

___. 2009b. "Martha Nussbaum's Capabilities Approach and Equality Rights for People with Disabilities: Rethinking the *Granovsky* Decision." *Supreme Court Law Review* 45.

Nussbaum, Martha C. 2006. *Frontiers of Justice: Disability, Nationality, Species Membership.* Cambridge: Harvard University Press.

O'Brien, Ruth. 2005. *Bodies in Revolt: Gender, Disability and a Workplace Ethic of Care.* New York: Routledge.

Oliver, Michael. 1990. *The Politics of Disablement.* London: Macmillan Press.

Peters, Yvonne. 2001. "Reflections on the Latimer Case: The Rationale for a Disability Rights Lens." *Saskatchewan Law Review* 64.

Pothier, Dianne. 2006. "Appendix: Legal Developments in the Supreme Court of Canada Regarding Disability." In Dianne Pothier and Richard Devlin (eds.), *Critical Disability Theory: Essays in Philosophy, Politics, Policy and Law.* Vancouver: University of British Columbia Press.

R. v. Latimer No. 1. 1997. *Supreme Court Reports* 1 at 217.

R. v. Latimer No. 2. 2001. *Supreme Court Reports* 1 at 3.

Reaume, Geoffrey. 2000. *Remembrance of Patients Past: Patient Life at the Toronto Hospital for the Insane, 1870–1940.* Toronto: Oxford University Press Canada.

Saxton, Marsha. 1987. "The Something That Happened before I Was Born." In Marsha Saxton and Florence Howe (eds.), *With Wings: An Anthology of Literature by and about Women with Disabilities.* New York: Feminist Press at City University of New York.

Shapiro, Joseph P. 1993. *No Pity: People with Disabilities Forging a New Civil Rights Movement.* New York: Random House.

Sheldrick, Byron. 2004. *Perils and Possibilities: Social Activism and the Law.* Halifax: Fernwood Publishing.

Sobsey, Dick. 1994. *The End of Silent Exploitation: Ending the Abuse of People with Disabilities.* Baltimore: Paul H. Brookes.

Steinstra, Deborah, and Enza Gucciardi. 2002. "Disabilities." In Donna E. Stewart, Angela M. Cheung, Lorraine E. Ferris, Ilene Hyman, Marsha M. Cohen and J. Ivan Williams (eds.), *Ontario Women's Health Status Report.* Toronto: Ontario Women's Health Council.

Thomas, Carol. 2007. *Sociologies of Disability and Illness: Contested Ideas in Disability Studies and Medical Sociology.* New York: Palgrave Macmillan.

Tremain, Shelley. 2005. "Foucault, Governmentality and Critical Disability Theory: An Introduction." In Shelley Tremain (ed.), *Foucault and the Government of Disability.* Ann Arbor: University of Michigan.

Turner, Bryan S. 2001. "Disability and the Sociology of the Body." In In Gary L. Albrecht, Katherine D. Seelman and Michael Bury (eds.), *Handbook of Disability Studies.* Thousand Oaks, CA: Sage Publications.

Valverde, Mariana, Linda MacLeod and Kirsten Johnson (eds.). 1995. *Wife Assault and the Canadian Criminal Justice System: Issues and Policies*. Toronto: University of Toronto Press.

Yoshino, Kenji. 2006. *Covering: The Hidden Assault on Our Civil Rights*. New York: Random House.

CHAPTER NINE

JUSTICE AND VICTIMIZATION IN THE INNER CITY
Notes from Central Winnipeg
Steven A. Kohm

Contrary to popular rhetoric, criminal victimization in Canada does not occur haphazardly. Victimization surveys consistently demonstrate that not all Canadians experience the same level of risk. In particular, those who are of a lower socio-economic status tend to suffer disproportionately from most types of victimization. For example, the 2004 General Social Survey (GSS) revealed distinct patterns of victimization (Gannon and Mihorean 2005). Canadians who are unemployed, single and who live in households with low incomes have significantly higher rates of violent victimization than those who are employed and who live in higher income households. Moreover, Aboriginal people reported rates of violent victimization three times higher than non-Aboriginal respondents. This long-standing pattern of criminal victimization is an opportunity to think broadly about justice. In a just world, we would not expect that the most vulnerable individuals would bear the brunt of social harms. However, the GSS makes it plain that being poor and a racialized minority means that you are going to be victimized by crime at a significantly higher rate than those who enjoy greater prosperity, suburban residence and membership in the dominant racial group.

While the patterns shown in the GSS are clear, it samples only Canadians who live in a relatively stable residence and have a telephone. A clearer picture of patterns of victimization should include those who would not normally be captured by a national telephone survey. A recent Winnipeg study did just that: the poor in Winnipeg's poorest neighbourhood were sought out on their own turf — in their homes, soup kitchens, drop-in centres and homeless shelters. In-depth interviews gave them the opportunity to describe and explain the daily experience of criminal victimization among a vulnerable population. Winnipeg's inner city is a diverse community that is both rich in cultural heritage and challenged by high crime rates, poverty and urban decline. In this context, residents in the inner city must navigate daily life in areas of the city characterized by high levels of crime, disorder and fear. The ways inner-city residents negotiate this precarious existence has important implications for the theme of justice.

WINNIPEG'S INNER CITY

Defining the inner city of Winnipeg appears to be akin to appreciating art. Most observers seem to know it when they see it, yet no authoritative definition exists. According to the City of Winnipeg, no official definition of the inner city exists, but for planning purposes, the city uses the boundaries established by the Winnipeg Core Area Initiative (CAI) in 1981. The CAI defined core area neighbourhoods by the age of the housing stock, proximity to the downtown core and a number of socio-economic indicators of distress. In practice, Winnipeg's inner city encompasses some twenty-five central neighbourhoods, most of which are low income, characterized by high rates of police-reported crime and have a higher than average visible minority and Aboriginal population.

Winnipeg's inner city is a comparatively large geographic area, nearly thirty square kilometers of populated neighbourhoods, representing 8.5 percent of the total populated land area of the city and accounting for close to 20 percent of the city's population. The inner city's population density is about two and a half times greater than non-inner-city areas. As Table 1 shows, there are key socio-demographic, economic and housing differences between the inner city and the rest of the city. Just more than 20 percent of inner-city residents are of Aboriginal ancestry, while only 9 percent of

Table 1: Inner City and Non-Inner City Winnipeg* Selected Characteristics from the 2006 Census

	Inner City	Non-Inner City	Total City
Total Population	121,615	503,980	633,451
Aboriginal Ancestry	25,045 (20.6%)	45,115 (9%)	11.2%
Visible Minority	28,145 (23.1%)	73,745 (14.6%)	16.3%
Recent Immigration	7,985 (6.6%)	15,825 (3.1%)	3.9%
Less Than High School Graduate	29,945 (29.9%)	89,080 (21.5%)	23.1%
Unemployment Rate, ≥15 years of age	7.8%	4.6%	5.2%
Reliance on Government Transfer Payments, Economic Families	17.1%	8.7%	9.7%
Median Total Household Income	$31,773	$55,812	$49,790
Lone Parent Families	9,130 (32.1%)	24,430 (17.0%)	19.5%
Renters	60.9%	27.7%	34.9%
Dwelling Constructed Before 1946	44.1%	12.6%	19.5%
Dwelling in Need of Major Repairs	14.4%	6.9%	8.5%
Moved 2001–2006	53.8%	37.9%	40.9%

*Data corresponds to the formal boundaries of the city of Winnipeg, not the larger CMA of Winnipeg used by Statistics Canada. Source: <http://www.winnipeg.ca/census/2006/City%20of%20Winnipeg/>.

non-inner-city residents reported Aboriginal ancestry. Nearly a quarter of inner-city residents self-identified as a "visible minority" compared with 14.6 percent in non-inner-city areas, and there are twice as many recent immigrants in the inner city than in the non-inner city. Furthermore, fewer inner-city residents have completed a high school education, unemployment rates are higher in the inner city, and the median annual household income in the inner city is $24,039 less than in the non-inner city. Nearly one third of all census families in the inner city are lone parent families, and most inner residents do not own their home. Moreover, homes in the inner city tend to be older and in greater need of major repair than homes in the non-inner city. Lastly, more than half of residents in the inner city moved within the last five years, while less than 40 percent of non-inner-city residents reported five-year mobility. In short, the inner city is characterized by a much higher degree of racial and ethnic heterogeneity and the area possesses many of the indicators of neighbourhood distress, social disorganization and socio-economic disadvantage. These neighbourhood conditions are further compounded by high levels of police-reported crime and self-reported victimization.

According to Fitzgerald, Wisener and Savoie (2004: 22), police-reported crime in Winnipeg is highly concentrated geographically. They point out that 30 percent of reported violent crime in 2001 occurred in just 3 percent of neighbourhoods while 30 percent of reported property crime incidents took place in only 7 percent of neighbourhoods. Moreover, Fitzgerald, Wisener and Savoie (2004: 22) demonstrate by using mapping techniques that the bulk of police-reported crime in Winnipeg is concentrated "in the core and north of the core." They note that the neighbourhoods with the highest levels of crime are characterized by high levels of socio-economic disadvantage, poor housing conditions, high rates of mobility, social disorganization and ethnic heterogeneity. In short, the same characteristics found in abundance in Winnipeg's inner city were all found to be strongly associated with high rates of violent and property crime. Furthermore, according to their analysis, the neighbourhoods with the highest rates of police-reported violent crime all fell within the City of Winnipeg's working definition of the inner city. In other words, location matters when it comes to crime in Winnipeg — especially crimes involving violence. What this means for residents is that living in the inner city means a higher likelihood of criminal victimization. For example, 68 percent of adult residents reported one or more incidents of criminal victimization in the previous twelve months in a 2007 victimization survey carried out in one high-crime, inner-city Winnipeg neighbourhood (Kohm 2009). In contrast, the 2004 GSS found only 28 percent of Canadians aged fifteen years or older had been criminally victimized one or more times in the previous twelve months (Gannon and Mihorean 2005). What this suggests is that national level victimization surveys tend to undercount inner-city populations who do not live in a stable residence or have a telephone. However, these undercounted individuals are of particular significance for criminological research, precisely because they appear to suffer disproportionately high levels of victimization and re-victimization. In fact, nearly one quarter of inner-city respondents reported five or more incidents of victimization in the previous year (Kohm 2009). This high level of repeat victimization of the inner-city poor begs us to think broadly about justice. As an instance of injustice, victimization of the most vulnerable in our society begs further analysis by delving more deeply into the experiences of the most disadvantaged inner-city neighbourhoods.

A recent study involving recipients of government transfer payments (such as welfare, government pensions, employment insurance and so on) living in and around Winnipeg's Main Street "skid row" area examined their criminal victimization.[1] Focusing on the experiences of crime and victimization among the most marginal of the urban poor, including those who live in homeless shelters, rooming houses and single-room occupancy (SRO) hotels in central Winnipeg, the study painted a detailed picture of crime and fear of crime in Winnipeg's inner city.

Marginalization, Exclusion and Victimization

A handful of empirical studies (Brunette, Kominsky and Ruiz 1991; Verheul, Singer and Christenson 1997; Li et al. 2007) and anecdotal observations by police and other emergency services personnel suggest that those times when social assistance is disbursed are accompanied by a rise in calls for emergency service, particularly in the skid row area. Thus, it was surmised that conditions for predatory victimization and social disorder were facilitated by the disbursement of government transfer payments on a predictable monthly basis. However, the Winnipeg study suggested that victimization and crime among the poor who lived in and around skid row were complex and often defied conventional definition and theoretical models.

Mainstream criminology focuses on various opportunity models of criminal predation — best typified by routine activities theory (Cohen and Felson 1979). According to this perspective, the volume of criminal incidents can increase irrespective of the number of motivated offenders when conditions fostering a greater number of criminal opportunities manifest. Thus, crime is viewed as the result of a convergence in space and time of motivated offenders and suitable targets with an absence of capable guardians against predation. This perspective is premised on the assumption that would-be criminals exercise rational choice when committing an offence. Motivation for offending is taken for granted and the question becomes: How can we influence an offender's rational decision to commit an offence? Such a perspective would look at crime among social assistance recipients as a simple problem of the timing or method of delivery of transfer pay-ments. When social assistance cheques hit the street, robberies, assaults, thefts and other forms of crime will flourish with this change to the opportunity structure. Change the way payment is made so that criminal opportunities are minimized and you can reduce the potential for crime. Routine activi-ties theory and the allied lifestyles-exposure theory (Hindelang, Gottfredson and Garofalo 1978) would explain the victimization experiences of skid row residents by the presence of structured opportunities and high-risk lifestyles that place the poor in harm's way.

Such perspectives, however, preclude broader questions about justice. Characterizing the life circumstances of the urban poor as a "risky lifestyle" suggests the poor are architects of their own misfortune. The conservative criminological adage "opportunity makes the thief" likewise neatly subverts questions about social justice. Instead, if we wish to contemplate questions of justice surrounding victimization in the inner city, we must re-conceptualize these experiences as the end result of a series of broad processes that mar-ginalize the poor spatially as well as socially and place them at a higher risk for victimization. Opportunity may indeed make the thief, but opportunity for victimization is not equally distributed throughout Canadian society.

By contrast, a theoretical approach based on a framework of social exclusion or marginality allows us to get at broader questions of justice (see Gaetz 2004; Lee and Schreck 2005). "Marginality" describes individuals who are "excluded from full membership in society" as a result of structural and personal circumstances (Lee and Schreck 2005: 1056). Gaetz (2004) argues that social exclusion may work to spatially exclude marginal individuals from places that are accessible to others, which could increase individual safety. For example, many homeless or street youth are routinely excluded from the warmth and safety of shopping malls or commercial establishments that most of us take for granted. In many urban downtowns, police or other security personal attempt to keep the homeless or marginal "moving along," and thus many are "pushed into places and circumstances that impair their ability to adequately ensure their safety and security and, consequently, increase their risk of criminal victimization" (Gaetz 2004: 428). While those who advocate a marginality or social exclusion explanation for victimization among street people do not dispute the main contours of opportunity theories of crime, they urge us to explore the broader factors that place vulnerable people in these precarious circumstances in the first place.

In order to appreciate the myriad ways victimization may manifest among the inner-city poor, it is necessary to take a less conventional view of victimization than is typical of most academic studies of crime victims. Gaetz (2004) points out that vulnerable populations like street youth may experi-ence a wide range of exploitation that may fall outside the official categories reported in most empirical research. Street youth are subject to exploitation and abuse from "petty criminals, sexual predators, unscrupulous landlords or employers" (Gaetz 2004: 444). This sentiment is echoed by Lee and Schreck (2005: 1058), who note that the people who victimize the homeless include "domiciled predators who cruise skid row, hotel managers who overcharge for illusory services, labour contractors who systematically underpay, and tavern and liquor store operators who run inflated tabs."

Marginality, Exclusion and Safety in Winnipeg

This framework of social exclusion leads to questions about the nature of social assistance, among others. Are social assistance recipients being pushed into situations and physical spaces that increase their spatial proximity to crime and victimization? Do the neighbourhoods and housing options available to social assistance recipients elevate their levels of personal risk of crime? In Manitoba, the benefits paid under the Employment and Income Assistance (EIA) program fall well short of the average cost of rental accommodations in Winnipeg. An individual EIA recipient considered employable (not disabled) receives $243 per month for basic rent. If the rental accommodations require the tenant to pay utility costs, then the maximum benefit increases to $285 per month. However, according the Winnipeg Census Metropolitan Area Rental Market Report (CMHC 2009), the average cost of a bachelor apartment in Winnipeg is $447 per month. This means that social assistance recipients are pushed into the most marginal neighbourhoods and the most marginal accommodation types, often rooming houses and residential hotels which set their rates to match the EIA housing allowance guidelines. In addition to the rental allowance, a single person without a disability receives $195 monthly in basic assistance. This sum must pay for all necessities — food, clothing and hygienic products — making it all but impossible for social assistance recipients to afford even the cost of transit fare ($2.45 per trip), meaning that they must navigate the inner city on foot. In combination, social assistance recipients typically find themselves relegated to the most marginal neighbourhoods of the inner city, forced to live in marginal accommodations, and unable to escape the streets even by public transit. There is no doubt that these broader forces of economic marginalization place the poorest of the poor into vulnerable situations where they are more likely to be exploited criminally.

The twenty-five participants in the study were selected by referrals from organizations dealing directly with the poor. There were seven females and eighteen males ranging from twenty-one to fifty-five years of age. All reported living in inner-city areas of Winnipeg near the skid row area. In terms of accommodation type, seven rented rooms at residential hotels, twelve were living temporarily at shelters, two lived in rooming houses, and the remaining four rented other types of accommodations. Most lived alone, but five reported living with children or roommates. All but two were unattached. Of those who were living in shelters at the time of the interview, most reported living in other parts of the inner city prior to ending up on the street. Only three people had lived in their present accommodations for longer than one year. One male reported living in a skid row hotel for approximately five years, while another male reported renting his accommodations in the inner city for the past seven years. Many of those who reported living in shelters had been there for a period of months and, in one case, nearly a year. Although shelters are designed to provide emergency accommodations, it appears as though some of Winnipeg's poor turn to these services as long-term solutions to personal housing crises.

Although more than half of the people interviewed were not, practically speaking, homeless, many of their personal characteristics and life experiences mirrored those reported by other homeless people. For example, many of those interviewed had no family connections in Winnipeg. Only two reported being married (common law) at the time of the interview. Many described experiences of pronounced disconnection from family and friends (see, for example, Lee and Schreck 2005). Many of the participants reported suffering from chronic illnesses or were disabled. Mental illness was reported in one case. Several individuals reported spending time in prison prior to ending up in their present circumstances. In short, participants were profoundly marginalized and socially excluded from the general Canadian population.

When the conversation turned to a discussion of their neighbourhood, most participants described these local spaces as filled with violence and exploitation. A thirty-eight-year-old single father of four children graphically described the potential for violence in his neighbourhood: "My neighbourhood is probably a rotten neighbourhood. Easy place to be dead. Murders, shootings and several beatings take place within a block radius of my home." Likewise, a fifty-two-year-old long-term residential hotel resident emphasized death in his description of the skid row area: "Rough. Deadly. There's been quite a few deaths in this area. Quite a few. And not only murders, but a lot of people die here, just from their habits." For a forty-two-year-old female hotel resident, racial tensions were also imbued within the day-to-day violence. When asked to describe her neighbourhood to an uninformed outsider she suggested that it was "better to be Native down this way." Moreover, she warned that it was important to be streetwise. She cautioned those who were not streetwise to stay out of the neighbourhood: "You'll get walked over, you'll get stepped on, you'll get beat up."

Many described feelings of spatial and social alienation from non-inner-city parts of the city. A fifty-five-year-old male resident of a downtown hotel expressed his desire to leave at the earliest possible time:

I mean now that I've looked at the other side, once I get on my feet, get something coming in steady, other than this crap, I'm the hell out of there. That's it. Just really depressing, truly is. I'm not suicidal or anything like that, and I attend church, thank God I have that. But, it's not a nice place to be. It's called downtown nowhere.

A number of participants described strategies to avoid the violence and crime in the area. A twenty-six-year-old single mother of two children had little to say about her neighbourhood because she rarely left her home out of fear: "I don't know really, cause I don't really go anywhere with my kids cause I stay home with them, cause there's too much drugs and that around. So I'd rather not take my kids anywhere." Likewise, a thirty-seven-year-old male participant described a distinctly spatial strategy of avoidance that was a central coping feature of life in his neighbourhood: "I personally like to hop on a bus and go somewhere else, for the afternoon or something. That's usually what I do."

Most respondents found themselves living in the inner city out of necessity and hoped someday that would change. Many expressed a desire to find a better place to live in a better neighbourhood. However, forces beyond their control ensured that these residents of Winnipeg's inner city were placed into situations where they felt vulnerable to crime and violence. Unlike the lifestyles-exposure perspective, the circumstances experienced by these men and women were not a result of a lifestyle choice, but were the end result of a process of social, economic and spatial marginalization. Most participants recognized that they were in a higher risk situation than other Winnipeggers, but they felt powerless to change their circumstances. As a result, many described extensive fear of crime and victimization.

When asked for their general thoughts about crime and being a victim of any type of crime, sixteen of the twenty-five interviewees indicated that they worried to some extent about being a victim of crime in their day-to-day life. When asked specifically if they worry more about crime at the time or times of the month when social assistance cheques are disbursed, seventeen indicated that they did worry more at those times. Often, individuals who reported worrying about crime at the time of cheque delivery did not worry about having their own money stolen as much as they worried about the general level of crime and disorder that resulted from money being placed into the hands of those with addictions. A fifty-five-year-old SRO resident described a typical day when social assistance cheques were disbursed at his hotel:

I don't go out at night for sure. And then there's usually scuffles all over the place. I keep my door shut, I don't care what's happening out there. I don't interfere at all. Even if I was physically fit, I wouldn't have, not my concern. It's a zoo. I don't even think police go there because they know it's the _____ hotel, they don't give a shit, unless it's a 911 call, then they'll show up.

A forty-seven-year-old skid row hotel resident described a similar but more graphically violent scenario around his hotel on the days that assistance cheques are distributed:

> Cheque day, any cheque day, I worry about it more than normal. I know it's easy to get caught up accidentally in a violent exchange with people, I've had enough experience to know that, just because you had nothing to do with it doesn't mean you're gonna get away with it by walking right past it. I'm just very conscious, I stop, I listen, I pay attention, if people are getting rowdy and they're a little bit drunk, I just stay in my room, till they move on. Well, hell, right outside my door four times, guys get loaded and beat each other right to death with claw hammers, with their head bouncing off my door. I can't even go to the bathroom sometimes because the stupid cops are doing the, taking the pictures and everything.

The interviewees seemed to fall into two categories in terms of their reaction to victimization experiences or fear of becoming a victim. The first group appeared to display a grudging acceptance of the persistently high level of violence in their day-to-day lives. These people took crime and violence in stride and regarded it as a fact of life in their neighbourhood. A twenty-five-year-old male shelter resident described a recent case of violent predatory victimization in rather fatalistic terms:

> Easy come, easy go. If they're hurting for money, to hell with it, I'm not gonna get myself killed over a few dollars. I told 'em no. I didn't think they would do anything, but they did. They got maybe twenty-five to thirty bucks out of me, but I still have the rest in my shoe, I didn't really care. Got a few kicks in the head for it, whatever. Like I said, easy come, easy go.

A similar characterization of predatory robbery was offered by a twenty-one-year-old resident of a downtown shelter. When I asked about any personal experiences she had with victimization around the time of her monthly social assistance cheque, she replied in a nonchalant manner: "I've been jumped for my money a few times when I just cashed my cheque, but things happen you know?"

In contrast to those who took their victimization in stride, a second group had very different reactions to their fear of victimization. This group took precautions and did not view the threat of violence in a fatalistic or light manner. In one case, the reaction of a fifty-two-year-old SRO resident was to become tougher on the street and react first before there was a chance the he might become a victim:

> You know what? I toughened myself up, and I hurt a few people who tried to do that, myself. I just got harder and harder and more hateful. When those people approach me, I don't give them a chance, I hit first now. Before, I just minded my own business. Those people get in my face, they are down before they even try. Cause, I hardened myself up to be like that. I don't like it, but it's the only way they'll leave you alone. They know that you're a person not to be dealing with. And word gets around on the street that, okay, this guy watch him. Sometimes it'll save your bacon, sometimes it won't. Some people may challenge you, they may have a weapon next time. That's life, you have to deal with it the best you can. If you back away, that's the worst thing you can do. Then they got you marked, you're a target, might as well just put an "X" right on your forehead. They know it, crack heads know it, the punks know it, you're just a walking victim.

Others described strategies of avoidance or even target hardening aimed at reducing their likelihood of victimization. Some would alter their walking routes on the day they received their cheques to avoid what they perceived to be dangerous areas. Some said they paid to ride the bus on the day they received their money because they felt it was safer than walking. Many described strategies of only carrying a small sum of money when on the street and never flashing money in public. One downtown SRO resident took steps to better secure his hotel room door against breaking and entering:

> I reinforced my door because I've seen guys get in with a butter knife. So I've fixed mine, I've put in four inch screws in mine, so they can't. They can knock the door in if they want to get in, but then they'll make one hell of a lot of noise.

In short, just like any victim of crime, the individuals interviewed had a variety of reactions to their experiences. However, what really stood out was the overall amount and the violent nature of crime that seemed to be all around the area. As if to punctuate the solemnity of the situation, toward the end of the interviewing process a man was stabbed and killed on the street right at the very heart of skid row. Most of those who were interviewed after this time spoke of this event. Many felt that it could have happened to any one of them as the dispute that led to the homicide involved something as minor as a pack of cigarettes and a few items of clothing. While this sort of violence is foreign and incomprehensible in suburban areas, some participants contextualized this as merely part of life in the inner city of Winnipeg. It is impossible to hear and see all this without the distinct impression that the experience of crime and victimization in the inner city is worlds away from the picture of victimization in other parts of the city.

It is important to place these findings into to a broader social context. Social and economic forces of exclusion place inner-city residents at greater risk of harm. Social assistance pays for only the most marginal housing, and, consequently, many of the urban poor have no choice but to live in the highest crime areas. Residents are further economically marginalized by the wholesale departure of mainstream financial institutions from most parts of the inner city (Buckland et al. 2004). Even where local bank branches remain, few interviewees had an account or proper identification and many preferred to deal with local businesses that would not look down on them. Residents turned to pawn shops, cheque-cashing businesses, hotels and payday lenders to cash their social assistance cheques. This opens to the door to a kind of economic victimization of the poor that falls short of criminality. Even though banks are obligated to negotiate government cheques without any fee, respondents reported paying between two and eleven dollars to cash their meagre assistance cheques at so-called "shadow banks" — cheque cashing businesses, pawn shops, rent-to-own stores, hotels and payday lenders (Buckland 2004). Worse yet, reliance on shadow banks opens up increased vulnerability to traditional forms of criminal predation. Without access to a bank account or credit, the poor are forced to deal only in cash. Thus, broader forces place many of the poor into a situation where they can be easily exploited economically and criminally. In the end, this raises questions about the shape of justice in a Canadian context which purports to uphold tenets of multiculturalism and equality for all its residents. The socio-economic and geographic sequestering of the persons interviewed suggests a lack of access to the basic socio-economic services that privileged citizens access on a daily basis. The absence of socio-economic justice, in this regard, is a matter to which the citizens interviewed seem somewhat resigned.

EXCLUSION AND THE CRIMINAL JUSTICE SYSTEM

For many Canadians, justice means involving the criminal justice system. However, most social assistant recipients do not turn to police when they have been a victim of crime. Moreover, for the minority that had dealt with police as a victim of crime, there were mixed feelings about the experience. For some, the experience was not a particularly memorable one but certainly not a negative one. A number of respondents who had reported victimization described the police as essentially respectful and professional. However, a handful of others described their experience in the opposite terms. Some felt that the police were suspicious of social assistance recipients in general and treated them as if they were the "bad guy." A fifty-one-year-old female respondent worried that the victims of crime from poor inner-city neighbourhoods might be treated differently than others, especially those who might have been drinking at the time of their violation: "Somehow, the police, when you phone them, somehow they turn it around on you. Even when you're sober." Several participants, irrespective of having any direct experience with the police as a victim of crime, felt that the police might not treat them fairly because of their racial background or their socio-economic status. A few respondents who identified as Aboriginal or Métis reported feeling that race was the main cause of their differential treatment by the police. One twenty-one-year-old EIA recipient felt that police might occasionally treat him differently because of his background:

> I would probably say because of my background. Not talking about rap sheet or anything, I'm talking about being an Aboriginal. I would think that, there's still a little bit of superiority among the white people. Especially with cops, because they just think, "he's just another bum, he's an Indian, he's just another bum." That runs through my mind a lot, but that's probably the only reason, one of the reasons why I wouldn't do it [report victimization to police].

Other participants felt that the police did not care about the plight of the poor in the inner city. A number of interviewees singled out their own poverty as a key reason why they were reluctant to report victimization to the police. One twenty-six-year-old male respondent felt that the police did not care about crime in and around skid row: "cops don't care... the only time they care if it's in a rich area, they don't care about people down here, they don't care." For another respondent, his address at a notorious inner-city SRO hotel meant that the police could easily overlook all but the most serious calls for service:

> They don't care, they figure it's from the [downtown SRO hotel], who cares? That's their attitude. It's discriminating against people that live there, even though some of the people down here might be decent people. Because you're generalized, right, and discriminated against just because the area you live in. I thought they were supposed to be here to protect and serve, instead of discriminate.

Like many victims of crime, respondents stated that their likelihood of reporting victimization to the police was dependent on the type and seriousness of the incident. Parents in the study reported a greater likelihood of reporting crime if it involved their children. Others suggested that they would be more likely to report violent crimes than non-violent ones. Those who did not report victimization to police were asked why they had not done so. Like those Canadians surveyed for the 2004 GSS, many indicated that they had not reported their victimization to the police (or would not in the future) because they did not feel that the incident was important enough or they felt that police would not be able to do anything (see, for example, Gannon and Mihorean 2005: 19). But while only a small fraction of those surveyed in the GSS (4 percent for property crime and 11 percent for violent offences) did not report their victimization out of fear (Gannon and Mihorean 2005: 13, 19), a considerable number of the inner-city residents, like the three below, reported fear as a key reason why they did not report to the police:

> Fear. I was worried that they'd ask me to testify in court. At that time I was hanging out at bars, and you become well known on the streets, and they know exactly where to come and find you. So, I would never report anybody that I've seen on the street before.

> I probably wouldn't [report victimization]. It seems like when you tell on someone, they're not going to stop bugging you, they're gonna come right back at you. So, I wouldn't bother with it, I know this city's gone crazy now.

> If I'm living in a neighbourhood like this, and I phone the police, then I get labelled a rat. People I don't even know are going to be coming up, punching me out, that's just kind of the way it goes down here… that's just something I guess I've learned, living on the street, you kinda learn to mind your own business.

Perhaps all Canadians have a measure of skepticism about the ability of the police or criminal justice personnel to bring about justice. However, in the context of the inner city and among the poorest of the poor, fear is a far more significant barrier to justice than it is in more affluent quarters of Canadian society.

Exclusion, Victimization and Justice

While justice can be conceptualized in a number of different ways, at base it implies a measure of fairness. When one group in society is consistently more likely to be harmed than another group, many would be likely to feel this is not fair. When that group most likely to be harmed has the fewest resources and structural conditions conspire to make it seemingly impossible to escape from the source of this harm, injustice seems an appropriate label. For residents of the inner city, and in particular for those marginalized residents of "skid row," this sort of injustice manifests in the day-to-day experiences of exploitation, violence and fear of crime. This experience of injustice is most acute for those who rely on the state to provide them with the basic necessities of life. Undoubtedly, the government social assistance scheme in Manitoba is probably not that different than in other parts of Canada. Rates for assistance are greatly outstripped by the high costs of decent housing in stable neighbourhoods. As a result, the poor experience a form of spatial marginalization to the most crime-prone neighbourhoods.

In addition, broader forces of the global market economy of the early twenty-first century have precipitated tremendous reorganization of the economy, including the local banking sector, for example. Banks have withdrawn from all but the wealthiest suburban communities, and the poor find it increasingly difficult to gain access to affordable and convenient financial services from the traditional banking industry. However, so-called entrepreneurs have stepped in to the fill the banking void. Shadow banks have flourished in the inner city where financial services and credit are scarce. The poor face financial exploitation on top of criminal victimization as a result of their marginalization from the economic mainstream.

For those who live in Canada's poorest neighbourhoods, the daily injustice of exploitation and victimization either blurs into a sort of day-to-day normality or underscores a constant level of fear, heightened at that time of the month when social assistance cheques are distributed. While their racial and economic marginality placed them into the high crime spaces of the inner city in the first instance, this same marginality lies at the heart of their feelings of apathy toward state agents of criminal justice. Setting right the injustices suffered by those who face high levels of crime and fear on a daily basis in the inner city can only begin by listening carefully to the voices of the marginalized and socially excluded. These voices allow us to understand that justice for our interviewees is not simply protection from the feared violence in the community that surrounds them, but extends to the socio-economic injustices they suffer by virtue of their geography and the lack of responses of the local business community in meeting their basic socio-economic service needs. Indeed, it just may be the case that those who live in areas of the city that have access to these resources, who may indeed experience less of the fearfulness of their surroundings, may be implicated in the geographic socio-economic dislocation of the interviewees. If that were the case, each resident of the city is implicated in the marginalization of more vulnerable communities, and each has a connection to the injustices experienced first hand by Winnipeg's urban poor.

Note

1. Here, we explore victimization and fear of crime in the inner city of Winnipeg by using interviews with twenty-five social assistance recipients from a previous study on crime among the poorest of Winnipeg's poor (Kohm 2006; Kohm 2007).

References

Brunette, D.D., J. Kominsky and E. Ruiz. 1991. "Correlation of Emergency Health Care Use, 911 Volume, and Jail Activity with Welfare Check Distribution." *Annals of Emergency Medicine* 20, 7.

Buckland, Jerry, B. Guenther, B. Bruce, G. Boichev, H. Geddie and M. Mutch. 2004. *"There are No Banks Here": Financial and Insurance Exclusion in Winnipeg's North End*. Winnipeg: Institute of Urban Studies, University of Winnipeg.

City of Winnipeg. n.d. "2006 Census: City of Winnipeg Census Profiles." At <winnipeg.ca/census/2006/City%20of%20Winnipeg/>.

CMHC (Canada Mortgage and Housing Corporation). 2009. *Rental Market Report, Winnipeg CMA: Fall 2009*. Ottawa: Canada Mortgage and Housing Corporation.

Cohen, Lawrence, and Marcus Felson. 1979. "Social Change and Crime Rate Trends: A Routine Activity Approach." *American Sociological Review* 44.

Fitzgerald, R., M. Wisener, and J. Savoie. 2004. *Neighbourhood Characteristics and the Distribution of Crime in Winnipeg*. Ottawa: Canadian Centre for Justice Statistics.

Gaetz, Stephen. 2004. "Safe Streets for Whom? Homeless Youth, Social Exclusion, and Criminal Victimization." *Canadian Journal of Criminology and Criminal Justice*. 46, 4.

Gannon, Maire, and Karen Mihorean. 2005. *Criminal Victimization in Canada, 2004*. Ottawa: Canadian Centre for Justice Statistics.

Hindelang, M.J., M.R. Gottfredson and J. Garofalo. 1978. *Victims of Personal Crime: An Empirical Foundation for a Theory of Personal Victimization*. Cambridge, MA: Ballinger.

Kohm, Steven. 2006. "'Welfare Is the Second Last Resort: The Last Resort Is Death.' An Exploratory Analysis of Social Assistance, Victimization and Crime." *Canadian Journal of Urban Research* 15, 1.

____. 2007. *Routine Activities, Opportunity and Crime in the Inner City: Investigating the Link between Monthly Income Assistance Payments and Crime in Winnipeg*. Winnipeg Inner-city Research Alliance. Winnipeg: Institute of Urban Studies.

____. 2009. "Spatial Dimensions of Fear in a High Crime Community: Fear of Crime or Fear of Disorder?" *Canadian Journal of Criminology and Criminal Justice* 51, 1.

Lee, Barrett, and Christopher Schreck. 2005. "Danger on the Streets: Marginality and Victimization Among Homeless People." *American Behavioral Scientist* 48.

Li, Xin, Huiying Sun, David Marsh and Aslam H Anis. 2007. "Impact of Welfare Cheque Issue Days on a Service for Those Intoxicated in Public." *Harm Reduction Journal* 4, 12.

Verheul, G., S.M. Singer, and J.M. Christenson. 1997. "Mortality and Morbidity Associated with the Distribution of Monthly Welfare Payments." *Academic Emergency Medicine* 4, 2.

CHAPTER TEN

SEX WORK AND THE LAW

A Critical Analysis of Four Policy Approaches to Adult Prostitution

Frances M. Shaver

What is justice and how does it apply to sex work and the law? In her lecture exploring a more generic version of this question, Mahoney (2010: 134) stated that, "while everyone is for justice, the content of justice is highly contested." This is unquestionably the case for prostitution. Guaranteeing justice for people working in the sex industry (PWSI)[1] is particularly problematic since it involves major discrepancies on political, social and moral grounds. Debates tend to be dominated by extreme claims about the activities associated with prostitution and its implications — both theoretical and empirical. In Canada, for example, we have been debating this issue for over twenty-five years. There have been two House of Commons Standing Committees (1983, 1990), a Federal-Provincial-Territorial Working Group (1998), a Special Committee on Pornography and Prostitution (Fraser Committee 1985) and a Subcommittee on Solicitation Laws of the Standing Committee on Justice and Human Rights (SSLR 2006). During the SSLR debates, the four federal political parties finally agreed that the prostitution laws are "unacceptable" and that the "status quo does more harm than good." Unfortunately they were unable to agree on changes and we are no closer to resolving the "prostitution problem" than we were twenty-five years ago (SSLR 2006). In a search for rational and pragmatic solutions to this problem, I critically analyze four common approaches: criminalization, the Nordic model, legalization and decriminalization.

CRITICAL TOOLS FOR A JUST AND FAIR ANALYSIS

In line with Mahoney, who argues that "decisions made in the abstract, outside of the messy, concrete reality of life are often too far removed from reality to truly understand what justice requires" (Mahoney 2010: 147), the analysis of each approach is grounded in the concrete, lived experiences of PWSI and residents in their everyday lives. It is also essential that it be structured to: 1) avoid the debate polarizing prostitution as either "victimization" or "sex work"; 2) rely on evidence-based information about the industry and the PWSI; and 3) adopt neutral language when describing both the workers and the industry (Shaver 2005; Weitzer 2010). Otherwise, understandings and perceptions about sex work are easily transformed into moral discourses that continue to reinforce the links between sex work, stigma and marginaliza-tion, and to hamper good policy development (Weitzer 2006, 2010; Sanders 2005; Shaver 1994, 1996). Together, these strategies will help determine the merits of each model for creating a socio-legal environment promoting the security, health and human rights of PWSI, residents and the communities in which they live and work.[2] In addition, they provide a useful framework for recognizing the diversity among PWSI and the complexity of the sex industry, traits often ignored in policy discussions and proposed solutions over the last twenty-five years (Sanders 2007).

REGULATING SEX WORK

The oldest and most common legal approach to prostitution is "criminaliza-tion." Sex work is usually regarded as an immoral activity that should be prohibited (as in most of the U.S. and South Africa) or tolerated (as it is in Canada and England). In the U.S. and South Africa, laws are designed to prohibit all elements of sex work, including the buying and selling of sexual services. In Canada, the exchange of sexual services for money does not violate any statutes of the *Criminal Code of Canada* (CCC 1985). However, activities associated with the buying and selling of sexual services violate several sections of the Criminal Code. Briefly stated, these include: keeping or being found in a common bawdy house (section 210); providing direc- · tions to or transporting someone to a bawdy house (section 211); procuring or living on the avails of prostitution (section 212); communication in a public place for the purpose of prostitution (section 213); and purchasing sexual services from someone under eighteen years of age (section 212(4)). Some forms of sex work are also affected by sections dealing with obscenity (section 163), engaging in an immoral theatrical performance (section 167), performing an indecent act in a public place (section 173) and public nudity (section 174). Although these laws are federal and apply in all provinces and territories, there is often a great deal of variation in how they are enforced (Shaver 1993, 2005a; van der Meulen and Durisin 2008).

Under criminalization, PWSI may also face charges through a number of other means such as drug and public nuisance charges. In San Francisco, for example, the possession of condoms may be used as circumstantial evidence of intent to commit prostitution (Lutnick and Cohan 2009: 38). In Canada, provinces may apply various kinds of legislation: highway and traffic (for example, vehicles used in prostitution-related offences can be seized and impounded); proceeds of crime (for example, the savings and investments of PWSI can be seized and confiscated); community safety (for example, buildings and properties can be closed in response to safety and prostitution-related concerns); and child protection (for example, authorizing the involuntary detention of minors engaged in prostitution) (Barnett 2008:

12–22). In addition, municipalities have independent power to control prostitution through municipal bylaws and other local measures. Police in most Canadian municipalities regularly use zoning laws to restrict prostitution and anti-jaywalking and loitering laws to hand out tickets in areas frequented by PWSI. Some municipalities (such as Calgary, Edmonton, Toronto, Victoria, Vancouver and Windsor) have enacted bylaws that require dating and escort services, exotic entertainers, massage parlours and others to obtain business licences. These mechanisms give municipalities some limited control over the sex industry without violating federal jurisdiction (Barnett 2008: 22–28).

Although still seen as a moral issue by many, the Canadian government has drawn a clear distinction between voluntary and non-voluntary prostitution. Barnett (2008: 2) points out that Canada did not sign the 1949 *UN Convention for the Suppression of Traffic in Persons and Exploitation of the Prostitution of Others* because it "strongly condemns all forms of prostitution as a violation of individual dignity and welfare, *whether that prostitution is voluntary or not*" (emphasis mine). Then, as now, "this position could not be reconciled with the law in Canada, where prostitution itself is legal and only offences associated with it are criminalized" (Barnett 2008: 2). This distinction permits the element of choice in adult prostitution to be recognized, facilitating the development of harm reduction programs.[3]

This is not the case in Sweden, where prostitution is regarded as a social ill and a form of men's violence against women. Under this model, the distinction between voluntary and non-voluntary prostitution is not relevant. The law — introduced in Sweden on January 1, 1999 — was the first in the world to criminalize the purchase, but not the sale, of sexual services. Based on a gender equality and human rights perspective, it shifts the focus away from the supply side (that is, prostitutes, who are seen to be exploited) to the demand side (that is, sex purchasers, procurers and traffickers). The assumption is that if there were no demand there would be no prostitution (SOU 2010: 30).

The proposal to criminalize the purchase of sexual services was part of a Swedish bill concerning violence against women. The bill proposed several measures in different social sectors to combat violence against women, prostitution and sexual harassment in working life. Thus, Swedish criminal law is used to regulate clients, managers and owners/operators, but not sex workers. Legislation criminalizes the purchase and procurement of sexual services, working indoors, working with others, advertising and profiting from the sexual labour of others. Similar laws have recently been adopted in Finland (June 2006), Norway (January 2009) and Iceland (April 2009); hence the term, "the Nordic model."

The remaining two options each make sex work legal but in very different ways. Under legalization — where sex work is generally regarded as a morally repugnant but inevitable activity — some forms of sex work are criminalized while others are licensed. Businesses and individuals involved in the sex industry face regulations and licensing procedures that other businesses do not, including the licensing of workers, compulsory medical check-ups, registration and size limitations on places of business (for example, bawdy houses), the maintenance of procuring and pimping criminal laws and limitations on street prostitution. In Nevada — where some prostitution activities are legalized — current practices require brothel workers to register with the police department, restrict brothel workers' mobility, stipulate working conditions and require mandatory weekly testing for gonorrhea and chla-

Table 1: Policy Approaches to Adult Prostitution — The Basic Tenants

Criminalization	The Nordic Model	Legalization	Decriminalization
Prostitution is an immoral activity	Prostitution is a social ill and a form of men's violence against women	Prostitution is a morally repugnant but inevitable activity	Sex work is a private matter between consenting adults
Voluntary and forced prostitution distinguished	Voluntary and forced prostitution not distinguished	Voluntary and forced prostitution distinguished	Voluntary and forced prostitution distinguished
Criminalizes PWSI, clients, managers, owners and operators	Criminalizes clients, managers, owners and operators	Regulates some PWSI, managers, owners and operators	Regulates PWSI and sex work activities; recognizes labour rights and responsibilities
Legislation criminalizes some aspects of sex work, such as negotiation in public, procurement and operating a bawdy house	Legislation criminalizes the purchase of sexual services and procurement	Practices include licensing, compulsory medical exams, registered and size limited bawdy houses, and laws against street prostitution	Includes labour and OHS standards, zoning regulations and access to unionization, professional associations and human rights codes
Disruptive and non-disruptive activities and abusive and non-abusive behaviours are regulated using criminal law	Disruptive and non-disruptive activities and abusive and non-abusive behaviours are regulated using criminal law	Disruptive and non-disruptive activities and abusive and non-abusive behaviours are regulated using criminal law	The most disruptive and abusive activities and behaviours are regulated using criminal laws explicitly designed to deal with them
Prostitution is a federal or state issue, severely limiting other levels of government	Prostitution is a federal issue, likely limiting other levels of government	Prostitution is a state issue, severely limiting other levels of government	Prostitution no longer a federal issue leaving fewer (if any) limits on other levels of government
Canada, the U.K., the U.S. and South Africa	Sweden, Iceland, Norway and Finland	Nevada, U.S.; the Netherlands and some states in Germany and Australia	New South Wales, Australia and New Zealand

mydia and monthly testing for HIV/AIDS and syphilis (Lutnick and Cohan 2009: 38). Prostitution activities are also legalized in the Netherlands and some states in Germany and Australia where criminal law is also a designated responsibility of the state (Jeffrey and Sullivan 2009: 61).

When sex work is seen as a private matter between consenting adults, "decriminalization" is the preferred model. It regulates PWSI and sex work activities without using criminal law, while recognizing labour rights and responsibilities. Prostitution activities are decriminalized in New South Wales, Australia and New Zealand, where workers, managers and business establishments are regulated using labour standards legislation, occupational health and safety codes and zoning regulations. These innovations are possible as, once decriminalized, sex work falls outside the federal domain, leaving fewer, if any, limits on the regulatory options available to other levels of government.

In New Zealand, the passage of the *Prostitution Reform Act* (PRA) in 2003 removed the offences of soliciting (that is, street-based sex work), brothel keeping, procurement of sex workers over the age of eighteen and living on the earnings derived from prostitution (Pérez-y-Pérez 2007: 11; Abel et al. 2010a: 76). In New South Wales, decriminalization began earlier and was implemented gradually. It is a partial, rather than a full, decriminalization of the industry. The law against public soliciting for the purposes of prostitution was repealed in 1979 and, although some restrictions were replaced in 1983, it is still not a criminal offence to solicit at a distance from residences, churches, schools and hospitals. Brothels were decriminalized in New South Wales in 1995 and there is no licensing of owners or any licensing fees. Brothels do, however, have to obtain consent under planning laws from municipal councils (Jeffrey and Sullivan 2009: 62). Table 1 summarizes the basic tenants of these four policy approaches.[4]

POLICY APPROACHES AND THEIR IMPACTS
Critically evaluating each of the four approaches to sex work requires assessing the extent to which each model supports the goals most often identified by the key stakeholders (PWSI and residents) and the likelihood each has for sustaining the social programs facilitating those goals. In the following section, we evaluate each model in terms of whether it provides a supportive, partially supportive or non-supportive environment for achieving these objectives (the arguments are summarized in Tables 2, 3 and 4).[5]

The Concerns of PWSI
We focus on five key areas of concern among PWSI, including fostering respect and reducing stigma, securing safe work locations, maintaining good health and well being, obtaining labour rights and gaining economic security. As

studies show, some of these benefits are possible under legislation grounded in criminal law, but most of the evidence indicates that support for their application is unlikely or very limited.

Fostering Respect and Reducing Stigma
First, it is difficult to foster respect and work with dignity when the activities surrounding the sale of sexual services are criminalized (Lewis et al. 2005a; Jeffrey and MacDonald 2006). PWSI, their managers and employers are treated differently and are more highly stigmatized than workers in other service industries. A longitudinal B.C. study comparing the working conditions, health and safety and experiences of stigma of PWSI to two other frontline service occupations — hair stylists and food and beverage workers — indicates that PWSI not only experience greater everyday suffering (Shumka and Benoit 2008), but they are also more likely to report poorer health and greater stigmatization from health care providers and the general public (Benoit et al. 2008; McCarthy et al. 2006). The stigma faced by PWSI can extend to their clients, who are criminalized and often "shamed" (Lowman 1990), and thus they too are treated differently from the clients of other service workers. Stigma by association, or courtesy stigma, can also extend to others who are associated with PWSI such as their health care and service providers and friends and families (Philips 2006; Philips and Benoit 2005; Abel et al. 2010: 244). Several studies have shown that these stigmas are often maintained and reinforced by the media, especially in the case of PWSI (see, for example, Hallgrimsdottir et al. 2006, 2008).

Given the stigmatization of sex work under criminalization, PWSI are often keen to maintain their anonymity. This is difficult. In Toronto, where some massage and escort activities are legal, confidential information regarding those who are legally licensed is compromised by having to be posted in a conspicuous place in the work environment (van der Meulen and Durisin 2008). In another Ontario study, Lewis and Maticka-Tyndale (2000) report cases where the police inappropriately used personal information provided for the purposes of municipal licensing to conduct criminal background checks or to facilitate charges and arrests under the Criminal Code.

The stigma associated with sex work is far-reaching. PWSI are often reluctant to report crime mainly because they believe that they will not be taken seriously by the police and courts (Lowman 2000; Jeffrey and MacDonald 2006; Campbell and Kinnell 2000/2001; Lewis and Maticka-Tyndale 2000; Pyett and Warr 1997). Other common reasons include their perceptions that the police think they get what they deserve (Lewis and Maticka-Tyndale 2000), fear that others will learn of their work (Campbell and Kinnell 2000/2001) and fear of arrest for sex work-related offences (Pyett and Warr 1997; Campbell and Kinnell 2000/2001).

Under the Nordic model, opportunities to foster respect and dignity

Table 2: Concerns of PWSI Within Policy Approaches

Concerns of PWSI	Likelihood of Support Under Each Legal Environment			
	Criminalization	Nordic Model	Legalization	Decriminalization
Fostering respect/ Reducing stigma: toward PWSI, clients, managers, employers and sex work	NS: Possible but unlikely. PWSI & managers stigmatized; clients often "shamed."	NS: Possible but unlikely for PWSI. Goal is to abolish prostitution & criminalize clients & managers.	NS: Possible but unlikely. PWSI & managers are stigmatized & marginalized.	P: Respect enhanced & stigma reduced for all given focus on labour rights & responsibilities.
Securing Work Locations: - Discretion regarding client-choice - Safe places to provide services - Secure working practices/locations	NS: Difficult. Laws negatively impact ability to maintain security; actions taken often contravene CC.	NS: Unlikely. It is more difficult to assess clients; must work underground to avoid detection.	P: Possible for legal workers but right to choose not guaranteed. Unlikely for the larger, unregulated illegal sector.	S: Enhanced. Safer work places available; PWSI better able to develop & promote safe/ secure working practices).
- Protection from all forms of violence & abuse	NS: Unlikely. Rights of PWSI are often ignored, have limited access to legal support, and are often unaware of their rights.	NS: Unlikely. Street-based workers report greater stress/danger & more risk-taking.	P: Possible for legal workers (easier to report violence/ abuse to police). Unlikely for the larger, unregulated illegal sector.	S: Possible. Police attitudes changed for the better; more appropriate sections of CC likely to be utilized. Easier for PWSI to report crime.
Health and Well-being: - Clean needles for drug users	P: Possible. Available as is a safe injection site but PWSI harassed.	NS: Unlikely. No state support for harm reduction programs.	S: Possible (already available).	S: Possible (remain available).
- Condoms easily available - Customers willing to use them	P: Both possible but difficult to enforce (no supporting OHS legislation & condoms used as evidence of prostitution).	NS: Unlikely (no state support for harm reduction programs).	P: Both possible (but mandatory testing may lead to a false sense of security and less condom use).	S: Both enhanced (safer sex seen as a general issue, not a prostitution issue & required by OHS regulations).
- Access to health and legal services	P: Possible. Health & social services for PWSI have increased but stigmatization is strong & inhibits access.	P: Possible. Sweden provides extensive health & social services to all, but stigmatization of PWSI is strong & may inhibit access.	P: Possible but only if willing to be licensed; ongoing stigmatization of PWSI may inhibit access.	P: Enhanced. Available to all regardless of licence but ongoing stigmatization of PWSI may still inhibit access. Emotional health still at risk.

Labour Rights & Protections: - Labour rights regarding workplace health and safety	NS: Overlooked. Sex work *not* seen as a viable occupation. Those with limited rights (dancers) often unaware of them.	NS: Impossible. Sex work seen as a social ill that must be abolished. No state support for harm reduction programs.	NS: Likely over-looked. Sex work still regulated using criminal law: no established working conditions. If paid as 'sub-contractor' no access to employment entitlements.	S: Possible. Sex work seen as a viable occupation. PWSI more aware of their rights.
- Access to Labour Unions/Cooperatives	NS: Unlikely. Yet some initiatives already in place.	NS: Impossible. Sex work seen as a social evil to be abolished.	NS: Likely over-looked. Sex work still regulated using criminal law.	S: Enhanced. Sex work seen as a viable occupation. Support for unions.
Economic Security: - Access to long-term economic security - Able to file taxes without risking assets	NS: Impossible on both counts as long as sex work activities are illegal (i.e., it is not a viable job).	NS: Unlikely. Swedish society supports economic & social equality but it's unlikely to apply to sex work.	P: Possible (but PWSI discouraged from investing, it can be used as evidence in criminal cases).	S: Enhanced opportunities to save and/or invest since sex work a viable occupation.

Note: NS = non-supportive; P = partially supportive; S =supportive

for PWSI and reduce their stigmatization are next to impossible. The law is built on the premise that prostitution is a social evil and a form of men's violence against women that must be abolished (SOU 2010). PWSI (referred to as "prostituted women") are perceived as victims or survivors who need help getting out of the industry, clients are labelled as social undesirables, and managers/employers are described as sexual predators. As Weitzer (2010: 17) points out, these descriptions — which "symbolize the [alleged] lack of choice women have over being used in prostitution" — render impossible any opportunity for PWSI to gain respect and dignity.

In the case of formalized legalization in Nevada and the Netherlands, licensed sex workers face regulations and licensing procedures that other service workers do not. PWSI can be "subject to mandatory finger printing and record checks, forced health evaluations, higher taxes and financial penalties, and constant police surveillance in addition to regulations on when and where one can work" (van der Meulen and Durisin 2008: 306). In Nevada, brothel workers must register with the police department. In addition to "restricted mobility and stipulated working conditions" they also face "mandated weekly testing for gonorrhea and chlamydia and monthly testing for HIV and syphilis" (Lutnick and Cohan 2009: 38–39). Sex-related businesses (such as bawdy houses and massage parlours) are also subject to additional regulation and surveillance beyond what would be expected for any other type of business, further undermining opportunities to foster respect and reduce stigma (Lutnick and Cohan 2009: 38). All of these conditions serve to reinforce stigma and undermine the respect and dignity of PWSI, their clients and their managers.

Fostering respect and reducing stigma is also difficult under the decriminalization approach. In a study conducted in New Zealand before and after decriminalization, Abel and Fitzgerald (2010a) found that PWSI continued to experience stigma well after the PRA had been put in place. The discrimination identified by many PWSI in the study was intense:

> It had a direct impact on the broader determinants of health, most notably on their employment options outside of the industry, their ability to both rent and purchase houses, their accessing of health and other essential services and for many, especially street-based workers, social networks, which were constricted and mostly comprised of other sex workers. (Abel and Fitzgerald 2010a: 240)

In response, they adopted strategies to manage stigma that were similar to PWSI operating under other legal approaches. These included: concealing and/or controlling information about their work; being selective about whom they disclosed this information to; and constructing different roles for the private and public spheres of their lives (2010a: 249, 245, 255). They also remained concerned about protecting family and friends from the consequences of their involvement in the sex industry and continued to fear reprisals in the form of abuse and negative judgments from others because of their job (2010a: 247).

In spite of the ongoing stigma, Abel and Fitzgerald (2010a: 241) report that most PWSI in their study "did not internalize shame and were angry at the perceived injustice and contravention of their human right to be able to choose and work within an industry without discrimination." They seemed to be very aware that social acceptance would not come automatically with changes to the legal system. They also recognized that the PRA had little or no impact on the public's perceptions of their job. As Petal, a private female worker, reported, "no laws have the power to do that. The people have to change" (Abel and Fitzgerald 2010a: 241). Thus, decriminalization on its own is not enough to foster respect and dignity or to remove stigma from sex work.

Securing Safe Work Locations

Job security is another major concern for PWSI. According to PWSI, job security is "physical safety on the job, securing a safe working environment, rights to protection, health and well-being, and economic security" (STAR 2006: 8). Participants in the Sex Trade Advocacy and Research (STAR) project also specified that when securing their work environment it was helpful to create solidarity with fellow workers, screen clients thoroughly, insist on discretion regarding the choice of clients and develop strategies for dealing with clients (STAR 2004).

Attaining safety and security on the job is extremely difficult under the first two models. In fact, several Canadian studies have shown that the law actually criminalizes actions that help keep PWSI safe and secure (Lewis and Shaver 2011; Shaver et al. 2011; STAR 2006; Lewis et al. 2005, 2005a; Benoit and Millar 2001; Lowman and Fraser 1996). For example, in-call workers[6] report that operating in a known space increases the control they can exercise over the environment and, consequently, their security. Physical security is also increased by being driven to work, by sharing in-call spaces with other workers and by working for someone who runs a massage parlour or brothel. Since the costs of advertising, attracting clients and providing the work location are either shared or carried by the owner/manager, this strategy also increases the worker's economic security. However, these strategies violate sections 210, 211 and 212 of the *Criminal Code of Canada* (Lewis et al. 2005, 2005a).

Sections 213 and 173 are particularly problematic for street-based workers. Section 213 criminalizes direct sex worker–client communication in a public place as well as using a cellphone or payphone to make worker-client arrangements. PWSI say this severely limits their capacity to screen for potential bad dates, aggressors and other risks. In addition, when conducting business in a car, for example, it is safer to select a semi-discrete location (for example, a dark parking lot) where people pass by occasionally (in case there is a need to call for help) but this still contravenes section 173 (indecent behaviour in a public place) and may contravene section 174 (public nudity). If a worker opts to rent a hotel room for the evening in which to entertain clients in order to avoid this risk, costs are increased, as is the likelihood of being charged under section 210 (keeping or being found in a common bawdy house) (Lewis et al. 2005, 2005a; see also van der Meulen and Durisin 2008).

Job security is also extremely difficult to achieve under the Nordic model. In spite of the desire to achieve gender equality by combating violence against women and sexual harassment at work, Scoular (2010) reports that the consequences for PWSI in Sweden are remarkably similar to those operating in a criminalized environment. The practical effects of the law led to a temporary reduction in street work, the displacement of women and men into more hidden forms of sex work and the worsening of conditions for those who remained on the streets (Scoular 2010: 18). Several studies reported that street-based workers were being forced to move into illegal brothels or to work alone from indoor locations, leaving them more isolated than before and subject to greater risks of violence and stress. Furthermore, despite the fact that purchasing sex was criminalized irrespective of location, Scoular's (2010: 19–20) research shows that the law is selectively enforced: the main focus is on the highly visible spaces of street-based prostitution, generating higher levels of risk and danger to street-based workers, those who are most vulnerable to risk.

In contrast, a report recently released by the Swedish Government (SOU 2010) concluded that the ban on the purchase of sexual services was successful. The report claims that the halving of street prostitution in Sweden — unlike in Denmark and Norway — represents a "real reduction in prostitution" and not simply a shifting of arenas to the Internet, that this reduction is mainly a result of the criminalization of sex purchasers, that the ban has countered the establishment of organized crime and that it has not had a negative effect on people exploited through prostitution (that is, on PWSI) (SOU 2010: 35–37). There have been a number of critiques of this report. Some focus on the extent to which the report simply ignores what "many sex workers say about how the law increases stigma and therefore their marginalization in society" (Agustin 2010). As well, the methodology is suspect. For example, the report lists PWSI as sources, but only a total of fourteen individuals from two organizations filled out the questionnaire. In addition, they are referred to in a discriminatory manner as "exploited persons." Agustin (2010) concludes that the report's conclusions are questionable.

Secure work locations are easier to achieve under legalization, at least for those working in the legal sector. Indeed, there is little doubt that workers in legally regulated brothels are safer and healthier than those who work in illegal venues or on the streets (Brents and Hausbeck 2005; Harcourt et al. 2001; Weitzer 2005; Wolffers and van Beelen 2003). Comparing sexual practices before and after legalization in Australia, Seib et al. (2008) found that the legal brothels were "smoke-free and alcohol- and drug-free, have a compulsory condom policy, and workers receive compulsory training in personal protection, safe sex negotiation, and visual screening for STIs" (Seib et al. 2008: 9). Nevada's legal brothels are similar in that they "offer the safest environment available for women to sell consensual sex acts for money" (Brents and Hausbeck 2005: 289). Evidence from these and other studies make clear that

> sex workers in brothels are much less vulnerable to violence and sexual assault because of the presence of other staff, increased possibilities for screening clients, and the provision of alarms. Where brothels are legal and subject to the normal requirements of operating a business, additional safeguards will also be in place as operators are required to pay attention to maximizing the occupational health and safety of workers — for example via the provision of adequate lighting, private areas for workers, and personal protective equipment such as condoms. (Jeffrey and Sullivan 2009: 65)

In addition, legal workers are more likely than their counterparts in the illegal sector to take assault and sexual assault complaints to the police (Prostitution Licensing Authority 2004 cited in Jeffrey and Sullivan 2009: 65).

However, Jeffrey and Sullivan (2009: 65) also identify the drawbacks to legalization, including the high costs in terms of workers' rights and the lack of established normal working conditions. One group of PWSI in their study described licensed brothels as "oppressive work environments":

> They are paid as independent "sub-contractors" rather than as "employees," which means that they do not have access to normal employment entitlements like sick leave, recreation leave, or employer contributions to pensions. [And] despite their status as "sub contractors," owners and managers of licensed brothels impose a wide range of controls on sex workers including the hours they can work, what they can wear to work and the prices they may charge for their services. (Jeffrey and Sullivan 2009: 66)

Furthermore, client choice is not always guaranteed, and workers who refuse to see particular clients are subject to sanctions that may include quiet shifts with fewer opportunities to earn money (Jeffrey and Sullivan 2009: 66).

Working conditions appear to be more enhanced under decriminalization. According to Jeffrey and Sullivan (2009), decriminalization in New South Wales has made a big difference, particularly in terms of improving safety and protecting rights. Street-based workers are less likely to sustain the criminal fines that tend to force them back into street work as they can legally solicit clients and take them to a local "safe house brothel" and they are more prepared to protect their rights and speak up about client and other violence (2009: 67). Decriminalization in New South Wales also permits a diverse range of working environments, including the choice to work in a large brothel (with the option of being an employee or a sub-contractor) or a smaller business, to establish their own brothel or escort agency (including co-operatives), or to work privately. As is the case with other workers, the availability of different working environments allows PWSI to optimize their own situation, maximize their safety and protect their rights (Jeffrey and Sullivan 2009: 68).

More recent research from New Zealand shows a similar pattern. Decriminalization there has enabled workers to become more aware of their occupational safety and health rights, increased their legal rights and afforded some legitimacy to their occupation. In addition, the legalization of employment and legal rights have given many sex workers the confidence to avert or react to situations that hold potential for violence. Participants from all legal sectors report that legal rights have improved since the PRA has been enacted. For example, PWSI can ensure their safety — without fear of entrapment — before going to a room or getting into a car by making clear to clients what to expect from a transaction (Abel and Fitzgerald 2010: 221–23).

Significantly fewer managed workers reported having to accept an unwanted client after decriminalization (Abel and Fitzgerald 2010: 225). And, "even when management was resistant to change, some participants talked of the knowledge of their rights and what they could insist on" (2010: 226). Although some reported that working on the street still meant having to accept the possibility of violence, they often clarified that the streets had become safer after decriminalization (2010: 226). "More than half… thought that police attitudes had changed for the better since the law had changed," and many maintained they were less hesitant to report adverse incidents to the police (2010: 228–29). However, street-based and private workers were significantly more likely than managed workers to report this. Overall, the evidence indicates that decriminalization provides the best possible environment for PWSI to achieve their first two objectives: more respect and dignity and secure work locations.

Health and Well Being
Since the passage of the *Prostitution Reform Act* in 2003, New Zealand's sex industry has been operating under health and safety regulations. Workers, managers and business establishments are regulated using regional labour standards legislation, occupational health and safety codes and zoning regulations. Only the most disruptive and abusive activities associated with some sex work — coercion, kidnapping, physical assault, sexual assault and unlawful confinement — are regulated using criminal law. This combination of factors has reinforced the ability of PWSI to ensure safe(r) sex practices (Abel and Fitzgerald 2010: 220) and secure their work environments through the provision of occupational, employment, and legal rights. They have not, however, served to fully address all health issues. Risks to emotional health as a result of the stigmatization attached to sex work still remain (2010: 234).

It must be noted that it is possible for PWSI to access health and legal services under the first three models (criminalization, the Nordic model and legalization), especially in settings where the state is committed to harm reduction programs, but it is not always to their advantage. For example, clean needles and condoms — and, in Vancouver, a safe injection site — are available to PWSI operating under criminalization, but research indicates that police sometimes "stake out" the facilities — particularly harm reduction programs that provide condoms and needle exchanges — and when workers exit, they are "harassed," "frisked for drugs" and "pulled into" police cars for background checks and "questioning" (Shaver et al. 2011: 58). In San Francisco, the possession of condoms may be used as circumstantial evidence of intent to commit prostitution (Lutnick and Cohan 2009: 38). Drawing on case studies in two industry sectors in Canada (massage and escorting), van der Meulen and Durisin (2008: 300) report that concerns regarding public health and safety (often built into bylaws requiring medical examinations for licensed PWSI) are premised on the assumption that sex workers transmit infection, thus reinforcing the stigma of being a "disease carrier." Contrary to this assumption, research conducted in Canada (Benoit and Millar 2001; Phillips and Benoit 2005; Johnston et al. 2006; Remple et al. 2006) and North America and Europe (Ward et al. 2004) shows that, under certain social and economic conditions, PWSI practise high levels of safer sex during commercial encounters and serve as a vital gateway to sexual health promotion for clients and non-paying sexual partners (Canadian HIV/AIDS Legal Network 2005; Sanders 2006). Sanders (2004) reports that PWSI in Britain view risks to sexual health as minor: they have well-maintained strategies to ensure condom use and view it as a controllable feature of their work.

In Sweden, where there is no state support for harm reduction, it would be very difficult to develop safe(r) sex practices and/or clean needle programs. State-run exit programs are available alongside poverty reduction measures aimed at women in order to prevent their entry into the sex industry. In addition, access to more traditional health and social services available to all Swedish citizens could well be available to PWSI. However, it is more likely that the ongoing criminalization of sex purchasers and the stigmatization of sex workers will make it difficult for PWSI to access these services without also participating in exiting programs.

Under legalization, workers in legal brothels are subject to compulsory health examinations. These rules seem unreasonable, since they do not apply to other vulnerable service workers (such as doctors, nurses and dentists), as well as inappropriate, since PWSI generally have a low incidence of STIs (Harcourt et al. 2005). In addition, the mandatory medical checks may lead to a false sense of security and less condom use if clients assume that a safe bill of health justifies not using a condom. Finally, regardless of the legal approach in place (criminalization, the Nordic model or legalization), studies also show that ongoing stigma and marginalization are likely to limit the access of PWSI to both health and legal services (Jeffrey and MacDonald 2006; STAR 2006; Scoular 2010). In addition, the greater the stigma and marginalization, the less likely PWSI are to be open about their occupation when discussing their health with a health care provider (Benoit and Millar 2001; Jeffrey and MacDonald 2006; STAR 2006; Scoular 2010). Decriminalization seems to provide the best environment for achieving the goals for health and well being set out by PWSI (see the summary on Table 2).

Labour Rights and Protections
Studies evaluating labour rights and economic security under each approach are small in number and few, if any, comparative studies have been conducted.

However, it is not unrealistic to conclude that labour concerns are likely to be overlooked under criminalization since sex work is not seen as a legitimate revenue-generating activity. As reported above, there is little capacity in the regulation of brothels under legalization to address the important workplace issues. There are no standardized working conditions, and workers — often paid as independent sub-contractors rather than employees — have "no access to... employment entitlements like sick leave, recreation leave, or employer contributions to pensions" (Jeffrey and Sullivan 2009: 65–66).

As has been argued above, labour rights and protections would be impossible under the Nordic model. Given that the goal is to abolish sex work altogether, the initiatives in place are designed to help PWSI exit the trade; labour rights and protections are not part of the plan.

Labour rights and protections were clearly part of the plan in New Zealand. The new legislation represented a shift to a public health and human rights approach that includes occupational health and safety for sex workers. The purpose of the PRA was to decriminalize prostitution (without morally sanctioning it) and to create a framework that would safeguard PWSI's human rights and promote their occupational health and safety (OHS) while being conducive to public health (Abel et al. 2010a: 77).

Many of the participants in the study by Abel and Fitzgerald (2010a) discussed how decriminalization facilitated OHS rights, and most were aware they now had such rights under the PRA. However, more work remains: only two-thirds had seen the Ministry of Health pamphlets giving information on the safe sex requirements situated under the PRA and "less than half had seen the occupational, safety and health (OSH) guidelines published by the Department of Labour" (Abel and Fitzgerald 2010: 219). As in other legal settings, however, those in managed sectors — in comparison to participants in other sectors — were more aware of their rights and significantly more likely to have seen both publications (2010: 219).

The reports on the New Zealand sex workers' fight for decriminalization (Abel et al. 2010) have little to say about access to labour unions and cooperatives, but it is likely that decriminalization would enhance these options. First, the approach itself is grounded in labour rights and responsibilities. Second, sex work is seen as a viable occupation.

Such initiatives would be impossible under the Nordic model and unlikely under criminalization. Nevertheless, I have reported elsewhere that some union and cooperative initiatives are already in place in spite of criminalization (Shaver 2008). There is an Exotic Dancers Union in San Francisco, the West Coast Co-op of Sex Industry Professionals in Vancouver (Davis 2008) and a Brothel Project in Victoria (Casey 2008). In addition, the Canadian Union of Public Employees supports the idea of there being a union for PWSI (CUPE 2005). While it is good to see that criminalization does not completely eliminate such initiatives, decriminalization would likely facilitate them more readily.

Economic Security

A final and key concern of PWSI is economic security. This includes access to long-term economic security, opportunities to invest and the ability to file taxes based on their work in the industry without risking their assets. Since there is little research on sex worker economic security, I can really only speculate on this aspect.

Under criminalization, such security is jeopardized through proceeds of crime legislation that hinders workers' capacity to save or invest for the future (Lewis et al. 2005: 17). Short-term economic security is threatened as well, through the fines and legal costs often associated with the illegal activities associated with engaging in the legal activity of selling sexual services. This cycle can lead to a revolving door situation — especially for street-based workers — that greatly increases their economic vulnerability.

Economic security for all may be possible in Sweden given the greater amount of economic and social equality built into their extensive social programming; however, it is unlikely that this would apply to PWSI. As mentioned earlier, the underlying goal of the ban on the purchase of sexual services is to abolish the industry. Thus, economic security would only become possible on exiting the industry. Opportunities for economic security are more likely under legalization, although only for registered brothel workers. On the other hand, they would be significantly enhanced under decriminalization, in part because it is recognized as a viable, revenue-generating activity.

Overall, with respect to all nine concerns identified by PWSI, the evidence indicates that decriminalization is likely to provide PWSI with the most supportive environment for addressing their concerns. Of the nine concerns listed in Table 2, seven have already achieved various levels of support and the remaining two are only partially supported. No other regime does as well.

Concerns of Residents

People who live in the areas where sex work occurs have two key concerns: the nuisance and noise associated with street-based prostitution and indecent acts taking place in public (both signs of disrespect), and specific concerns that have to do with ensuring the safety and security of their neighbourhoods. In the latter case, this usually means eliminating the danger of used needles and condoms along with the risk of abuse and/or violence directed to them or their children. Unfortunately, there is little data currently available about the degree these concerns are adequately addressed under any of the legal approaches. However, the evidence that is available, most often provided by key informants, such as municipal politicians and service practitioners, suggests that the initiatives usually designed to resolve these concerns are more likely used to penalize individual PWSI than to address the disturbing behaviour.

For example, in Montreal and Toronto, problems related to street-based prostitution are to be addressed, in part, through programs such as the Projet-Pilote, John School and Cyclope, Streetlight and Temps d'Arrêt and community or targeted policing (Shaver et al. 2011: 54). These projects were considered largely unsuccessful by both key informants and PWSI. The conflicting perceptions of "the problem" and therefore "the solution" were paramount on their lists. Many noted that the definition of the problem was based on residents' concerns, excluding PWSI who lived and worked in the same neighborhood. As a result, a common program goal was to rid the streets of prostitution entirely. Other participants argued that the initiatives seemed to be designed primarily to ensure the security of the public, while ignoring security concerns of PWSI.

Key informants also argued that the projects were grounded in a simplistic understanding of the sex industry and of the people working in it. The industry was seen as a danger to residents and PWSI were perceived to be a homogenous group "in need of saving," rather than diverse individuals with dissimilar needs (Shaver et al. 2011: 55). Informants also anticipated

Table 3: Policy Approaches and the Concerns of Residents

Concerns of Residents	Likelihood of Support Under Each Legal Environment			
	Criminalization	Nordic Model	Legalization	Decriminalization
Nuisance & Noise: - Eliminate nuisance & noise of street-based prostitution - Prevent indecent acts in public - Eliminate disrespect toward residents	P: Possible and there have been initiatives (but not to resolve these problems; when implemented, the focus is on the individual PWSI and not the disruptive activity).	P: Possible (but success for residents under this model puts PWSI at greater risk since sex work must operate underground).	P: Some residential locations protected(for example, brothels in isolated rural areas or industrial zones) Public perceptions of PWSI are more positive.	S: Most protected (more PWSI will be able to work inside and some municipalities have bylaws limiting brothel locations).
Safe/Secure Neighbourhoods: - Eliminate the danger of dirty needles and used condoms - Protection for residents and their children from the risk of violence/ abuse	P: Possible (but the Projet-Pilote initiative in Montreal failed due to lack of support from the residents; anti-client legislation makes the situation worse for PWSI).	P: Possible (but success for residents puts PWSI at greater risk since sex work must operate underground).	P: Possible (but some disruptive and dangerous activities not addressed (not all are related to prostitution activities).	P: Most concerns addressed (focus on the disruptive and dangerous behaviours regardless of link to the sex industry). No increase in street-based sex work.

Note: NS=non-supportive; P=partially supportive; S=supportive negative and unexpected outcomes from several of these programs. For example, Cyclope and John School increased working hours for PWSI since they resulted in a decrease in clients. Residents' complaints to the police led to increased crackdowns on strolls and the creation of zones of tolerance; these actions dispersed and relocated workers, increasing their vulnerability and limiting their access to resources (2011: 12–13). Thus, while partially resolving the resident-identified problems, these initiatives actually worsened the situation for street-based sex workers.

The ban on purchasing sex in Sweden had a similar effect. Although there is no supporting research, residents may well have noticed fewer disturbances on the streets and perhaps less danger for themselves and their families. However, possible success for the residents comes at the expense of PWSI, who are at greater risk since they must operate underground (Scoular 2010; Agustin 2010).

Legalization addresses some resident concerns since most of the legally sanctioned brothels in Nevada, for example, are located in isolated rural areas. In Queensland and Victoria (Australia), the location of a brothel "has to be approved by the local (municipal) council and most licensed brothels are therefore located in industrial or commercial zones," far away from residential areas (Jeffrey and Sullivan 2009: 62). Such policies may serve to eliminate the alleged nuisance, noise and dangers linked to prostitution, but they do not address disruptive and dangerous behaviours linked to other street-based activities (whether perpetrated by residents, street children or late-night traffic, for example), nor do they address the safety and security concerns expressed by PWSI. Nevertheless, according to a report by the Prostitution Licensing Authority (2004), opening legal spaces for sex work in Queensland has had a positive impact on public perceptions that "sex workers are entitled to the same rights as others (as human beings, citizens and workers) and on sex worker advocacy in defense of these rights" (cited in Jeffrey and Sullivan 2009: 65).

This positive change in public perception is likely to be even more enhanced under decriminalization. Together with the positive changes in police attitudes toward PWSI, more attention is likely to be paid to the disruptive activities, rather than the individuals alleged to be creating the disruption. In addition, enabling PWSI to work inside may well reduce (although not eliminate) street-based activities. Although there are only a few restrictions on street-based prostitution in New South Wales (for example, soliciting is not permitted near schools or places of worship) and none in New Zealand, street-based prostitution did not increase with the advent of decriminalization nor become more disruptive (Jeffrey and Sullivan 2009: 63–64; Abel, Fitzgerald and Brunton 2009). In fact, population estimates of street-based sex workers in Christchurch, New Zealand, were marginally less after the PRA (100 versus

106), while the number of private workers increased slightly, the number of managed workers dropped, and there was no significant increase in the total number of sex workers (Abel, Fitzgerald and Brunton 2008: Table 2-2).

In sum, residents' concerns are more or less addressed regardless of the legislative environment in place. However, it is obvious that decriminalization provides the only environment with the potential for addressing the concerns of residents without jeopardizing those of PWSI (see the summary in Table 3).

The Viability of Critical Social Programs

Social programs are essential components to all four approaches. Whether they are designed to address sex work as work, eliminate stigma and marginalization in police and court responses, educate the public and policymakers about the diversity within the sex industry, provide economic and organizational support for sex work organizations, facilitate the provision of education and job training for (exiting) PWSI or support national and international research, all have been identified as essential components of a well rounded approach to sex work. The key question is under what regimes are these goals likely to meet with the least amount of resistance? This issue has not been widely studied; thus the evaluation is limited to programs where some comparative evidence or logical arguments are available: labour, health and safety standards; the elimination or reduction of stigma; and the education of the public, police and policymakers.

For example, common sense suggests that it would be difficult to respond positively to labour, health and safety standards under criminalization when PWSI carry an outlaw status. Using similar reasoning, it would be impossible to implement such standards under the Nordic model (the objective is to abolish prostitution) and complicated to implement them under legalization (sex work is regulated, for the most part, using criminal law).

Eliminating stigma and discrimination in police and court responses and improving relations between the police and PWSI are also difficult goals to achieve under these three approaches. Sex workers continue to be very apprehensive about the police under the first two — as is reflected in their reluctance to report crimes to the police (Lowman 2000; Jeffrey and MacDonald 2006; Pyett and Warr 1997; Campbell and Kinnell 2000/2001; Lewis and Maticka-Tyndale 2000; Abel et al. 2010) — and, although possible, there is no clear evidence that relations with the police improve under legalization. On the other hand, there is some evidence that opening the legal space for sex work in Australia also had a positive impact on public perceptions that PWSI are entitled to the same rights as others and on sex worker advocacy in defence of these rights (Jeffrey and Sullivan 2009: 65). This has not been the case under criminalization, where there is evidence indicating that relations between PWSI and residents have deteriorated (Shaver et al. 2011).

These three program goals seem to be most viable under decriminaliza-tion. In New South Wales and New Zealand, health and safety standards applicable to PWSI are already built into labour code legislation and are having a positive impact on the workers (Abel and Fitzgerald 2010, 2010a). The New Zealand study also provides evidence that police attitudes toward PWSI are more positive (Abel and Fitzgerald 2010: 228–29). However, there is no clear evidence that public attitudes have changed in New Zealand or that relationships between PWSI and residents have improved. In addi-tion, evidence from media studies suggests that educating the public and policymakers will be a difficult task. The print media coverage of sex work post-PRA was neutral towards the Act overall, but there were many negative

Table 4: Policy Approaches and the Viability of Social Programs

| Critical Social Programs | Likelihood of Support Under Each Legal Environment | | | |
	Criminalization	Nordic Model	Legalization	Decriminalization
Labour, health and safety standards: - Ensure industry operates un-der the same health and safety rules as other businesses - Ensure PWSI have rights and protections	NS: Difficult to promote. PWSI carry an outlaw status and continue to be stigmatized.	NS: Impossible to promote. PWSI seen as victims and sex work as exploitation.	NS: Difficult to promote. Sex work regulated using criminal law. Limited access to labour rights.	S: Possible. Outlaw status is removed. OHS for PWSI built into labour code legislation.
Eliminate/reduce stigma - Eliminate stigma & dis-crimination in police & court responses - Improve police-PWSI relations	NS: Difficult (sex work stigma-tized & workers apprehensive of police).	NS: Difficult (sex work stigma-tized & workers apprehensive of police).	P: Possible (sex work still stigmatized; no evidence that relations have improved).	S: Possible (stigma reduced). Some evidence that police at-titudes are more positive.
Educate the public & policy-makers - Dispel myths about sex work & PWSI - Improve resident-PWSI relations	NS: Difficult. It is generally assumed that ste-reotypes are ac-curate. Programs designed to improve relations failed.	NS: Difficult. Stereotypes about clients and managers remain & are reinforced in the law.	P: Possible. There is some evidence that public perceptions are more positive.	P: Possible and essential in order to counteract residents' con-cerns, but no clear evidence that relations have improved.
Overall support of each ap-proach for the concerns of all stakeholders (PWSI, residents and social programs).	Non-supportive in nine areas. Partially support-ive in five areas. None likely to be supported.	Non-supportive in eleven areas. Partially sup-portive in three areas. None likely to be supported.	Non-supportive in four areas. Partially sup-portive in nine areas. Supportive in one area.	Non-supportive in zero areas. Partially sup-portive in three areas. Supportive in eleven areas.

Note: NS = non-supportive; P = partially supportive; S = supportive themes. The most common was that "sex work was a threat to the dominant morality, even though there was no empirical evidence to support this theme" (Fitzgerald and Abel 2010: 209). Politicians' views were overrepresented in the media while those of sex workers were underrepresented (Fitzgerald and Abel 2010: 203, Table 12-1), and letters to the editor rarely expressed positive views to the PRA (2010: 202). This is regrettable in a decriminalized context, given that the media are an important conduit through which to normalize relationships between PWSI and the rest of society (Silverstone and Georgiou 2005 cited in Fitzgerald and Abel 2010: 198). However, on a positive note and with respect to justice personnel and policymakers, when a number of local bodies (city councils in Christchurch, Auckland and Hamilton) attempted to regulate street-based sex work in particular settings, they were overturned for contradicting the human rights and public health aims of the PRA (Knight 2010).

DECRIMINALIZATION IS THE MOST PROMISING POLICY ALTERNATIVE

What can be concluded from the above discussion? Answering this question rests on whether the concerns of PWSI and residents are supported and the social programs are deemed feasible. Clearly, the model currently in place in Canada — criminalization with tolerance — does not adequately address these issues: nine of the fourteen objectives identified in Tables 2 to 4 are likely to go unsupported and only five are partially supported. The Nordic model does no better: objectives are unsupported in eleven of the fourteen areas of concern and only partially supported in three. None are unequivocally supported. In contrast, legalization and decriminalization fare much better, but the support for all stakeholder goals is highest under decriminalization, where all fourteen of the concerns identified are either partially supported (three) or fully supported (eleven). Under legalization, only ten of the fourteen areas are partially supported (nine) or supported (one). There were no non-supported areas in decriminalized environments in comparison to four under legalization.

As argued above, residents' concerns are more or less addressed regardless of the legislative environment in place. Their concerns are only partially supported under all but one model — that of decriminalization — where it is likely that concerns regarding nuisance and noise are likely to be successfully addressed. However, it is clear that decriminalization provides the only environment with the potential for addressing the concerns of residents without jeopardizing those of PWSI.

Three areas remain problematic for PWSI in a decriminalized environment: the lack of respect for PWSI, clients, managers and employers; the ongoing stigma and marginalization experienced by PWSI; and the challenges to developing education programs designed to dispel myths and misunderstandings about sex work and PWSI. In fact, these three areas were unsupported or only partially supported under all four models. These results highlight the importance of combining legal reforms with social policy programs involving education, support and advocacy under all circumstances. Such programs are likely to facilitate the recognition and acceptance of PWSI as full citizens and sex work (involving consenting adults) as a legitimate revenue-generating activity.

Labour rights and access to labour unions and cooperatives — both overlooked under legalization — provide another indication of how and where to begin program initiatives. In addition to recognizing these rights, it will also be essential — when modifying labour codes — to seek input from a full range of people, including sex workers, managers and employers, clients (a group whose concerns were not considered in this analysis), residents and policymakers. Only rarely have sex workers or their allies been represented in policy discussions regarding approaches to prostitution. This must change if the codes are to be modified to reflect the wide diversity of workers in the industry.

My second intent when writing this chapter was to provide readers with the tools necessary for conducting a just and fair analysis on their own. Such an analysis depends on a critical approach to the claims being made, the evidence (or lack of evidence) supporting those claims and a willingness to remain open to all options in spite of personal morality. In addition, the search for rational and pragmatic solutions to the so-called prostitution problem must be grounded in an understanding of justice and fairness that is context-based (that is, grounded in the lived experiences of individuals in their everyday lives).

Will these tools be sufficient? Some say no, arguing that justice must also be compassionate. Brian Dickson, the late chief justice of Canada, urged his colleagues to practise compassionate justice. It was his belief that,

> for the law to be just, it must reflect compassion. For a judge to reach decisions that comport with justice and fairness, he or she must be guided by an ever-present awareness and concern for the plight of others and the human condition. (Cited in Mahoney 2010: 150)

This is good advice for researchers and laypeople alike. Following it requires a shift away from moral discourses and stigmatizing terminology and a willingness to critically weigh the validity and reliability of all available evidence. Similar to our counterparts in New South Wales and New Zealand, we should stop moralizing about sex work and adopt legal and social reforms grounded in rational and pragmatic solutions to concrete problems that are both just and fair. Decriminalization, I would argue, provides the most appropriate environment for achieving this goal.

Notes

1. PWSI refers to adults involved in the exchange of sexual services, or explicitly sexual fantasies, for money, goods or services. The term "sex workers" is also used for this group of people.
2. For a lengthier discussion of these analytic tools see Shaver (2012).
3. Harm reduction is any program or policy designed to reduce or minimize the adverse health and social consequences related to risky behaviours (such as substance use or unsafe sex) without requiring the cessation of that behaviour. Interventions may be targeted at the individual, the family, the community or society.
4. A condensed version of this table appears in Table 2 in Lewis and Shaver (2011).
5. A condensed version of Tables 2 to 4 appears in Table 1 in Shaver (2012).
6. In-call work involves the client coming to the worker's place of business (such as a brothel or sex work establishment). Out-call work involves the worker going to the client (for example, a hotel room, home or office).

References

Abel, G., and L. Fitzgerald. 2010. "Risk and Risk Management in Sex Work Post-Prostitution Reform Act: A Public Health Perspective." In G. Abel, L. Fitzgerald and C. Healy with A. Taylor (eds.), *Taking the Crime Out of Sex Work: New Zealand Sex Workers' Fight for Decriminalisation*. Briston: Policy Press.

___. 2010a. "Decriminalisation and Stigma." In G. Abel, L. Fitzgerald, and C. Healy with A. Taylor (eds), *Taking the Crime Out of Sex Work: New Zealand Sex Workers' Fight for Decriminalisation*. Briston: Policy Press.

Abel, G., L. Fitzgerald and C. Brunton. 2008. "The Impact of the PRA on the Health and Safety of Sex Workers." Invited presentation at the University of Victoria in conjunction with the WHRN Workshop: Strategies to Reduce Violence and Promote the Health of B.C. Sex Workers (April).

___. 2009. "The Impact of Decriminalization on the Number of Sex Workers in New Zealand." *Journal of Social Policy* 38, 3.

Abel, G., L. Fitzgerald, and C. Healy with A. Taylor (eds.). 2010. *Taking the Crime Out of Sex Work: New Zealand Sex Workers' Fight for Decriminalisation*. Briston: Policy Press.

Abel, G., C. Healy, C. Bennachie and A. Reed. 2010a. "The Prostitution Reform Act." In G. Abel, L. Fitzgerald, and C. Healy with A. Taylor (eds.), *Taking the Crime Out of Sex Work: New Zealand Sex Workers' Fight for Decriminalisation*. Briston: Policy Press.

Agustin, Laura. 2010. "Behind the Happy Face of the Swedish Anti-Prostitution Law." At <lauraagustin.com/behind-the-happy-face-of-the-swedish-anti-prostitution-law>.

Barnett, Laura. 2008. "Prostitution in Canada: International Obligations, Federal Law, and Provincial and Municipal Jurisdiction." Ottawa: The Library of Parliament, Parliamentary Information and Research Service (PRB 03-30E).

Benoit, Cecilia, and Alison Millar. 2001. *Dispelling Myths and Understanding Realities: Working Conditions, Health Status, and Exiting Experiences of Sex Workers*. Prostitutes, Education, Empowerment and Resource Society (PEERS). At <peers.bc.ca>.

Benoit, C., K. Vallance, M. Jansson and B. McCarthy. 2008. "Inequalities in Health

Status and Access to Health Services among Frontline Services Workers."
Presented at the International Sociological Association Research Committee
on the Sociology of Health (RC15) and the Canadian Medical Sociology
Association Inaugural Meeting, Montreal.

Brents, B., and K. Hausbeck. 2005. "Violence and Legalized Brothel Prostitution in
Nevada." *Journal of Interpersonal Violence* 20.

Campbell, R., and H. Kinnell. 2000/2001. "'We Shouldn't Have to Put Up with
This': Street Sex Work and Violence." *Criminal Justice Matters* 42.

Canadian HIV/AIDS Legal Network. 2005. *Sex, Work, Rights: Changing Canada's criminal
laws to protect sex workers' health and human rights.* At <aidslaw.ca/EN/publications/
index.htm>.

____. 2007. *Not Up to the Challenge of Change: An Analysis of the Report of the Subcommittee
on Solicitation Laws.* At <aidslaw.ca/EN/publications/index.htm>.

Casey, Lauren. 2008. "Behind Closed Doors: An In-Depth Look at the Indoor
Sex Industry." Presented at the Canadian Sociology Association, 43rd Annual
Meeting Sociological Perspectives — Thinking Beyond Borders: Global Ideas,
Global Values. University of British Columbia (June 3–6). Summary at <peers.
bc.ca/images/BehindClosedDoors.pdf>.

Criminal Code of Canada (CCC), R.S.C. 1985, c. C-46.

CUPE (Canadian Union of Public Employees). 2005. "Sex Work: Why It's a Union
Issue." *CUPE*, 1-5. At <cupe.ca/updir/BackgroundPaper-SexWorkEng.doc>.

Davis, Susan. 2008. "Sex Industry Stabilization/Safe Work Environments." Presented
at the Canadian Sociology Association, 43rd Annual Meeting. Vancouver:
University of British Columbia (June 3–6). Also at <wccsip.ca>.

Farley, M. 2004. "Bad for the Body, Bad for the Heart: Prostitution Harms Women
Even if Legalized or Decriminalized." *Violence Against Women* 10.

Federal–Provincial–Territorial Working Group on Prostitution (F–P–T). 1998. *Report
and Recommendations in respect of Legislation, Policy and Practices Concerning Prostitution-
Related Activities.* Ottawa: Department of Justice Canada.

Fitzgerald, L., and G. Abel. 2010. "The Media and the Prostitution Reform Act." In
G. Abel, L. Fitzgerald, and C. Healy with A. Taylor (eds.), *Taking the Crime Out of
Sex Work: New Zealand Sex Workers' Fight for Decriminalisation.* Briston: Policy Press.

Hallgrimsdottir, H., R. Phillips and C. Benoit. 2006. "Fallen Women and Rescued
Girls: Social Stigma and Media Narratives of the Sex Industry in Victoria,
BC, from 1980 to 2005." *Canadian Review of Sociology and Anthropology* Special
Issue 43, 3.

Hallgrimsdottir, H., R. Phillips, C. Benoit and K. Walby. 2008. "Sporting Girls,
Streetwalkers, and Inmates of Houses of Ill Repute: Media Narratives and
the Historical Mutability of Prostitution Stigmas." *Sociological Perspectives* 51, 1).

Harcourt, C., I. van Beck, J. Heslop, M. McMahon and B. Donovan. 2001. "The
Health and Welfare Needs of Female and Transgender Sex Workers in New
South Wales." *Australian and New Zealand Journal of Public Health* 25.

Harcourt, C., and B. Donovan. 2005. "The Many Faces of Sex Work." *Sexually
Transmitted Infections* 81.

Jeffrey, L.A., and G. MacDonald. 2006. *Work, Stigma, and Resistance: Sex Workers in the
Maritimes Talk Back.* Vancouver: UBC Press.

Jeffrey, L.A., and B. Sullivan. 2009. "Canadian Sex Work Policy for the 21st Century:

Enhancing Rights and Safety, Lessons from Australia." *Canadian Political Science Review* 3, 1.

Johnston C., V.P. Remple, V. Bungay, R. Leclair, D.M. Patrick, M.W. Tyndall, A.M. Jolly, J. Barnett and G. Ogilvie. 2006. "Condom Use of Indoor Commercial Sex Workers (CSW) in Vancouver, BC: A Quantitative and Qualitative Analysis." Poster presentation, 15th Annual Canadian Annual Conference on HIV/AIDS Research, May, 2006, Quebec City, QC.

Knight, Dean. 2010. "The (Continuing) Regulation of Prostitution by Local Authorities." In G. Abel, L. Fitzgerald, and C. Healy with A. Taylor (eds.), *Taking the Crime Out of Sex Work: New Zealand Sex Workers' Fight for Decriminalisation.* Briston: Policy Press.

Lewis, J., and E. Maticka-Tyndale. 2000, "Licensing Sex Work: Public Policy and Women's Lives." *Canadian Public Policy* 26, 4.

Lewis, J., E. Maticka-Tyndale, F.M. Shaver and K. Gillies. 2005. "Health, Security and Sex Work Policy." Invited presentation to the House of Commons Subcommittee on Solicitation Laws (SSLR), Ottawa Canada. At <uwindsor.ca/star>.

Lewis, J., E. Maticka-Tyndale, F.M. Shaver and H. Schramm. 2005a. "Managing Risk and Safety on the Job: The Experiences of Canadian Sex Workers." *Journal of Psychology and Human Sexuality, Special Issue* 17, 1/2.

Lewis, J., and F.M. Shaver. 2011. "The Regulation of Adult Sex Work and its Impact on the Safety, Security, and Well-Being of People Working in the Sex Industry in Canada." In Rochelle L. Dalla, John DeFrain, Lynda M. Baker, and Celia Williamson (eds.), *Global Perspectives on Prostitution and Sex Trafficking: Europe Latin America, North America, and Global.* Lexington Books.

Lowman, J. 1990. "Notions of Formal Equality before the Law: The Experience of Street Prostitutes and Their Customers." *Journal of Human Justice* 1, 2.

____. 2000. "Violence and the Outlaw Status of (Street) Prostitution." *Violence Against Women* 6, 9.

____. 2009. "Deadly Inertia: A History of Constitutional Challenges to Canada's *Criminal Code* Sections on Prostitution." Unpublished manuscript, School of Criminology, Simon Fraser University. At <mypage.uniserve.ca/~lowman/>.

Lowman, John, and Laura Fraser. 1996. *Violence Against Persons Who Prostitute: The Experience in British Columbia, Technical Report No. TR1996-14E.* Ottawa: Department of Justice Canada.

Lutnick, A., and D. Cohan. 2009. "Criminalization, Legalization or Decriminalization of Sex Work: What Female Sex Workers Say in San Francisco, USA." *Reproductive Health Matters* 17, 30.

Mahoney, K. 2010. "What Is Justice?" *The Trudeau Foundation Papers*, Volume 11: 130–59. At <trudeaufoundation.ca/resource/public/trudeaupapers/trudeaupapers_2010pdf>.

McCarthy, B., C. Benoit and M. Jansson. 2006. "Occupational Stigma and Health." Stigma and Global Health Research Networking Meeting. Rosslyn, Virginia, U.S.

Occupational Safety and Health Service (OSHS). 2004. *A Guide to Occupational Health and Safety in the New Zealand Sex Industry.* New Zealand, Occupational Safety and Health Service, Department of Labour. At <osh.dol.govt.nz>.

Pérez-y-Pérez, Maria. 2007. "The Struggle to Minimize Risk and Harm for Sex Workers in New Zealand: The Prostitution Reform Act 2003." *Te Awatea Review* (August).

Phillips, R. 2006. "Courtesy Stigma, Health Service Providers and Vulnerable Populations." CIHR National Student Research Poster Competition. Winnipeg, Manitoba.

Phillips, R., and C. Benoit. 2005. "Social Determinants of Health Care Access among Sex Industry Workers in Canada." *Sociology of Health Care* 23.

Pyett, P., and D. Warr. 1997. "Vulnerability on the Streets: Female Sex Workers and HIV Risk." *AIDS Care* 9, 5.

Raymond, J. 2003. "10 Reasons for Not Legalizing Prostitution." Coalition Against Trafficking in Women International (CATW). Retrieved June 20, 2006 from <rapereliefshelter.bc.ca/issues/prostitution_legalizing.html>.

___. 2004. "Prostitution on Demand." *Violence Against Women* 10, 11.

Remple, V.P., D.M. Patrick, M.W. Tyndall, C. Johnston and A.M. Jolly. 2006. "Sexual Networks of the Indoor Commercial Sex Industry: Implications for HIV and STI Propagation." (Abstract).

Sanders, Teela. 2004. "The Risks of Street Prostitution: Punters, Police and Protesters." *Urban Studies* 41, 9.

___. 2005. "Blinded by Morality? Prostitution Policy in the UK." *Capital and Class* 86.

___. 2006. "Female Sex Workers as Health Educators with Men Who Buy Sex: Utilizing Narratives of Rationalizations." *Social Science and Medicine* 62.

___. 2007. "Protecting the Health and Safety of Female Sex Workers: The Responsibility of All." *BJOG* 114.

Scoular, Jane. 2010. "What's Law Got to Do with It? How and Why Law Matters in the Regulation of Sex Work." *Journal of Law and Society* 37, 1.

Seib, Charrlotte, Michael P. Dunne, Jane Fischer and Jackob M. Najman. 2008. "Commercial Sexual Practices Before and After Legalization in Australia." *Archives of Sexual Behavior.* Published online, 30 December.

Shaver, F.M. 1993. "Prostitution: A Female Crime?" In Ellen Adelberg and Claudia Currie (eds.), *In Conflict with the Law.* Vancouver: Press Gang Publishers.

___. 1994. "The Regulation of Prostitution: Avoiding the Morality Traps." *Canadian Journal of Law and Society* 9, 1.

___. 1996. "The Regulation of Prostitution: Setting the Morality Trap." In B. Schissel and L. Mahood (eds.), *Social Control in Canada.* Oxford University Press.

___. 2005. "Sex Work Research: Methodological and Ethical Challenges." *Journal of Interpersonal Violence* 20 (3): 296–319. At <uwindsor.ca/star>.

___. 2005a. "Sex Work Policy: An Integrated Approach." Invited presentation to the House of Commons Subcommittee on Solicitation Laws (SSLR), Ottawa Canada. At <uwindsor.ca/star>.

___. 2008. "Legal Approaches to Sex Work: Opportunities for Positive Action." Invited presentation at the WHRN Workshop *Strategies to Reduce Violence and Promote the Health of BC Sex Workers,* Victoria, BC (April 30).

___. 2012. "Legislative Approaches to Prostitution: A Critical Introduction." In *Reading Sociology: Canadian Perspectives.* Second Edition by the Canadian Sociology Association, Lorne Tepperman and Angela Kalyta. Oxford University Press.

Shaver, F.M., J. Lewis and E. Maticka-Tyndale. 2011. "Rising to the Challenge: Addressing the Concerns of People Working in the Sex Industry." *Canadian Review of Sociology* 48, 1.

Shumka, L. and C. Benoit. 2008. "Social Suffering and Gaps in Alternative Health

Care for Vulnerable Women Workers." *Sociology of Health Care* 25.

SOU (Statens offentliga utredningar). 2010 "Evaluation of the Ban on Purchase of Sexual Services." (English summary). Ministry of Justice, Government Offices of Sweden. At <sweden.gov.se/content/1/c6/14/92/31/96b1e019.pdf>.

Special Committee on Pornography and Prostitution (The Fraser Committee). 1985. *Pornography and Prostitution: in Canada, Volume II*. Ottawa: Department of Supply and Services.

Standing Committee on Justice and the Solicitor General. 1983. Report to the House, *Solicitation for the Purposes of Prostitution*.

___. 1990. *Report of the Standing Committee on Justice and the Solicitor General Concerning the Three-Year Review of Section 213 of the Criminal Code*.

SSLR (Subcommittee on Solicitation Laws of the Standing Committee on Justice and Human Rights). 2006. *The Challenge of Change: A Study of Canada's Criminal Prostitution*. Ottawa: Government of Canada.

STAR (Sex Trade Advocacy and Research). 2004. *Security Matters*. At <uwindsor.ca/star>.

___. 2006. *Safety, Security and the Well-Being of Sex Workers: A Report Submitted to the House of Commons Subcommittee on Solicitation Laws (SSLR)*. Windsor, ON. At <uwindsor.ca/star>.

van der Meulen, E., and E.M. Durisin. 2008. "Why Decriminalize? How Canada's Municipal and Federal Regulations Increase Sex Workers' Vulnerability." *Canadian Journal of Women and the Law* 20.

Ward, H., S. Day and J. Weber. 2004. "Declining Prevalence of STI in the London Sex Industry, 1982–2002." *Sexually Transmitted Infections* 80, 5.

Weitzer, Ronald. 2005. "Flawed Theory and Methods in Studies of Prostitution." *Violence Against Women* 11.

___. 2006. "Moral Crusade against Prostitution." *Society* (March/April): 33–38.

___. 2010. "The Mythology of Prostitution: Advocacy Research and Public Policy." *Sex Research Social Policy* 7.

Wolffers, I., and N. van Beelen. 2003. "Public Health and the Human Rights of Sex Workers." *Lancet* 361.

CHAPTER ELEVEN

SCARECROWS AND CANARIES
Justice and the Youthful Other
Bryan Hogeveen and Joshua Freistadt

In the late spring of 2010, two youth were stabbed within hours of each other outside the Stanley Milner Library in downtown Edmonton. In the weeks that followed, these events and this space became a lightning rod for public disdain regarding all that is wrong with the downtown area and the marginalized young people who frequent it. Such events afford an opportunity to understand and think through contemporary understandings of justice for youth. In this chapter, we show that city officials reacted to these events by concentrating more police officers in this space, encouraging police to detain more young people for minor offences and instructing police to stop and search anyone appearing suspicious (read: harassing Aboriginal youth). This proposal is curious given that library staff claim that disorderly incidents in the downtown library decreased nearly 50 percent from the previous year and the number of patrol officers in the downtown were increased twofold a few months earlier (Kent 2010b; Anonymous 2010). Such tenuous suggestions make a just response difficult. That is, efforts that might welcome youthful others are brushed aside in favour of resolutions that close down and expel youth from prime urban space.

City responses to this event clearly evidence the dominant approach to justice for young people. Instead of amelioration and emancipation of the marginalized Other, officials have put more police on the streets and ensured that young people who do not appear to fit middle class standards of acceptability are expunged from inner-city space. Unfortunately, far too many contemporary politicians and media outlets consider padding police budgets and buoying the prison industrial complex as the *sine qua non* of contemporary justice while monies for essential helping services continue to erode. In this chapter, we question such hegemonic discourses. Instead of perpetuating Otherness and exclusion through contemporary processes and tactics that close down upon and exclude the Other, we argue for a just hospitality that would fashion future spaces of welcome for those young people coercively expunged not only from downtown city space, but the social world.

Encounters with strangers, particularly marginalized young people in inner city space, raise an important question about justice: How should we relate to the Other? We begin to address this important question via Jacques

Derrida's (2005, 2002b, 2000, 1999) unique understanding of "hospitality." Following Derrida, we argue for an ethic of hospitality that creates spaces of welcome for the Other and ameliorates the suffering of marginalized populations. In the context of a violent exclusion of the Other (often, but not exclusively, in the form of policing practices), whereby policies of risk management, privatization, self-governance and policing, precaution and populist will (what we would call neo-liberal rationalities put into policy practices) shunt the marginal into spaces of confinement far removed from the economically privileged, creating spaces of welcome and a corresponding ethic of hospitality for marginalized populations is critical — for their survival, for their dignity and, most of all, for justice.

This chapter emerges out of our study of homelessness in the inner city of Edmonton and draws on interviews with social service providers and young people, newspaper accounts, city and not-for-profit group reports and homeless counts.[1] We rely heavily on interviews we conducted with two social workers — Sam and Tim.[2] Both individuals have worked in the social service industry for many years and, as such, are ideally situated to provide insight into how contemporary strategies of governing difference in the inner city impact marginalized young people. Sam says that he has seen things that would "scare the shit out of you."

In contrast to the police and political response, a group of organizers, including iHuman Group Society (a not-for-profit group that provides programming for at-risk youth), is attempting to carve out a hospitable space for inner city young people through an urban-style Olympics. Held in a space that is typically foreclosed to young people (Churchill Square), the Games are an attempt to showcase the talents and interests of marginalized young people (such as skateboarding, hip hop and pow-wow dancing).

"HOSPITALITY": DERRIDA AND JUSTICE

Using Derrida's theorizing when addressing questions of justice may seem odd given his insistence that "there is nothing outside the text" (Derrida 1997: 158), but this would be to dismiss his political and discursive engagements. That Derrida was fundamentally concerned with justice inside and outside of academia and its intersection at the political and ethical levels is not always obvious. It may come as a surprise to many that Derrida struggled for human rights in Prague, railed against apartheid in South Africa and addressed the thorny issue of immigration and amnesty in France (Jennings 2006). His prose was similarly dedicated to questions of ethical being and justice (see, for example, Derrida 2002a, 1992, 1995, 2000).

Derrida (2002a) was convinced that justice was not, like every other idiom, deconstructable. He (2002a: 237, emphasis in original) argues:

That is how I would like to employ myself here: to show why and how what one currently calls deconstruction, while seeming not to "address" the problem of justice, has done nothing else while unable to do so directly but only in an oblique fashion. I say *oblique*, since at this very moment I am preparing to demonstrate that one cannot speak *directly* about justice, thematize or objectivize justice, say "this is just," and even less "I am just," without immediately betraying justice, if not law.

Derrida often (re)turns to questions of justice in his writings, but he reminds his readers that these queries remain deferred fundamentally because justice does not lend itself to equations that take the form of "justice = x" (Jennings 2006).

The English language employs justice in a variety of ways: we have a justice system; there are justices of the peace; Canada boasts a federal Department of Justice; it is used in law and legislation to imply the impartiality of the system (for example, the *Youth Criminal Justice Act*); and it is even a village in Manitoba (located northwest of Brandon) (Hogeveen and Woolford 2009). If these are all instances of justice, how can Derrida say that it is constantly deferred? Primarily because Derrida seeks justice beyond a right, a justice "finally removed from the fatality of vengeance" (Derrida 1994: 21). As John Caputo (1997: 131) explains:

> Justice is not a present entity or order, not an existing reality or regime; nor is it even an ideal eidos towards which we earthlings down below heave and sigh while contemplating its heavenly form. Justice is the absolutely unforeseeable prospect in virtue in which the things that get deconstructed are deconstructed.

For Derrida, then, "justice appears as a promise, beyond law, and is itself incalculable, infinite and undeconstructable" (Pavlich 2007: 989). It is not a thing or person or even a law to which we may point or hold up as exemplary.

There is a fundamental opposition between justice and law that makes the latter incapable of fabricating justice. Consider, for example, the gross over-representation of the Indigenous and marginalized Other in Canada's courts of law and centres of detention (Minaker and Hogeveen 2009; Calverley et al. 2007; Corrections Investigator of Canada 2006). The arrest of Aboriginal youth for violence and property crimes by the nation's police forces is not fundamentally injudicious in its relation to law, nor is their incarceration inept under law. Quite the opposite, their frequent arrest and detention are faithful to the letter of law. However, when considered in the context of structural patterns of discrimination and centuries-old racism toward the

Other that is manifest in arrest and detention records (detention in both jails and residential schools), it becomes clear that there is a problem with law as justice (Jennings 2002). Such an intrusion into the life of the Other is legal, but fundamentally unjust because Aboriginal youth are being condemned and subjected to pain and deprivation through law. Such youth are charged by agents of the state, as individuals rather than as members of a collective culture. The law is left in place, uninterrogated and unquestioned, and the notion that justice is synonymous with law is undisturbed. The oppression of the Other seemingly supports this notion.

Derrida (2005, 2000, 1995) was convinced that justice is grounded in an impossible ethical and hospitable being with the Other that is always deferred and to come. In other words, whatever hospitability is imagined and afford-able to the Other is forever put off to another speculative end point. This notion speaks to the seeming impossibility of justice through law.

The inevitable critique is that being hospitable is futile and nihilistic. This is a charge often levelled at Derrida and his interlocutors. This critique, however, is easily answered. Deconstruction promotes disquiet in thinking about laws implicated in marginalizing the Other. Our provocation of the ethical over the legal, with justice over law, occurs at a time of increasing levels of pain being administered to the poor and marginalized in an effort to whet the public's appetite for revenge and retributive justice (Wacquant 2009). Under Stephen Harper, the Conservative Party of Canada is rallying for more prisons and more severe punishments (Curry 2010; Lunau 2010). In Edmonton, the police force is employing law toward the further mar-ginalization of the Indigenous Other. Sam provided the following example of how Kron initially came to police attention in large part because of the colour of his skin:

> So Kron is sitting at a bus stop and he is Native. The police drove by and just said "Oh, who are you?" So he says his name and they say, "Well what are you doing here?" And he says, "Well what do you think? I am waiting for a bus." But he is a Native kid, so they run him on the system. And they said, "Oh, you have some warrants for not complying, you have a ticket for drinking, you are this and that." So he has five warrants. In the system four warrants you can get a PTA [promise to appear]. Five warrants you maybe get a no-cash bail. Six warrants you are gonna go to jail. So they cops give him a charge of a breach. So he has six and the justice of the peace gives him three months in the slammer and they ship him out.

Marginalized Others suffer most dramatically at the hands of this cruelty administered by agents acting on behalf of the state. By refusing to accept arbitrary coercion and the harassment of the Other that is justified through and in law, we seek increasingly more just ways of being that would necessarily provoke political action in the name of justice to come (or justice deferred). This move towards justice needs to be translated into entrenched socio-legal, political and economic systems in order to move further away from state-sanctioned violence.

Because over-policing young people has more to do with those who benefited most from colonialism, we insist on interrogating the question of "hospitality" alongside and through questions of justice. Hospitality pertains to our sense of "us" and "them." It concerns how we relate to ourselves, our home, our country and the marginalized Others who seem alien, foreign and dangerous. It pivots on questions of justice and involves an unfettered openness to the Other (Derrida 2000; Molz and Gibson 2007; George 2009). Openness moves beyond the idea of tolerance, because tolerance suggests merely accepting an Other in privileged spaces, but those spaces are still not for or of the Other in that they are not the Other's spaces.

In an ethos of a violent exclusion of the Other, whereby state practices shunt the marginal into spaces of confinement far removed from the economically privileged, questions inspired by hospitality to and for the marginalized Other are urgent: where the gravest interest concern life and death, well being and destruction (Hogeveen and Freistadt forthcoming). Such an ethic demands pushing beyond imposed limits by shredding conventions that are manifest in tensions between visitor and owner, stranger and host, poor and affluent. Such an undertaking is no doubt difficult and even dangerous. Even if unconditional hospitality is seemingly impossible or beyond contemporary ontological limits, we should nevertheless continue to push established limits beyond current iterations toward a welcome of the Other without reservation or calculation — "an unlimited display of hospitality to the new arrival" (Derrida 2005: 66).

Hospitality is politics and ethics rooted in reverence for the unnamed and always potentially dangerous Other. It is, as David Carroll (2006: 823) maintains, "a politics whose ultimate horizon is unlimited." Hospitality demands acts of total munificence and an opening of space to an unknown and unknowable other (Carroll 2006). It is a politics that does not accept limits imposed upon itself, but always asks "What's next?" and in response relentlessly pushes against established exclusionary boundaries of being. It is in the name of hospitality to the marginalized, the excluded and incarcerated Other that we articulate an unrelenting ethical and political demand for and to justice (Carroll 2006). Taking the ethical demand embedded in hospitality seriously provokes such queries as: How can we fashion spaces of and for the Other in an ethos of intolerance and hatred?

THE INHOSPITABLE POLITICS OF EDMONTON

Efforts to constrain marginalized young people by increasing police presence must be situated in the context of concerted city council attempts to revitalize Edmonton's downtown. Recently, efforts to this end have taken many forms, including the provision of financial incentives to real estate investors, re-zoning and plans to build a new arena and accompanying entertainment district (City of Edmonton 2010; Kent 2010a, 2010c; McKeen 2010). Churchill Square and the Stanley A. Milner Library are very much at the centre of the city's ambitions (City of Edmonton 2010). Predictably, the marginalized and excluded who frequent this city centre space do not appear to figure into the city's plans other than as obstacles to profitable revitalization.

Since 1997 (and perhaps even before), several proposals have been forwarded and reports commissioned with an eye to redeveloping Edmonton's downtown into "a high-density residential, employment, education and entertainment centre" with a distinct "pedestrian orientation" that situates the downtown core as "the only truly urban retail destination within the metropolitan region" (City of Edmonton 2010: 148, 9, 65). As it stands, the area surrounding the Milner Library and Churchill Square are only intermittently frequented by the consumer classes. In recent months the municipal government released a blueprint (the *Capital City Downtown Plan*) for the future development of downtown that will put the pieces in place to reverse this trend. The city calls its formula "a bold vision for Edmonton's downtown that is... sustainable. Vibrant. Well Designed. Accessible" (City of Edmonton, n.d.). City council's goals are to fashion a showcase for Edmonton and increase revenues from this downtown space. According to the report, if fully implemented, it would result in increased urban densification, increased economic activity, increased tax revenues and, but not limited to, higher land values that would ostensibly benefit the entire city and capital region (City of Edmonton 2010: 49).

The report, however, conveniently neglects to mention anything concrete about the needs and concerns of the marginalized Others who currently call the downtown streets and public spaces home. Current conditions of life for those living and existing on downtown streets are disregarded and conveniently omitted from the report. Thus, the downtown core, now inhabited by society's most marginalized groups, is treated as an open and empty space simply awaiting redevelopment. Indeed, it is now considered a space of wasted economic potential that could be exploited to capitalist ends. Such an outcome is to be expected when the overwhelming majority of report advisors were government officials and members of Edmonton's business community, with only a sprinkling of social service representatives. Furthermore, there was no representation from among the homeless or youth population on the advisory board (see City of Edmonton 2010: vi).

Despite the exclusion of the young, marginalized Other from the consultation process, several references are made in the report to disinfecting the disordered space of downtown. For example, it bemoans, "the existence and perception of a crime problem that can cause a vicious cycle — residents move from Downtown, lowering the desirability of the area, making it a more attractive locale for criminal or socially undesirable behaviour" (City of Edmonton 2010: 33). Enhancing the "overall aesthetic quality of Sir Winston Churchill Square and nearby properties" (City of Edmonton 2010: 162) takes centre stage in the report. Excluding young marginalized people from both the planning and the words of the report itself make it loud and clear that these disenfranchised youth are Other to the image the city hopes to foster through revitalization.

The report proposes two strategies to address the allegedly threatening disorder that is said to haunt downtown. First, all major downtown streets will be designed with continuous street-level retail, featuring storefronts at uniform distances facing wide sidewalks. Increasing "natural surveillance" through foot traffic and "eyes on the street" is the intended goal (City of Edmonton 2010: 82, 102). Second, the report suggests that increasing the number of festivals occurring in Churchill Square would attract crowds of the economically privileged (City of Edmonton 2010; see also Sands, 2010). Festivals are typically highly planned city-permitted events that cordon off Churchill Square, surround it with food vendors and fill it with suburban residents and security officials. Churchill Square's usual inhabitants are routinely chased away. To date, festivals for the marginalized Other that attend to their unique interests and welcome them into the city centre are conspicuous by their absence. While city officials consider this space open for the economically privileged and middle class suburbanite, it is closed to the marginalized Other.

Consumer spaces set aside for the privileged exclude the homeless and youthful Other. They are unwelcome intruders in places of economic potential where the beacons of the neo-liberal economy spend, earn and invest. Marginalized populations, who are set apart by their economic destitution and inability to participate fully in a consumption-driven economy, are excluded from planning sessions and city centre space. Blemishes on the space reserved and set out for economic investment, they are shooed away through scarecrow policing and shunted into jails in order to make room for capitalist expansion.

Canaries in the Hospitality Coalmine: Young People in Edmonton's Inner City

Young people expunged from the space surrounding the Milner Library and Churchill Square are overwhelmingly society's most marginalized and traumatized. They are also most likely to be Aboriginal. Canada's Aboriginal population is younger, less well educated, less likely to be employed, more likely to be homeless and exceedingly more likely to be incarcerated than any other group (Statistics Canada 2006). Furthermore, Indigenous young people are grossly overrepresented among the homeless population. Aboriginal people comprise roughly 19 percent of Edmonton's population. Tragically, a conservative estimate advises that they constitute 40 percent of the city's homeless (Homeward Trust 2008). Discussions with social service providers suggest that this number might be misleading. The long time executive director of an inner city agency told us that these numbers reflect the older homeless group. She maintains that up to 70 percent of the young homeless population (under twenty-four years old) she encounters claim Aboriginal heritage.

Fetal alcohol spectrum disorder (FASD) is also overrepresented among the Aboriginal population. FASD has lasting and significant effects. According to the Edmonton Fetal Alcohol Network people living with FASD have brain damage for which there is no current cure (EFAN 2010). Janine Hutson (2006: 2) claims that approximately "50 percent of children in care in Alberta have [FASD]." Although no accurate statistics on incidence are available, Square (1997) argues that prevalence among the entire population is about 1 to 3 cases per 1,000 live births, while among Aboriginals is believed to be between 55 and 101 per 1,000 live births (Fuchs et al. 2010).

Individuals with FASD are often afflicted with learning disabilities, chronic health issues, alcoholism and mental illness (EFAN 2010). Both Tim and Sam confirmed that it is a significant issue among street-involved youth. Sam complained that the "[FASD] thing is rampant." Because of FASD, Tim suggests that these young people "can't deal with stressors in a normal way. So they are always being victimized, or they are victimizing." Sam routinely encounters FASD's many deleterious effects. He maintains that while FASD is certainly significant, it is important that we understand the disease in the context of the street. For instance, Sam recounts that Katherine, a street teen

> has a beautiful heart and when she is not on drugs or drunk, is a beautiful person, but she has no coping skills having severe [FASD] and she is all brain damaged from being beaten up as a youth. She has problems. And that is all that matters.... [As a result,] her coping skills are so low that if you come up to Katherine and say something to her, she doesn't care how big you are, she can throw you across the room. She has got that much shit inside her and she uses that.

Street-involved Aboriginal youth face countless barriers and circumstances that too often result in their entrenchment on the street (Minaker and Hogeveen 2009). In addition to FASD, many marginalized young people, like Katherine, face vulgar family environments that consequently result in significant pathways to the street. As Tim argues:

A lot of them just can't live at home because there is too much chaos. It's not large enough. There are infrequencies in the areas of basic needs. Like food comes and goes, comes and goes; clothing. There is lots of violence, alcohol and drugs. So they gravitate towards the streets.

Many young people, Tim explains, are looking for spaces of inclusion. However, the traditional space of hospitality for many middle class young people, the family home, is too often a hostile space that marginalized young people find filled with violence and ravaged by addiction. Faced with violence, abuse and general disorder, the street becomes a refuge. Phil's story is illustrative. The twenty-seven-year-old former gang member, who is now involved in social service work, cannot recall at time when his life was not disrupted by fighting and abuse. Since his father never took an active role in his life, his relationship with his mother largely shaped his childhood experience, and it is through her relationships with abusive men that he became intimate with violence. He remembers:

One time she came home and her shirt was all bloody. She finally passed out in her bedroom and I sat by her bed all night because her nose was all messed up, eh? I don't know if I found out what had happened at that age or if it was somewhere down the road that I found out that my cousin punched her out. My cousin weighs between 350 and 400 pounds. This was all because she wouldn't buy any more beer at the bar. So he broke her nose. She couldn't really breathe, so I stayed up with her all night, sitting by her bed, wondering if she would be okay.

Violence coloured Phil's childhood. His mother, like many other Aboriginal women in Canada, suffered at the hands of her male partners. Not only are Aboriginal women three times more likely than non-Aboriginal women to suffer domestic violence, but 90 percent of federally sentenced Aboriginal women report having been sexually abused (Canadian Association of Elizabeth Fry Societies 2006; Amnesty International 2004). Further, the past two decades have witnessed over 500 Aboriginal women go missing. Most are presumed dead (Amnesty International 2009). Aboriginal families once ripped apart by the residential school system continue to be destroyed through violence and death (Armitage 1993; Kline 1992). Is it any wonder, then, that increasing numbers of Aboriginal youth come to call the streets home?

Like Phil's mother, these growing numbers of marginalized street youth experience severe and often traumatizing victimization. Tim explains that "they can always point to where they have been victimized either physically, or sexually, or, they don't understand emotionally, but its there too." By contrast, the youth worker claims:

> If I went to Holy Trinity school [a school that caters primarily to the middle class] and talked to ten random adolescents and say, "Have you ever been victimized?" you know, maybe one or two would identify. But if I went to Churchill Square and I talked to ten adolescents of the same age, I am looking at nine or ten [that] can point to something fairly traumatic.

Research confirms that street-involved young people experience an elevated risk of violent victimization (Baron 2009, 2003; Erickson, Butters and Bruno 2009). On the afternoon that Sam talked to us, he had spent his morning attending to a girl who had been raped the previous evening. Sam conveys the brutality of life on the streets for young women and the magnitude of the problem:

> He [the rapist] flipped her over and she tried to resist, because she is so small, and he raped her, you know…. No is no. I never heard anybody say no is yes. So that is the problem you are facing. This is a huge problem.

Substance use constitutes a significant part of street youth's daily routine (Baron 1999). Tim argues, "There is normalization of alcohol consumption. There is this normalization of cannabis. There is this normalization of ecstasy or Crystal Meth, or crack, or even heroin now. I mean it just doesn't ripple them anymore. It's a given." And street-involved young people go to whatever lengths necessary to secure resources for their drug of choice. Tragically, as a result of cuts in the 1990s that relegated many helping services to the social welfare dustbin (Laxer and Harrison 1995; Harrison 2005), too few treatment beds are currently available in Edmonton to handle street-entrenched young people (CBC News 2009a). Awaiting assistance, these young people too often continue along a self-destructive path. Sam provides a telling example: "That is what the girls do. I had a girl sell herself last week for some booze. Get a hundred dollars from a guy. She calls it a trade, but it is selling herself."

Unwanted and expunged from contemporary society and with insufficient resources reserved for them, many marginalized young people never receive the help they need or want. Conversely, political officials are all too ready to release the most coercive (and costly) forms of social control to govern their conduct. Resources that deliver pain, which are the most expensive and least effective, are seemingly the only investment in marginalized young people that political officials are willing to make (Hogeveen 2005; Wacquant 2008).

Government cuts to welfare and social services during the 1990s have meant fewer young people in need are benefitting from social services (Lafrance 2005; Kinjerski and Herbert 2000; Kline 1997; Freistadt 2010). In the name of "fiscal tightening," the 1993 Alberta Government cut social assistance rates to the lowest in the country, especially for single parents (Lafrance 2005). Despite over fourteen years of significant budgetary surpluses, these rates have never fully rebounded. Instead, the province has chosen to hoard its surplus money into stock market "heritage funds" (which have since lost much value) to pay off debts it incurred bailing out failing private businesses, and to provide all citizens, regardless of need, with $400 rebate checks (Harder 2003; CBC 2006; Parkland Institute 2004, 2006). While social assistance rates and public spending were cut, Alberta instituted the country's most regressive income tax scheme (Parkland Institute 2009). These measures benefit only the wealthiest Albertans.

The trouble remains that there are far too many children and young people in need and too few helping resources. Indeed, only half of all homeless youth have access to emergency shelters (Homeward Trust 2008), while the other half are left to fend for themselves on unforgiving city streets that, incidentally, claimed the souls of fifty-seven homeless people in 2010 (Liewicki 2011). Many of these individuals lost their lives simply because they were unable to secure services that would meet their basic needs. The situation has worsened over the most recent economic downturn. Over a three-month period in 2009, Edmonton's Youth Emergency Shelter, the city's largest youth shelter, turned away countless kids due to bed shortages (CBC News 2009a).

Policing as Social Service
In contrast to helping services, resources dedicated to policing and incarcerating marginalized populations have been fortified. Recently, and at a time when the city is cutting many departmental budgets, the Edmonton Police Service (EPS) has demanded and been awarded an $11 million windfall. To this end, police officials threatened politicians and the public that failure to grant the increase would result in one hundred fewer officers on the street and more crime (CBC News 2009b). Armed with this information and considerable public support, politicians eagerly opened the public coffers to bolster police services. Such willingness to support the police, Tim states, is the result of an entrenched ideology where we have been told that "we are safer with more police. And no one has really challenged that." Indeed, the same level of hyperbole was not found or heard when urban Aboriginal programs, nonprofits and a homeless initiative were on the "chopping block" (McKeen 2009).

Policing, it seems, is our primary and most well funded resource for dealing with the excluded Other. Sam observes how his organization lacks the necessary funding to do effective helping work or provide his staff with much needed health benefits:

> Our staff doesn't get shit and they have no benefits.... We don't have any fucking money. Our budget is like $300,000 buddy. The police of Edmonton get a budget of $120 million last year, that is escalating every year by 10 percent. And more cops are being hired.

While countless dollars are being pumped into police budgets to bolster coercive interventions, social services and non-profit agencies are suffering under the weight of neo-liberal government restructuring. Sam maintains that while citizens eagerly approve budget increases for police and prisons, when it comes to social services they are much more reticent. He complains, "Nobody wants to pay for that stuff. So there again, I paid for medicines for half the kids in the city, nobody will pay for them. I bought a girl who got raped today, I bought her an after-pill because nobody paid for the damn thing, you know?" Those interested in justice will find it disappointing that citizens and government officials are keen to increase police annual budgets by millions but are absent when it comes to providing essential helping services. Predictably, the EPS has decided against deploying these resources to ameliorate the Other's suffering. They did, however, spend two million dollars to purchase a second helicopter to "provide... the opportunity to improve police efficiency and catch criminals and make more arrests" (EPS 2009; CBC News 2008).

Scarecrow Policing: Closing Inner City Space

The EPS has employed their resources to close down upon and exclude the Other. In the wake of the Milner Library stabbings, police officials have tightened their grip on this inner city space. To this end, they have increased the number of officers who patrol this area. This comes after the EPS had already doubled the number of beat officers downtown a few months earlier (Anonymous 2010). According to Police Chief Mike Boyd, the "extra police will patrol the square and interact more with the public, plainclothes officers will visit the area regularly and police will work with other security officials to make sure troublemakers are removed" (Sands 2010).

Marginalized young people are feeling the effects of increasing numbers of police on the street. According to Sam, "You can't even go anywhere. They are up your ass." One young person informed the *Edmonton Journal* that "there's lots (more police). We always get talked to, every single day" (Sands 2010). Tim bemoans how young marginalized youth are

> the canaries in the coalmine.... They are the first to experience, you know, knee-jerk reactions [of] the justice system. Even if it is

informal — example being that stabbing in the library where the young person was stabbed in the neck and, of course, there was this instant reaction by the police, by city council, by peace officers, by security, to become very aggressive towards young people. Not just in the library, but around the downtown area where they became very forceful and searching and harassing.

In addition to increasing police harassment and questioning of youth, police presence was rendered more obvious and prominent. Although seemingly benign, expanding police presence in this downtown public space effectively renders it inhospitable to marginalized youth. Tim describes this crackdown as "scarecrow policing": "They just want this really expensive piece of pine wood that they hire, and then they put on all sorts of body armour, and black gloves, and hats and they pound them in wherever they think crime is and scare the ravens away." Scarecrow policing involves a very visible police presence. Tim states: "They literally had a cop car parked in the middle of Churchill Square. Like sitting there, with a cop with his air conditioner on."

The goal is to not only deter criminality but to impress upon the affluent that something is being done about crime and disorder. Despite his critical attitude, Tim agrees that scarecrow policing is proving quite effective. He says: "You go there right now and there is no one there because, again, it's that scarecrow approach where they have been harassing young people to the extent of saying, "Why are you here?" I mean, to me, why would anyone ever ask me why am I here? Especially in a public place." Scarecrow policing obviously signifies that marginalized youth are unwelcome and thus contrasts sharply with the ideal of hospitality.

Scarecrow policing remains a band-aid that attempts to cover over the festering sores left over from centuries-old oppressions that are moving ever more dangerously close to the surface. Colonialism, FASD, poverty and chronic substance abuse are entrenched in our social world and demand attention, yet are perpetually neglected in favour of quick fixes and sound bites. For his part, Mayor Stephen Mandel claimed that the city could effectively solve the problems these young people were causing by simply moving the Milner Library entrance from where it now stands to quieter and less populated space. He argued: "(The Plaza) gives you more space. People aren't going to be as crowded" (Kent 2010b). How this proposal addresses structural inequalities that reproduce generational problems in the first instance is unclear. Perhaps this is the point. Focusing media and public attention on the triviality of the library's door as the cause and site of social disorder effectively shifts blame and public attention from stubborn antecedent conditions to relatively trivial, yet infinitely more pliable, objects. In the process, inequality and marginalization shamelessly continue undaunted.

Altering the door's location, or putting more officers on the street, for that matter, is inapplicable toward fashioning just spaces of hospitality for marginalized young people. Closing down space for the Other does not ameliorate suffering. It does nothing to address marginalization — such practices only entrench disadvantage. When police close the Milner Library space, young people will simply move. Let us be clear, however, this does not mean that the problem has been effectively solved. Tim says that when this inevitability occurs, the whole process will begin again. "And, of course, then we will just pick up these fence posts and we will pound these scarecrow cops somewhere else, and these ravens fly away and they just land on another tree. I mean that, it's simplistic, it's stupid." Displacing social problems leaves the foundation firmly rooted and the doors that open onto structural inequalities securely fastened. The question remains: How do we open space for the Other?

URBAN GAMES: RENDERING HOSPITABLE PUBLIC SPACE AND INSTITUTIONS

> The Urban Games are about at-risk youth engaging at-risk youth, youth, and the general public in activities and events that showcase their talents, gifts, and abilities and promote social change. It challenges pre-existing stereotypes and provides the opportunity to create compelling futures. (iHuman, 2010: 1)

How is it even possible to fashion a just and hospitable welcome to the marginalized youthful Other in an ethos where justice is primarily defined by violent exclusion and intrusive penalty? How should we receive these youth and carve out space for their difference? Given the increasing numbers of homeless youth and the ramping up of coercive state controls that further entrench marginality, these questions are urgent.

Youth workers, like Sam and Tim, recognize the urgency with which we must respond to the exclusion of young marginalized Others and provide spaces of welcome that open out to, rather than close down upon, youth. Toward this end, Tim and Sam have worked diligently with street involved youth to buck exclusionary trends and exploit the city's vision of Churchill Square as a cultural festival centre. While established, city-sponsored celebrations held in Churchill Square almost exclusively cater to the needs and interests of the affluent, what has been dubbed "the Urban Games" showcased the unique expertise of marginalized populations.

Collaboration on the Urban Games was distinctly unique. Instead of adults dictating the scope and nature of the games, youth were their catalyst and engine. The idea emerged after a particularly frustrating conference on the *Youth Criminal Justice Act* (YCJA), where the young people in attendance felt excluded from the conversations despite having been invited to provide a youth perspective. As is often the case, the young people were silenced and relegated to a supporting role. Time and again, young people are invited to criminal justice events to enter their concerns and unique perspective into the record only to be banished to the shadows (Hogeveen 2006). Young people are routinely silenced at such events and become frustrated at the lack of adult interest. An attendee at a criminal justice conference in 1994 complained about the almost complete disregard for youthful voices when he said, "Probably the biggest issue for most of the youth I spent time with was finding a voice and being 'heard' by the experts and the professionals" (National Crime Prevention Council 1997). Given their chronological age, level of maturity and apparent lack of relevant experience, young people are too often considered inferior (Minaker and Hogeveen 2009).

After the conference, Tim sat down with ten of the marginalized youth to discuss solutions and possible ways that youthful diversity might be celebrated. Championed by these enterprising young people were events that celebrated their distinct interests and showcased their inimitable talents. Although their interests and skills diverge from and are not always valued in the mainstream, these young people wanted to demonstrate that they are talented and that their interests require skill and are socially productive (iHuman, 2010). They proposed an event modelled after the Olympics that would feature less formally structured competitions that would nevertheless showcase activities marginalized young people enjoyed — hip hop and pow-wow dancing, hacky-sack, rap and skateboarding. However, they were adamant that the Urban Games not be a one-off event.

Tim's interest was piqued. He describes his meeting as an "ah-ha moment." Such an event would make marginalized "young people feel that this is their community as well; it is not just soccer clubs and hockey, it is also hip-hopping, and hacky-sack and those kinds of activities." Further, he now understood that it was about "allowing them a forum where they take centre stage in our community for a day or two." Toward this end, he approached his department for funding to support the youths' vision. The department, not needing ministerial approval for the limited amount he requested, obliged. To date, the funds have been used to hire seven marginalized young people at $17.50 an hour — twice the current minimum wage and well above the $13.25 determined to be the necessary living wage in Alberta (ESPC 2008) — to make the Urban Games a reality. After securing the necessary funds, the adults stepped back and encouraged these "at-risk" young people to "make themselves at home" and "take over the place."

Tim explains that working with young people to just ends necessarily means "allowing marginalized people more involvement, not just as the recipients of the justice system or the health care system or the transportation system, but being the deliverers of this model and encouraging them to be part of meaningful boards and programs where they have a real say." Young people involved in establishing the Urban Games "weren't just a steering committee, they were the rudder and the wheel of this project." A space of welcome and a corresponding ethic of hospitality for the marginalized young Other was carved out. Here young people could express themselves and have their proposals not only heard, but realized in form. The Urban Games will allow marginalized young people to exhibit not only their unique talents, but also their abilities to conceive and implement the products of their creativity.

In a twist of irony, the group solicited the City of Edmonton Administration to host the Urban Games in Churchill Square — the site of youth expulsion. In September 2010 Churchill Square hosted Canada's first-ever Urban Games to celebrate the activities of the at-risk youth that are regularly chased away from this space. Contrary to the contemporary patterns of closure around the Square, the Games opened this space to the Other in a celebration of the youth and the activities that city, police and justice officials regularly deem signs of disorder.

Despite carving into established hegemonic spaces of exclusion, there are limits to the Games' hospitality. While the Games challenge the borders of previously closed and unjust spaces and institutions, the Games expose two limits to a sense of justice to come. First, organizers must always remain cautious that they too do not alienate and disregard persons for whom the Games are intended. It must remain an open and hospitable space. Some of the evidence suggests that many young people felt excluded in the planning. Sam, for example, deplores the fact that only a select few marginalized young people were hired to work on the Games, while others are forced to either continue eking out a living through illicit means or working in dead-end jobs at minimum wage. He states:

> The Urban Games was a great idea but they paid them too much. All the other kids are mad. Pissed off. Why did they get all this fucking money? You hired seven kids. What about us? Kelsey, you know, working at KFC, can't keep it up, she was fired. She was in my car today and says, "I need a job, I need something."

Adult organizers should be commended for having secured seven spaces that would pay young people for their talents and efforts. Nevertheless, justice demands an open hospitality for all youth to benefit. Some will argue that this is an impossible demand. We agree. But the call to justice and for justice is infinitely demanding. Should we be contented that a select few are being rewarded while scores of others remain on the street and sell their bodies for alcohol? Justice demands pushing beyond imposed and imagined limits by abolishing conventions; hospitality requires an unconditional welcome to all.

Second, the Urban Games remains a festival and, like many such events, constitutes a temporary reversal of established rules. Measures ought to be taken to continually allow youth involvement in the development and delivery of not only the revitalization of Churchill Square but, more importantly, the justice system. Indeed, Churchill Square ought not to have returned to an exclusionary site after the Games. Permanent spaces of welcome that cater to the interests of marginalized Others must be fashioned. Hospitality requires that all doors remain open.

CONCLUSION

Our discussion of the Urban Games offers a glimpse into what a possible future that welcomes the marginalized Other in the name of justice might entail. Nevertheless, as it is here, and everywhere, justice is deferred. It is not yet. It is to come. The Urban Games could not go nearly far enough. Our vision is for a welcome unfettered by logistics and preconceptions — one that is brimming with respect for the Other who is encountered in, but too often excluded from, public space. The Urban Games pushes the limits of adult authority, but in the effort confirms and reaffirms their hegemony. While for two days in September 2010 marginalized youth culture was on display in the bastion of white hegemonic power, the same young people will no doubt continue to be banished from Churchill Square for the very same conduct. Police and security were close by to ensure that the guests did not overrun the space and overstay their welcome. The adult overseers were then, and are now, very much in control.

Such limited hospitality clearly demarcates boundaries established between self/Other, host/guest and included/excluded. Our suggestion is to move beyond this limited sense to an unlimited welcome of the Other in the name of justice. No one must be refused. Certainly, this form of ethical being and openness to Otherness creates the possibility that the space may be overrun and destroyed. But this is a situation that must be abided when we fashion spaces of welcome for those who inhabit a cruel and violent world. Are we content with current ontologies of being wherein the Other is held in cells and rigorously policed because of difference? Those who arrive and those now appearing on the horizon may conceal injurious intentions, but if we are to exclude them on the basis of this expectation there is no hospital-ity — no justice for the Other.

There is risk associated with this opening out to the Other, but it is a risk that must be accepted in the interests of pushing current limits of being and contemporary understandings of justice as punishment. Justice does not come at the end of an officer's gun, nor is it found in a prisoner's bunk, it is to be located in our infinite responsibility to all Others — especially those marginal-ized through racism, colonialism and market forces. Such an undertaking is no doubt difficult and even dangerous. Even if unconditional hospitality is seemingly impossible or beyond contemporary ontological limits, we should nevertheless continue to push beyond these limits toward a welcome of the Other without reservation or calculation.

Today, when young marginalized Others are victimized, drug addicted, homeless, unemployed and overrepresented in centres of incarceration, there is an urgent need for spaces of welcome. Supporting epistemologies of justice backed by the promise of more pain only serves to solidify contemporary patterns of exclusion. Rather, the need for a new ethic of hospitality without limits and without being constantly deferred is dire. It would not be intermittent, but would rather take the form of an unbroken space and time of welcome where boundaries between self/Other and included/excluded would necessarily become blurred.

Today there is a pressing need to reflect on and challenge systemic processes which (re)produce the Other, expunge them from public space and entrench them in state systems of control. We must work tirelessly in the name of a justice to come to welcome the marginalized Other with reverence and respect for their being.

Notes

1. Given its intimate ties to world energy markets, Edmonton is tightly integrated into processes that we describe in our forthcoming work as neo-liberal globalism (Hogeveen and Freistadt forthcoming).
2. To protect anonymity all names in this piece have been changed.

References

Amnesty International. 2004. *Stolen Sisters: Discrimination and Violence Against Indigenous Women in Canada.* Ottawa: Amnesty International. <amnesty.ca/campaigns/sisters_overview.php>.

____. 2009. *No More Stolen Sisters: The Need for a Comprehensive Response to Discrimination and Violence against Indigenous Women in Canada.* London: Amnesty International Publications.

Anonymous. 2010. "Moving Entrance No Solution." *Edmonton Journal,* May 11.

Armitage, Andrew. 1993. "Family and Child Welfare in First Nations Communities." In Brian Warf (ed.), *Rethinking Child Welfare in Canada.* Toronto: McCelland and Stewart.

Baron, Stephen. 1999. "Street Youths and Substance Use: The Role of Background, Street Lifestyle, and Economic Factors." *Youth and Society* 31, 1.

____. 2003. "Street Youth: Violence and Victimization." *Trauma Violence Abuse* 4, 1.

____. 2009. "Street Youths' Violent Responses to Violent Personal, Vicarious, and Anticipated Strain." *Journal of Criminal Justice* 37, 5.

Calverley, Donna, Adam Cotter and Ed Halla. 2007. "Youth Custody and Community Services in Canada, 2004/2005." *Juristat* 27, 2. Ottawa: Canadian Centre for Justice Statistics.

Canadian Association of Elizabeth Fry Societies. 2006. "Aboriginal Women." <eliza-bethfry.ca/eweek06/pdf/aborig.pdf>.

Caputo, John. 1997. *Deconstruction in a Nutshell: A Conversation with Jacques Derrida*. New York: Fordham University Press.

Carroll, David. 2006. "'Remains' of Algeria: Justice, Hospitality, Politics." *Modern Language Notes* 121, 4.

CBC (Canadian Broadcasting Corporation). 2006. "Boom Times: Alberta's Red-Hot Economy." *CBC News in Review*. Toronto: CBC Learning. At <newsinreview.cbclearning.ca/wp-content/uploads/2006/05/alberta.pdf>.

CBC News. 2008. "Edmonton Police Commission Calls for 2nd Chopper." *CBC News Online*, April 18. At <cbc.ca/canada/edmonton/story/2008/04/18/police-helicopter.html>.

____. 2009a. "Edmonton Street Children Turn to Emergency Shelters." *CBC News Online*, July 21. At <cbc.ca/canada/edmonton/story/2009/07/21/edmonton-youth-shelter-homeless-wards.html>.

____. 2009b. "Police Budget Still Over Recommended 3 percent Hike." *CBC News Online*. December 3. At <cbc.ca/canada/edmonton/story/2009/12/03/edmonton-police-budget.html.>

City of Edmonton. n.d. *Capital City Downtown Plan Website*. Edmonton: City of Edmonton. At <edmonton.ca/city_government/planning_development/capital-city-downtown-plan.aspx>. July 7, 2010.

____. 2010. *Capital City Downtown Plan*. Edmonton: City of Edmonton.

Corrections Investigator of Canada. 2006. *Annual Report of the Corrections Investigator of Canada, 2006*. Ottawa: Queen's Printer.

Curry, Bill. 2010. "Burgeoning Prison Budgets Spared the Axe." *Globe and Mail*, March 29.

Derrida, Jacques. 1992. *Given Time: I. Counterfeit Money*. Trans. Peggy Kamuf. Chicago: University of Chicago Press.

____. 1994. *Specters of Marx: The State of the Debt, the Work of Mourning, and the New International*. Trans. Peggy Kamuf. New York: Routledge.

____. 1995. *The Gift of Death*. Trans. David Wills. Chicago: University of Chicago Press.

____. 1997. *Of Grammatology*. Trans. Gayatri Spivak. Baltimore, MD: John Hopkins University Press.

____. 1999. "Hospitality, Justice and Responsibility: A Dialogue with Jacques Derrida." In Richard Kearney and Mark Dooley (eds.), *Questioning Ethics: Contemporary Debates in Philosophy*. New York: Routledge.

____. 2000. *Of Hospitality*. Stanford: Stanford University Press.

____. 2002a. "Force of Law: The 'Mystical Foundation of Authority.'" In Gil Anidjar (ed.), *Jacques Derrida: Acts of Religion*. London: Routledge.

____. 2002b. "Hostipitality." In Gil Anidjar (ed.), *Jacques Derrida: Acts of Religion*. London: Routledge.

____. 2005. "The Principle of Hospitality." In Rachel Bowbly (trans.), *Paper Machine*. Stanford: Stanford University Press.

EFAN (Edmonton and Area Fetal Alcohol Network). 2010. *Edmonton Area FASD – Home*. At <region6fasd.ca/home.php> August 7.

EPS (Edmonton Police Service). 2009. "Air 2 Takes to the Skies." *EPS News*. At <edmontonpolice.ca/News/SuccessStories/Air2TakesToTheSkies.aspx>

September 14.

Erickson, Patrica, Jennifer Butters, and Tara Bruno. 2009. "Victimization and Predatory Violence Among Street Youth in Toronto, Canada." *International Annals of Criminology* 47, 1/2.

ESPC (Edmonton Social Planning Council). 2008. *We Can Do Better: Toward an Albertan Child Poverty Reduction Strategy for Children and Families.* Edmonton: Edmonton Social Planning Council.

Freistadt, Joshua. 2010. "Navigating Potentially Competing Political Rationalities: Discursive Strategies about "Family" in Alberta's Child Welfare Law." *Canadian Journal of Family Law* 26, 1.

Fuchs, Don, Linda Burnside, Sheila Marchenski and Andria Mudry. 2010. "Children with FASD-Related Disabilities Receiving Services from Child Welfare Agencies in Manitoba." *International Journal of Mental Health and Addiction* 8, 2.

George, Siby. 2009. "Hospitality as Openness to the Other: Levinas, Derrida and the Indian Hospitality Ethos." *Journal of Human Values* 15, 1.

Harder, Lois. 2003. *State of Struggle: Feminism and Politics in Alberta.* Edmonton: University of Alberta Press.

Harrison, Trevor (ed.). 2005. *The Return of the Trojan Horse: Alberta and the New World (Dis)Order.* Montreal: Black Rose Books.

Harrison, Trevor, and Gord Laxer (eds.). 1995. *The Trojan Horse: Alberta and the Future of Canada.* Montreal: Black Rose Books.

Hogeveen, Brian. 2005. "'If We Are Tough on Crime, If We Punish Crime, Then People Get the Message': Constructing and Governing the Punishable Young Offender in Canada During the Late 1990s." *Punishment and Society* 7, 1.

____. 2006. "Unsettling Youth Justice and Cultural Norms: The Youth Restorative Action Project." *Journal of Youth Studies* 9, 1.

Hogeveen, Bryan, and Joshua Freistadt. Forthcoming. "Spaces of Neoliberalism: Hospitality in Edmonton's Inner City."

Hogeveen, Bryan, and Andrew Woolford. 2009. "Contemporary Critical Criminology." In Rick Linden (ed.), *Criminology a Canadian Perspective*, sixth edition. Toronto: Nelson Education.

Homeward Trust. 2008. *A Count of Homeless Persons in Edmonton, 2008.* Edmonton: Homeward Trust Edmonton Homeless Count Committee. At <intraspec.ca/HTE_2008FinalHomelessCountReport.pdf>.

Hutson, Janine. 2006. "A Prenatal Perspective on the Cost of Substance Abuse in Canada." *Journal of FAS International* 4, 9.

iHuman. 2010. *What Is the Urban Games?* Edmonton: iHuman Youth Society.

Jennings, Theodore. 2006. *Reading Derrida/Thinking Paul: On Justice.* Stanford: Stanford University Press.

Kent, Gordon. 2010a. "'Bleak' Edmonton Pedway Networks Needs an Overhaul." *Edmonton Journal,* July 15.

____. 2010b. "Library Doors Not Issue, CEO Says." *Edmonton Journal,* May 12.

____. 2010c. "World Beats Path to City Hall's Door Over Edmonton Airport Redevelopment." *Edmonton Journal,* July 15.

Kinjerski, Valerie, and Margot Herbert. 2000. *Child Welfare Caseload Growth in Alberta: Connecting the Dots.* Edmonton: Alberta Children's Services.

Kline, Marlee. 1992. "Child Welfare Law, 'Best Interests of the Child' Ideology, and

First Nations." *Osgoode Hall Law Journal* 30.

___. 1997. "Blue Meanies in Alberta: Tory Tactics and the Privatization of Child Welfare." In Susan Boyd (ed.), *Challenging the Public/Private Divide: Feminism, Law, and Public Policy.* Toronto: University of Toronto Press.

Lafrance, Jean. 2005. "Does Our Path Have a Heart? Children's Services in Alberta." In Trevor Harrison (ed.), *The Return of the Trojan Horse: Albert and the New World (Dis)Order.* Montreal: Black Rose Books.

Liewicki, Nathan. 2011. "Homeless Memorial Casts Light on Forgotten Deaths; Boyle Street Observance Remembers 57 Who Died on Street Last Year." *Edmonton Journal,* Jan. 23.

Lunau, Kate. 2010. "What Is the Agenda Behind the Tory Prison Budget Boost? Prison Ombudsman Howard Sapers Makes Sense of the Proposed Influx of Money." *Macleans.* March 30 <2.macleans.ca/2010/03/30/whats-the-agenda-behind-the-tory-prison-budget-boost>.

McKeen, Scott. 2009. "Annual Police Budget Hyperbole Intolerable." *Edmonton Journal,* November 11.

___. 2010. "Katz Returns to $100M Edmonton Arena Offer." *Edmonton Journal,* July 14.

Minaker, Joanne, and Bryan Hogeveen. 2009. *Youth, Crime and Society: Issues of Power and Justice.* Toronto: Pearson.

Molz, Jennie Germann, and Sarah Gibson (eds.). 2007. *Mobilizing Hospitality: The Ethics of Social Relations in a Mobile World.* Burlington, VT: Ashgate.

National Crime Prevention Council. 1997. *Young People Say: Report from the Youth Consultation Initiative, National Crime Prevention Council.* Ottawa: National Crime Prevention Council.

Parkland Institute. 2004. *A Time to Reap: Re-investing in Alberta's Public Services.* Edmonton: Parkland Institute.

___. 2006. *Fiscal Surplus, Democratic Deficit: Budgeting and Government Finance in Alberta.* Edmonton: Parkland Institute.

___. 2009. "Giving Away the Golden Egg: Alberta's Tax Giveaway and the Need for Reform." *Fact Sheet.* 16 December. Edmonton: Parkland Institute. At <parklandinstitute.ca/research/summary/giving_away_the_golden_egg/>.

Pavlich, George. 2007. "Deconstruction." In George Ritzer (ed.), *The Blackwell Encyclopaedia of Sociology.* Malden: Blackwell Publishing.

Sands, Andrea. 2010. "Library Loiterers Given Lesson in Crime and Punishment." *Edmonton Journal,* May 15.

Square, David. 1997. "Fetal Alcohol Syndrome Epidemic on Manitoba Reserve." *Canadian Medical Association Journal* 157.

Statistics Canada. 2006. *Persons Charged by Type of Offence.* Ottawa: Queen's Printer.

Wacquant, Loïc. 2008. *Urban Outcasts: A Comparative Sociology of Advanced Marginality.* Cambridge, UK: Polity Press.

___. 2009. *Prisons of Poverty.* Minneapolis: University of Minnesota Press.